The Internationalisation of Higher Education

We are in the middle of a fundamental transformation of the global order which is challenging the supremacy of the USA, and to a certain extent of Europe, in economic and also in normative terms. The financial crisis has further accentuated this shift in the post-Cold War architecture, with emerging economies becoming an engine of globalisation. The chapters in this volume examine the role of higher education and its internationalisation in this context, focusing on the different regions of the world and on the new role of international organisations like UNESCO. The empirical findings of these studies are part of a new research agenda in higher education studies, one that goes beyond a 'higher educationism' limiting itself to a simple description of institutional changes in the light of internationalisation. The different case studies advance an interdisciplinary perspective, drawing on accounts from critical and postcolonial theory, international relations and international political economy. They shed light on the struggles related to this major transformation of higher education characterised by specific strategic selectivities. The empirical findings illustrate how this transformation underpins the emerging global architecture.

This book was originally published as a special issue of *Globalisation, Societies and Education*.

Eva Hartmann is a Lecturer of International Relations in the Institute of Political and International Studies at the University of Lausanne, Switzerland. Her current research focuses on the internationalisation of higher education and labour market policy, state theory, International Political Economy and Postcolonial Studies.

The Internationalisation of Higher Education
Towards a new research agenda in critical higher education studies

Edited by
Eva Hartmann

First published 2011
by Routledge
2 Park Square, Milton Park, Abingdon, Oxfordshire OX14 4RN

Simultaneously published in the USA and Canada
by Routledge
711 Third Avenue, New York, NY 10017

First issued in paperback 2014

Routledge is an imprint of the Taylor and Francis Group, an informa company

© 2011 Taylor & Francis

This book is a reproduction of *Globalisation, Societies and Education*, volume 8, issue 2. The Publisher requests to those authors who may be citing this book to state, also, the bibliographical details of the special issue on which the book was based.

All rights reserved. No part of this book may be reprinted or reproduced or utilised in any form or by any electronic, mechanical, or other means, now known or hereafter invented, including photocopying and recording, or in any information storage or retrieval system, without permission in writing from the publishers.

Trademark notice: Product or corporate names may be trademarks or registered trademarks, and are used only for identification and explanation without intent to infringe.

British Library Cataloguing in Publication Data
A catalogue record for this book is available from the British Library

ISBN13: 978-0-415-67227-6 (hbk)
ISBN13: 978-0-415-75470-5 (pbk)

Typeset in Times New Roman
by Taylor & Francis Books

Disclaimer
The publisher would like to make readers aware that the chapters in this book are referred to as articles as they had been in the special issue. The publisher accepts responsibility for any inconsistencies that may have arisen in the course of preparing this volume for print.

Contents

Notes on Contributors	vii
1. Introduction: The new research agenda in critical higher education studies *Eva Hartmann*	1
2. The structure and silence of the cognotariat *Christopher Newfield*	7
3. Corporatisation, competitiveness, commercialisation: new logics in the globalising of UK higher education *Susan L. Robertson*	23
4. Current internationalisation: the case of France *Annie Vinokur*	37
5. Brazilian higher education from a post-colonial perspective *Denise Leite*	51
6. Soft power and higher education: an examination of China's Confucius Institutes *Rui Yang*	65
7. The Bologna Process as a hegemonic tool of Normative Power Europe (NPE): the case of Chilean and Mexican higher education *Francis Espinoza Figueroa*	77
8. The selectivity of translation: accountability regimes in Chilean and South African higher education *Barbara Junge (formerly Dickhaus)*	87
9. Re-orienting internationalisation in African higher education *Mala Singh*	99
10. Small world: access to higher education between methodological nationalism and international organisations *Gaële Goastellec*	113
11. Singapore: bridgehead of the West or counterforce? The s[t]imulation of creative and critical thought in Singapore's higher education policies *Ingrid Hoofd*	125

12. The United Nations Educational, Scientific and Cultural Organisation: pawn or global player?
   Eva Hartmann   135

   Index   147

Notes on Contributors

Francis Espinoza Figueroa is a Researcher/PhD candidate in the Department of Political Sciences and International Studies (POLSIS) of the University of Birmingham, UK and a Lecturer in the Catholic University of the North (Universidad Católica del Norte), Chile. She is interested in international relations and higher education policies. Her recent work analyses the European influences on the higher education policies of Chile and Mexico.

Gaële Goastellec is a Researcher in the Observatoire Science, Policy and Society, University of Lausanne, Switzerland. She is a former Fulbright New Century Scholar. Her work focuses on comparative higher education, notably on equity, identities, organisations and policies. She is the author of *Understanding inequalities in and by higher education. Global perspectives on higher education* (2010).

Eva Hartmann is a Lecturer of International Relations in the Institute of Political and International Studies at the University of Lausanne, Switzerland. Her work focuses on the internationalisation of higher education and labour market policy, state theory, international law and International Political Economy. Her most recent book analyses the global dimension of the Bologna Process from a state-theoretical and postcolonial perspective. She has also written on *The Difficult Relation between International Law and Politics: The Legal Turn from a Critical IPE Perspective* forthcoming in *New Political Economy*.

Ingrid Hoofd is an Assistant Professor in Communications and New Media at the National University of Singapore. Her research interests are the transformation of higher education, feminist and critical theory, and philosophy of technology. Her current book project *Between activism and academia: The complicities of alter-globalist resistances in speed* discusses the ways in which alter-globalist academics mobilise divisions in an attempt to overcome oppressions. Ingrid Hoofd did her master's degree in Women's Studies at Utrecht University in The Netherlands.

Barbara Junge (formerly Dickhaus) is a PhD candidate, teaches and works at the research unit 'Globalisation & Politics' at the Department of Social Sciences, Kassel University, Germany. Her research interests are global governance and public policy with a focus on public service provision (esp. higher education), trade in services (GATS) and European studies. She teaches in the Master programme 'Global Political Economy'.

NOTES ON CONTRIBUTORS

Denise Leite received her master and doctoral degrees in Education and Human Sciences from UFRGS, Brasil. She is currently an invited professor at the Graduate Program on Education, UFRGS, Brazil; a senior researcher (level 1B CNPq, National Research Council); and coordinator of the Research Study Group Innovation & Evaluation (CNPq-UFRGS), in charge of inter-institutional and international research projects. Her main research interests are university innovation and evaluation and university pedagogy.

Christopher Newfield is Professor of English at the University of California, Santa Barbara. His current research focuses on higher education history, funding, and policy, culture and innovation, and the relation between culture and economics. He is the author of *Ivy and industry: Business and the making of the American university, 1880–1980* (2003), and *Unmaking the public university: The forty year assault on the middle class* (2008).

Susan L. Robertson is Professor of Sociology of Education, Centre for Globalisation, Education and Societies, University of Bristol. Her current research interests are processes of globalisation and regionalisation as they are mediated by education. She has published widely on these issues. This research was funded by the ESRC's Centre for Learning and Life Chances in Knowledge Economies and Societies (LLAKES).

Mala Singh is Professor of International Higher Education Policy in the Centre for Higher Education Research and Information at the Open University in the United Kingdom. Previously, she was the founding executive director of the post-1994 national quality assurance system for higher education in South Africa. She has a doctorate in philosophy and has published in the fields of philosophy, higher education and quality assurance. She serves on the editorial boards of *Higher Education Policy* and the *Journal of Higher Education in Africa* and is a member of the Academy of Science of South Africa. Her current research interests relate to higher education and social change, higher education regulation, and higher education in developing country contexts.

Annie Vinokur is Emeritus Professor of Economics at the University of Paris-Ouest Nanterre La Defense. Her main field of research is the economics of education. She has also worked as a consultant for international organisations in Europe and in several developing and transitional countries.

Rui Yang is Associate Professor and Director of the Comparative Education Research Centre, Faculty of Education, The University of Hong Kong. He has worked in different higher education systems, with particular interest in crossculturalism in education policy, higher education, and sociology of education. He has written extensively in the field of comparative and international education. His current interest is focused on comparative and global studies in education policy and higher education internationalisation.

INTRODUCTION
The new research agenda in critical higher education studies

The establishment of the Bologna Policy Forum, on the occasion of the Bologna follow-up meeting in Leuven in 2009, marked a turning point. It is no longer the establishment of a European Area of Higher Education alone that is at the top of the European agenda. The extra-European dimension of the Bologna Process has become a second important issue. Europe is about to become a major promoter not only of a European, but also of a global knowledge society. This new focus is reflected in the title of the second meeting of the Bologna Policy Forum, 'Building the global knowledge society: Systemic and institutional change in higher education'. This second meeting took place on 12 March 2010 on the occasion of the 10th anniversary of the Bologna Process, which was celebrated in Vienna. 30 non-European countries were invited to gather in Vienna and to enter into a dialogue with the 46 countries participating in the Bologna Process. Developed countries such as Australia, New Zealand, Israel, Japan and the US accepted the invitation, as did emerging economies such as Brazil, China, Mexico, Egypt and Morocco. Other participants in the forum included education ministers from developing countries such as Ethiopia and Kyrgyzstan. Hence Bologna is going global. This new extra-European emphasis of the Bologna Process is to be seen in the context of a general transformation of the global architecture challenging the supremacy of the US, and to a certain extent of Europe, in economic but also normative terms. The current crisis is further accentuating the transformation of this post-Cold War architecture, since the crisis has hit high-income countries more severely than many developing countries.

This special issue focuses on the internationalisation of higher education (HE), situating the trend in this broader context.[1] It advances an interdisciplinary perspective drawing on accounts from higher education studies, international relations (IR) and international political economy (IPE). It suggests a research agenda that goes beyond a simple description of the institutional change of HE in the light of internationalisation, and also beyond measuring the volume of the flow of international students. Roger Dale (2009) has coined the term 'higher educationism' for this kind of narrow perspective. As a number of contributors to this issue outline, such an analysis overlooks the broader context and the strategic selectivity, transformation and struggles within which the object of analysis is to be placed and, as a consequence, depoliticises the internationalisation of HE. A broader research agenda draws attention to the very different functions of HE depending on the socio-historical context. They may differ from each other so fundamentally that the name 'university' just becomes an empty signifier for very different objects. We thus need to further develop a theory of the university and education in more general terms, one that takes into account the role of the context, including time and scale. What are the implications for the function of higher education when the flow of global students is about to become part of a vision according to which each student, regardless of his or her origins, should have access to all the universities of the world?

Research on higher education needs to overcome a methodological nationalism that has dominated the field of study so far. Methodological nationalism takes the national state as the unquestioned analytical unit, and runs the risk of overlooking the interdependency between different countries and reifying the equation between nation, state and society. The need to overcome this methodological nationalism does not take place in a historical vacuum. Globalisation challenges the imaginary of the national state as a sovereign unity, with consequences for the role of universities. For around 200 years, universities have been instrumental in underpinning the construction of the nation as imagined community and in enabling the national bureaucracy to administer society. The massification of higher education is to be seen in the context of the further extension of the state as a welfare state, which went hand-in-hand with a scientification of politics. The current internationalisation strategy of higher education challenges this national orientation and highlights the role of higher education in building a global knowledge society as an imagined community. Symptomatic of this reorientation is the last world conference on higher education of the United Nations Educational, Scientific and Cultural Organisation (UNESCO) that took place in June 2009. A first draft of the conference's communiqué emphasised that 'Higher education plays an important role in nation-building' (2009, para 2). However, the reference to this function of higher education was deleted in the final communiqué. Hence, universities have become an integral part of the endeavour to establish an international framework. The constitution of Europe as a post-national imagined community which aims to establish its own higher education area has become a major point of reference for similar undertakings in other regions of the world aiming at establishing regional areas of higher education. However, we should be careful in our analysis of internationalisation not to substitute too hastily methodological globalism for methodological nationalism as a new normative orientation. Studies are needed which examine *whether* the nation state remains the main organising principle. In other words, the nation state is no longer the *explanans* but the *explanandum*. Such a differentiated perspective points up how internationalisation strategies may significantly change in different institutional contexts. Drawing on Michel Foucault's concept of the strategic dispositif, we can understand the internationalisation of higher education as a bundling of very different, often conflicting strategies at local, national and post-national levels whose specific rationales, intentions and also institutional settings are still identifiable (1980, 194). The more the different strategies are related to each other, the more the imaginary of an international area of higher education takes shape. Such an imaginary can no longer be attributed to one single intention or one single institutional framework.

The case studies on the US and the UK outline how these two major destinations of students from other countries have been drastically hit by the financial crisis. Christopher Newfield shows in his study that the crisis has exacerbated an already existing tension between the official demand for highly-qualified knowledge workers and the reluctance of the public system to provide the necessary funding. The lack of funding has been detrimental to quality, notably the quality of those study programmes that have absorbed most of the new demand in the course of the massification of higher education. By contrast, other study programmes have managed to remain rather exclusive. As a consequence, graduates of these programmes can be sure that they will not meet the same competition in the labour market as the graduates from overcrowded degree courses. As a consequence, the latter are much more likely to find themselves in highly casualised working conditions, being part of a new proletariat, the cognitariat. The study shows that this situation is further aggravated by an internal struggle over the redistribution of the revenues from tuition fees, which is taking the form of a bottom-up redistribution. Those study programmes attracting most students tend to subsidise the more exclusive courses with their revenues from tuition fees. Accordingly, a struggle for access to tax money and people's savings, without equally sharing the benefits afterwards, can be seen not only when it comes to the bailing out of banks but also in the microcosm of higher education.

In the light of public spending cuts, the role of foreign fee-paying students has become crucial in the US and also in the UK, the second largest destination for students, as Susan Robertson's contribution outlines. The case study of the UK outlines how the selling of Britain's reputation, language skills and knowledge within the UK, but also abroad through offshore campuses, is increasingly part of the overall economic strategy aiming at positioning the UK at the upper end of the global value chain. This overall economic strategy has further gained in importance in the light of the aggravation of global competition where emerging economies have taken the lead in exporting industrialised goods, at least in net terms (WTO 2009, 13). However, the international provision of higher education through pure market mechanisms is likely to exacerbate fragmentation and fractures, as it does not constitute an institutional arrangement that mediates between long-term and short-term interests. As a consequence, such fragmentation risks undermining the endeavour to establish a global information society.

The situation in France is quite different, as Annie Vinokur outlines in her case study. A different university–industry nexus prevails in this country, promoting a reform of the higher education sector with a view to improving research and development. In this context, the HE sector is seen as an infrastructure requiring major investment in order to improve the overall economic performance of the country. As a consequence, funding by taxpayers' money continues to be the main funding mechanism while tuition fees remain rather nominal. Accordingly, universities have less interest in establishing offshore campuses with a view to increasing their revenues. The study shows that this situation is now changing. HE is increasingly being seen as a commodity in France too, which has led to more aggressive exporting strategies on the part of French universities. The current public budget cuts are likely to strengthen this trend. Hence, we can see a certain convergence in the different countries paving the way for a trans-nationalisation of higher education through the establishment of offshore campuses. However, the government in France continues to play a key role in initiating projects.

Denis Leite identifies an even stronger role of the government in her case study on Brazil, as does Rui Yang in his study of China. Both of these emerging economies have started to promote the internationalisation of HE through some public but also private universities in the case of Brazil, and through Confucius Institutes in the case of China. Accordingly, China is about to develop a soft power strategy comparable to that of the Alliance Française, the Goethe Institut, the British Council or the Japan Foundation. This new Chinese strategy indicates a major shift in the global architecture with China as a major player, and highlights the role of (higher) education in this transformation. But the case study of the internationalisation strategies of emerging economies reveals a more complex picture of the interaction between internalising external norms and externalising internal norms. In her comparison of Chile and

Mexico, Francis Espinoza Figueroa develops a concept of normative power that draws on accounts from post-colonial studies with a view to analysing the normative influence of the Bologna Process and the EU in Chile and Mexico. Her study sheds light on a major competition between the US and the EU over normative influence in Latin America.

Barbara Dickhaus's study, comparing adoptions of an external quality assurance system in Chile and South Africa, provides a framework which enables us to understand the adoption of international norms as a translation process, characterised by a specific selectivity. This study examines how structure, agency, discourse and scales interact with each other, paving the way for a social compromise. The establishment of a social compromise at a national level has thus a truly international dimension without being limited to it.

Mala Singh's study of the reorientation of the internationalisation strategy in Sub-Saharan Africa also emphasises the importance of mediation between international, regional, national and local levels to ensure that international norms are adequate for the objectives being pursued. Her study discusses the potential and the risk of adopting the Bologna framework with a view to creating a common African higher education and research space, bridging the gap between disparate education systems. Her study outlines how the asymmetries of power in the North–South partnership and the lack of local mediation capacity reduce the possibility of using this framework for an alternative internationalisation politics in African HE.

Would the situation be different if the international norms themselves had an emancipatory meaning? Gaële Goastellec's study shows that international norms can also include elements that are usually seen as the result of a national social compromise: the move from the norm of inherited merit to the norm of equality of opportunities. This raises fundamental questions about the meaning of emancipation and the internationalisation of a specific kind of critical thinking that questions the *status quo*. Ingrid Hoofd takes up this question in her contribution, while reflecting on her position as a white European teacher at the National University of Singapore. Her study highlights a recent tendency of emerging economies to employ research and teaching staff from western countries at their universities. Is this trend the outcome of a new assertiveness of these countries, or just another strategy aimed at reinforcing western supremacy? Hoofd, drawing on Martin Heidegger's reflection on originary thinking, shows that there is no easy answer to this question. The critical and creative thinking promoted within the Singaporean context is not *per se* questioning of power relations or transformative, but neither can it be reduced to a simple imitation of a western way of thinking. This insight also has major repercussions for the attempt to use critical theory, which was mainly developed by western philosophers, to analyse the current shift of the global architecture. To what extent is such an endeavour part of an effort to reinforce western supremacy? This question is at the core of post-colonial studies, which will help us to further develop critical studies in HE. A close examination of who actually has a say in defining the function of higher education is the first requirement. The meaning of a norm or a concept cannot be detached from its underlying social structure. Consequently, even emancipatory norms risk being detrimental to emancipation as long as the social groups addressed by this political endeavour have not participated in the design of the project.

Eva Hartmann's case study examines the strategic selectivity of the norm-settings in the framework of UNESCO. It sheds light on a precarious alliance aiming at establishing international standards that facilitate the mutual recognition of higher education qualifications: a major precondition for ensuring students' mobility. This study shows that UNESCO plays an important role in mediating between conflicting interests at the global level. However, the organisation is no longer challenging North–South asymmetries as it did in the 1970s, when it was the mouthpiece for a new information order linked to a new economic order. The organisation rather risks becoming complicit in a political project aiming at establishing a global knowledge society that privileges the interests of the countries of the North. However, the overall picture is more complex, as the different contributions in this special issue show. We hope to contribute with this volume to a further clarification of the complexity of what we may call the dispositif of the internationalisation of higher education.

Eva Hartmann
University of Lausanne, Switzerland

Note
1. A number of the contributions were first presented at a workshop at the University of Lausanne in September 2009. I would like to thank the Swiss National Science Foundation and the *Fondation du 450e Anniversaire* for their generous financial support of this workshop.

References

Dale, R. 2009. What's 'Public' about the NPM in HE? The changing discourses of 'public' in the Bologna Process. Paper presented at the conference on L'Enseignement Supérieur entre Nouvelle Gestion Publique et Dépression Economique Analyse comparée et essai de prospective, Université de Paris Ouest Nanterre La Défense, December 11–12, in Paris.

Foucault, M. 1980. *Power/knowledge: Selected interviews and other writings, 1972–1977.* Harvester, London: Pantheon.

World Conference on Higher Education. 2009. World Conference on Higher Education: The New Dynamics of Higher Education and for Societal Change and Development (Unesco, Paris, July 5–8, 2009), Draft Communique (1st Draft June 26, 2009), Para 2.

World Trade Organisation. 2009. *World Trade Report.* Geneva: Author.

The structure and silence of the cognotariat

Christopher Newfield

University of California, Santa Barbara, USA

> This paper describes the most likely social structure awaiting 'knowledge workers' in the knowledge economies of high- and medium-income nations. Commentators from across the political spectrum and in diverse institutional positions have been noting that the source of new products and industries is increasingly 'cognitive'. They have been concluding from this that knowledge workers are in effect knowledge capitalists who will either own, and/or control, the economy, and will gradually acquire the economic power historically allotted to owners, shareholders and top executives. The paper analyses the discourse of 'knowledge management' in conjunction with the structure of higher education's primary disciplines to argue that in fact knowledge workers are divided into traditional social groups. Only a small 'creative class' will achieve control or creative freedom, and they will achieve this largely because of their direct institutional connections to the owners and executives who run the knowledge economy. There are no signs that the current economy is redistributing economic authority in a more egalitarian way, nor are knowledge workers showing signs of political mobilisation against this traditional stratification.

Introduction

Many Americans assume that because business and political leaders agree that the US is a 'knowledge economy', they therefore support an increase in knowledge production and support the university systems that perform the majority of this basic research in the US and other wealthy countries. The reality is something quite different. American leaders are preoccupied with reducing public expenditures on higher education and with lowering the cost of each degree produced. They are containing and cheapening the research and educational systems on which they say the future of their economies depends. This raises the core question I'll discuss here: why would wealthy societies cut back on the sources of high-tech knowledge when they believe their future lies with high-value, high-tech industries? Isn't this contradictory, and also fairly dumb?

Well yes: some of it is ordinary human myopia and selfishness. Some of it is the result of the artificially created general hostility towards universities and towards the politically independent and racially diverse middle classes that had been produced by public universities after World War II.[1] Some of it is the result of a business reflex in the US, which is to address all revenue issues with downsizing and layoffs.[2]

But looking at this basic reflex only deepens the sense of contradiction. Mainstream experts estimate sustainable 'efficiencies' to amount to perhaps 3% savings a year for the first few years, not the 5%, 10%, or 20% cuts being imposed by state governments. They also agree the real crisis in American higher education is that it is producing perhaps half as many college degrees as it needs, not that it is spending too much money.[3] What, then, is the logic of cuts that contradict the knowledge economy's apparent requirement of a *mass* middle class, a society that has a majority of college graduates and of knowledge workers?

The contradiction exists only if we assume that today's leaders of the knowledge economy actually seek a mass middle class, desire high standards of living for the vast majority of their population, and believe that the knowledge economy needs armies of college graduates. But if, instead, we posit that the political and business leaders of the knowledge economy seek a smaller elite of knowledge-based star producers, then the unceasing cheapening of public higher education in the US and elsewhere makes real sense.

Many authors have pointed out over the years that knowledge capitalism obligates firms to seek rents and a monopoly position in their markets.[4] Clear support for this thesis comes from the oligarchic structures of the information technology and biotechnology industries in the US and elsewhere. A companion thesis has been that there is a fundamental contradiction between capitalism and the knowledge economy, clearly described by André Gorz, since knowledge is abundant and capitalism artificially forces its scarcity.[5] In fact, the US experience suggests that this contradiction is productive of the system of cognitive capitalism in Foucault's sense of a productive contradiction: the appropriation of abundant knowledge, the privatisation of public and socially-created goods – that is, the famous 'enclosure of the knowledge commons' – is the set of operations that cognitive capitalism exists to perform, with full knowledge that it is forcing knowledge out of its creative collective habitat.

In this article I will look at several aspects of this process. One is a systematic stratification within knowledge workers as a class or group. The second is the development of a structural basis for this stratification – proprietary knowledge – that gives the powerful system of financial capital a direct stake in stratifying knowledge workers. The third is the system of unequal universities and disciplines within universities that reproduces the labour hierarchy of knowledge work and that makes opposition psychologically difficult. Finally, there is the practice of 'open innovation' in which a firm defines value-creation not as the output of its own workforce, but as the output of proprietary knowledge workers from a whole network of firms. I suggest that this leads to a new version of the ancient regime's Three Estates, and that this structure needs to be confronted directly by knowledge workers in academia and industry alike.

Managing and dividing

For nearly four decades, a range of American commentators thought knowledge work meant a kind of independence, creativity, even liberation. Clark Kerr's landmark *The uses of the university* (1963) described the centrality of the university and its knowledge workers to advanced capitalist economies. John Kenneth Galbraith saw the college-trained middle classes forming a 'technostructure' that ruled large corporations in *The new industrial state* from 1967. In 1979 Barbara and John Ehrenreich defined the 'professional–managerial class' (PMC) as a new and dominant force in previously binary class dynamics. The decline of the industrial state only fed the claims that knowledge workers were the rulers of the new economy. Robert Reich's 1991 *The work of nations* defined 'symbolic analysts' as a new ruling class, one that Richard Florida would rechristen the 'creative class' in 2002, to which all-important social resources would flow.

The fullest endorsement of this idea of a self-determined knowledge class that could make the rules of its own work life came from the moderate, corporatist dean of management studies in the US, Peter Drucker. In the immediate aftermath of the fall of the Berlin Wall, Drucker (1993, 8) offered this vision of knowledge work leading to 'post-capitalism':

> The basic economic resource – 'the means of production', to use the economist's term – is no longer capital, nor natural resources (the economist's 'land'), nor 'labor'. *It is and will be knowledge.* … The leading social groups of the knowledge society will be 'knowledge workers' – knowledge executives who know how to allocate knowledge to productive use, just as the capitalists knew how to allocate capital to productive use; knowledge professionals, knowledge employees. Practically all these knowledge people will be employed in organizations. Yet, unlike the employees under Capitalism, they will own both the 'means of production' and the 'tools of production' …[6]

But this is not the destiny actually achieved by brainworkers in knowledge companies.

The old industrial goliaths may have needed armies of college graduates to operate themselves, and universities were producing armies of managers, majors in economics, social psychology and related fields who would perform complicated tasks while supporting the company's priorities and the economic system that favoured it. But do knowledge companies now want these armies of brainworkers?

There is much evidence to suggest that they do not. The first indication is that high-tech industries have famously stratified workforces and pay structures in which their blue-collar workers do not make living wages. The second is that when they grew large, they hired as many temporary workers as possible. Microsoft, one of the wealthiest companies in history, was sued for its practice of hiring 'permatemps', second class employees with different coloured badges and lower wages and benefits who would nonetheless often work with the company for years.[7] A third piece of evidence is that they are as inclined towards mass layoffs as any other industrial sector.[8] A fourth is that the large majority of occupational sectors within 'high tech employment' in Silicon Valley declined during the 2000s (Mann and Nunes 2009). A fifth piece of evidence is that total direct employment in high-tech fields (science, technology, engineering and mathematics or STEM occupations) was 5.2% of all jobs in the US in 2007, which means that high-tech firms cannot see themselves as sources of mass employment, and must see themselves as employing only a fraction of college graduates (Bureau of Labor Statistics 2007, Figure 44).

There are about seven million STEM jobs in the US, while the higher education system produces about 2.3 million bachelors, masters, professional and doctoral degrees every year (in all fields) (National Center for Education Statistics 2008, Table 186). This means that the US university system could reproduce the entire STEM workforce in three years (two years if we include associate degrees). If a normal STEM career lasts about 30 years, we can conclude, using very rough figures, that the US university system produces about 10 times more graduates than the economy needs in its technical workforce.

The issue for knowledge industries, then, is *not* how they can create armies of knowledge workers. The issue is the opposite: how can they limit their numbers and manage their output? What happens to the nine-tenths of college graduates who, according to our simplified numbers, work in a knowledge economy but who do not directly produce its technical knowledge?

Stratification through knowledge management

A big part of the answer is that they are demoted to a lower class of worker. The mechanism is a form of sorting that emerged in the 1990s as large numbers of college students who'd grown up with computers entered the workforce with tastes and skills ideally suited to building the Internet and related industries. One term was 'knowledge management' (KM), and it received particularly clear codification in a book by Thomas A. Stewart. At the time, Stewart was a member of *Fortune* magazine's Board of Editors; he later became editor-in-chief of *Harvard Business Review*. KM was part of a system that hoped against hope (and against the economic evidence) that: 'The greater the human-capital intensity of a business – that is, the greater its percentage of high-value-added work performed by hard-to-replace people – the more it can charge for its services and the less vulnerable it is to competitors'. The reasoning here was that a company could thrive when it was, 'even more difficult for rivals to match those skills than it [was] ... for the first company to replace them' (Stewart 1997, 92). KM was thus not window-dressing, but the life-or-death creation of the human capital that would allow a firm to survive in the cutthroat New Economy.

Stewart distinguished between three different types of knowledge or skill. Type C (my label) is 'commodity skills', he wrote, which are 'readily obtained' and whose possessors are interchangeable. This category includes most 'pink collar' work that involves skills like 'typing and a cheerful phone manner'. Type B is 'leveraged skills', which require advanced education and which offer clear added value to the firm that hires such skill, and yet which are possessed by many firms. Computer programmers or network administrators are examples of essential employees who worked long and hard to acquire their knowledge, and yet who are relatively numerous. Ironically, they may have entered the field because it was large: its size may have signalled to them when they were picking a major in college – and to their stability-minded parents – something like 'the high-tech economy will always need computer support specialists'.[9] Yes, but not any particular computer support specialist, and not at a very high wage.

Type A consists of 'proprietary skills', which Stewart defined as, 'the company-specific talents around which an organization builds a business' (1997, 89). The knowledge manager must nurture and cultivate only the skills that directly contribute to the firm's proprietary knowledge, and stamp out (or radically cheapen) the first kind of knowledge worker, whose skills are interchangeable commodities. Only the star producers – those who create proprietary knowledge – enable the firm to seek rents, and only they are to be retained, supported, cultivated and lavishly paid.

Of particular interest is Type B, the large group caught in the middle, those with 'leveraged skills'. Part of this group is not generally associated with four-year college degrees: it includes 'skilled factory workers, experienced secretaries' or back-office bookkeepers. The latter, for example, have accounting skills as well as plenty of informal knowledge about how the particular company works. They have experience-based cultural knowledge that cannot be easily codified and transferred, and that helps them figure out what anomalous figures mean since they've seen them before, or which routes of project approval are slow and which are fast. Such knowledge directly improves efficiency and profits in various ways. Tough luck: they may be trained, intelligent, valuable and even necessary, but they are not perceived to contribute directly to the firm's main sources of profit. Thus a good knowledge manager should try to codify some of their informal knowledge, disregard the rest as irrelevant and outsource as many of these workers as possible.

The other part of this middle group consists of college graduates who produce much added value with high-end skills. They are people with expensively acquired, difficult knowledge, like code writing in a particular computer language, but who nonetheless are similar to their counterparts in other companies. KM will treat these workers as it treats their non-college colleagues: they must be transformed into distinctive specialists who directly contribute to the firm's proprietary knowledge, or they must be fired and their functions outsourced to a company that specialises in such skills. These employees followed the post-war college path to success: they finished school, did well, are reliable, hard-working, adaptive and intelligent, but are too similar to their counterparts from other universities to add unique value. They are 'excellent' but they are not 'unique': they are productive, but not proprietary. KM insisted that good college grads are no different from other production workers: there is nothing wrong with them, exactly, but they do not contribute the only thing that counts in the knowledge economy – unique comparative advantage through proprietary innovations. KM codified the major development in attitudes about white-collar labour in the 1990s, which was that, for the most part, they were as interchangeable and disposable as their blue-collar brethren before them.

Once KM had slotted knowledge workers according to their relevance to the firm's proprietary goods, its other major goal followed rather easily. That goal was to convert human to structural capital. Most experts offered the knowledge manager the kind of advice that Stewart did: recognise them and their importance. Give them the resources they need (Stewart 1997, 98–9). But don't get permissive and go too far. 'Fund them too much, and you'll start to want deliverables. You won't get what you want. You'll get what the community wants to deliver' (Valdis Krebs, cited in Stewart 1997, 100). Too much independence for knowledge workers would become a threat to the process by which knowledge was put to productive use. Toward the end of the 1990s, as elite knowledge workers became scarce or mobile enough to strike good deals for themselves, they caused all sorts of corporate complaining about the pampering of coders who acted like teenagers and the rise of a bratty class of 'gold-collar workers' (Munk 1998). Granting any bargaining power to knowledge workers – to say nothing of self-management – interfered with the task of maximising their knowledge's value to the firm.

Only satisfied knowledge workers could satisfy the firm's need for proprietary knowledge that would allow rent-like profits, and yet self-management, the central source of knowledge workers' satisfaction – as for all workers – could not be permitted in any general way. Self-managed workers posed permanent loyalty problems; they needed knowledge managers as much as or even more than, in this view, industrial workers had needed Taylorisation. Management in the knowledge economy consisted of separating employees with proprietary knowledge from the vast majority of knowledge workers, and then minimising this latter group's independence and social protections as thoroughly as had happened to industrial workers in an earlier age.

A three-tiered university

Meanwhile, the US university was following an uncannily similar path. Faculty members are knowledge workers par excellence; nearly all faculty members in four-year universities have doctoral degrees, and most conduct some amount of research. Nonetheless, over the past 30 years, the share of instructors lacking full-time and/or permanent contracts has doubled. The US system now operates with a teaching staff that is 70% temporary.[10] Even in the best-funded science and technology fields, 'the share of full-time faculty declined from 87% in the early 1970s to 75% in 2003' (National Science Foundation 2006a, Chapter 5). These non-tenurable faculty members have no say in university governance and little input if any into their own departments. They are on short-term contracts – from one semester to five years – and are distinctly second class in relation to the tenure-track faculty; in most cases they can be fired during times of financial stress.

The splitting of faculty into different strata is matched by a growing inequality between private and public universities. The wealth gap is the best known of these differences: one of my budget colleagues calculated that Harvard was spending $60,000 per undergraduate at a time, around 2005, when the University of California was spending about one tenth that amount on its undergraduates. Other gaps have grown as well – graduation rates, student–faculty ratios, acceptance rates and faculty salaries.[11] It is fair to say that the US now has a three-speed system of higher education. At the top is the Ivy League Plus, which educates about 1% of the 18 million people currently enrolled in some kind of higher education institution in the US. Europeans will have heard of all of these universities, from Harvard and Stanford to Duke, MIT and Cal Tech, and they dominate world rankings as well. There are around 20 of these universities. Next comes a group of about 150 colleges and universities that are 'selective' and have good reputations outside of their local area. This includes public research universities like Wisconsin, Michigan, North Carolina, Texas, Florida and many others.

This leaves over 3500 institutions of higher learning that admit more or less everyone who applies, are often focused on regional needs and vocational training, and that must make do with far fewer resources than is the case with the upper two tiers. These third tier institutions are often 'community colleges'. Whatever good things happen for these students in their classrooms, these schools confer mass degrees that offer their possessor no special advantage in the job market. Though their graduates have acquired meaningful cognitive skills and some focused credentials, they have obtained no social advantage. These institutions are about basic employability, but not about social mobility. They are increasingly seen as the only destination for knowledge training that the society's leaders are willing to pay for (see College Board 2008). They are the training grounds of the true 'cognotariat', knowledge workers and rarely knowledge managers, and are in fact heavily managed, starting with curricula oriented towards immediate job skills in their first year in college.

Similar tiers have long been part of European higher education, and modernisation is only making them worse. France already had a two-speed system of universities and grandes écoles; the recent legislation passed by the Sarkozy administration – *la loi relative aux libertés et responsabilités des universités* (LRU; passed in August 2007) – uses the concept of university autonomy to increase an inequality of funding that will lead to a intensified tiering of campuses within the national university system (see Charle and Soulié 2007, especially the chapters by Chris Lorenz and Frédéric Neyrat; also Cottet, Zubiri-Rey, and Sauvel 2009). The German 'Elite 10' competition is another example, and was a response to the increased prominence of international rankings of universities – generally from incommensurate national educational traditions and with diverging social missions – in the creation of educational policy.

Tiering blocks a direct response to the real problem of these university systems, which is their gross underfunding – France and Germany spend about one eighth per student of what those elite American universities spend that appear at the top of international lists.[12]

The stark and growing inequality within universities and within the 'creative class' of knowledge workers actually isn't good for knowledge. One simple indicator is the lack of growth in American scientific publications from the mid 1990s on (National Science Foundation 2006b), and this stagnation has not only produced a series of high-level reports sounding the alarm (National Academies 2007) but has recently been traced specifically to declining funding for public universities (Adams 2009). A more important indicator is that a country's educational attainment is measured by the percentage of a country's population that achieves a certain level of education – not just the level achieved by a small elite. The US has lost the educational leadership it had throughout the twentieth century, and is in the process of falling even further behind (Goldin and Katz 2008, Chapter 1).

An obvious response would be to reverse the decline of higher education funding, defined for example as a share of personal income, and to do so on the traditional capitalist economic grounds that higher education is an essential investment in future prosperity. This argument certainly circulates in the US. But this kind of argument is not prevailing. Why isn't it, even as the educational damage done through stratification becomes more obvious?

Cognitive capitalism as open innovation

One reason, once again, is that the rich and famous like paying lower rather than higher taxes. The cost for the median California family to restore University of California funding to its relatively strong 2001 level would be a ridiculously low $32 dollars per year – but much more for those with annual incomes measured in the millions of dollars. The wealthy are continuing a long tradition of opting-out of support for public services which they believe they do not need (see Newfield 2009c).

Another reason is the general form that power takes today with American-style corporatist government, which is an internally-conflicted, variably institutionalised hegemony that expends enormous resources in constant efforts of self-mobilisation (Greenwald 2009; Poulantzas 1976; Hartmann 2009). There is also an emerging structural reason that is built into knowledge industries themselves. These now have an innovation strategy that rejects the managerial cadres and white-collar armies of the industrial age. They have a strategy that they believe benefits their own innovation without requiring major 'sunk costs' in a fixed knowledge infrastructure. This innovation strategy depends on leveraging rather than investing, and on a disruptive rather than a curatorial relation to one's own workforce.

The current situation of the high-tech university–industry reciprocity can be summarised via the influential paradigm known as 'open innovation' (Chesbrough 2006). It is called open because it tries to respond to the genuine insight in the theory of the knowledge worker, which is that knowledge is common rather than scarce, widely rather than narrowly distributed in the population, and mobile in ways that even the most powerful corporations cannot control. As Henry Chesbrough, the business scholar most associated with the concept, has put it, technology-driven businesses must learn to operate a 'landscape of abundant knowledge' (2006, xiv).

The lead intellectual property strategist first for IBM and then for Microsoft, Marshall Phelps, has claimed:

> Whereas some 80% of major innovations during the 1970s had come from inside a single company's own R&D labs, by the dawn of the twenty-first century, studies now showed, more than two-thirds of major new innovations involved some sort of interorganisational collaboration – either between private firms, or between firms and federal laboratories or research universities. (Phelps and Kline 2009, 4–5)

'Open' innovation systems accept high labour mobility and value collaborations outside their institutional boundaries, particularly with universities. Open innovation theory tends to understand that value is created by individual intellectual labour within complex social networks, and puts collaboration across boundaries at the heart of the knowledge economy.

And yet the purpose of open innovation strategy is to absorb the value created by social collaboration into a given firm. Microsoft's Phelps notes that open innovation rests on intellectual property (IP) (as did 'closed' innovation). The difference is that 'intellectual property could no longer be viewed solely as a negative right' to block someone else's use of your IP or to extract a tax on that use in the form of licensing fees.

> From now on, IP's greatest value would lie not so much in being a weapon against competitors, but rather in serving as a bridge to collaboration with other firms that would enable companies to acquire the technologies and competencies they needed to compete successfully. (Phelps and Kline 2009, 5)

The lead firm, such as Microsoft, would create networks of smaller firms, subcontractors and clients whose own products would depend on Microsoft's through a system of cross-licenses that would bind the whole together as one large 'ecology' with Microsoft as its constitutive legal and technological *standard*.

Phelps and other open innovation gurus had figured out that true market dominance didn't come from open warfare for control waged against competitors, since this meant that you alienated customers and allies, soured your public image, lost the chance to access other people's inventions and lost big chunks of real estate. On the other hand, if you could convince your potential competitors to give you access to their inventions in exchange for something of yours, you could influence – if not directly control – a much larger business ecosystem than before. Moving from sovereignty to governance in Foucault's sense, open innovation companies like Microsoft used open not to undermine their monopolies but to extend them, precisely by making them more flexible. Open innovation gave small companies the chance to access established markets by participating in the Microsoft brand, as well as acquire some IP and financial support. For the bigs, open meant Ottoman-like expansion of a polyglot empire that nonetheless had their code written into all of its operations.[13]

The most successful knowledge corporations, then, are those who are best at using other people's money *and* other people's inventions. The name of the game is *leverage*. Intel, for example, the world's dominant manufacturer of computer processors, approaches an existing lab, already fully funded and staffed with a combination of federal grants and university contributions, suggests topics and personnel, funds a project for far less than what it would cost to perform (informal estimates among technology transfer personnel suggest that a company like Intel pays the university lab between 5% and 10% of what it would cost for Intel to conduct the research internally). This is of course money the university would not otherwise have, and it is sometimes accompanied with state-of-the-art equipment and excellent scientific input from Intel staff. For its sponsorship, Intel gets access to research results, often exclusively for a set period, and first pick of inventions that may turn into useful intellectual property. Universities do not generally disclose financial terms – they are not favourable to the university (see Newfield 2008, Chapter 12) – but they do publicise the alliance with a prestigious firm like Intel and trumpet interim research results. The strategy works for Intel because it can absorb other people's inventions, turning them into its own IP at a discounted cost.[14]

Intel has sponsored a number of interesting and very advanced research projects at various universities. One of these is research into a Hybrid Silicon Laser that in very general terms seeks to use light as well as electricity to continue to multiply the speed and performance of the integrated circuits used today to run computers' central processing units, among many other things.[15] Some of the research on this project was conducted at the University of California at Santa Barbara, where one of its laboratories participated in a survey and follow-up interviews conducted by my research group. One of our concerns was whether the members of the laboratory are aware of how the lab activity is funded. We felt that awareness of funding was a key indicator of full membership in a research group – of sufficient status in the group to have some real control over the future. Given the overwhelming importance of funding to contemporary research, between forty and fifty percent of research time is devoted to grant administration, including the writing of additional grant applications. The survey had shown that only about one-quarter of respondents knew about the structure of laboratory funding. In follow-up interviews with graduate students working on projects associated with the Intel grant, all expressed a combination of enthusiasm for the research and uncertainty about their own future in relation to it. High-quality performance would help keep them employed in one lab or another, but did not for any of this small sample lead to direct control over their careers.[17]

Open innovation has a clear implication for knowledge workers. They are not more valuable to a company just because they work for that company. Intel might find a graduate group at a university that does something that is relevant to a product development project and replace their own group that was doing that work before. Since profitable knowledge can come from anywhere at any time, management has no incentive to be loyal to its brainworkers as opposed to the brainworkers at a start-up or government lab or competitor who have just done something interesting. Any individual or group of employees, even if their work is excellent, will be evaluated in some version of KM terms: can they be automated, outsourced with cheaper workers, or turned into sources of proprietary knowledge? Only the latter group will be supported and protected; the rest will often be retained, but with the kind of second-tier pay, resources, and working conditions that have become normal in the university world. Open innovation logically tries to keep the vast majority of its knowledge workers as liquid as possible. This means retaining the absolute loyalty only of that minority of employees who produce proprietary knowledge, while minimising commitments to the rest.

Management through inequality

Like other theorists of cognitive capitalism, André Gorz anticipated the rise of political tensions between knowledge workers and knowledge managers. Gorz wrote:

> Le conflit qui se développe et s'exacerbe entre le capital immatériel des firmes et les acteurs de cette résistance est, à bien des égards, une lutte des classes déplacée sur un nouveau terrain: celui du contrôle du domaine public, de la culture commune et des biens collectifs. (Gorz 2003, 70)

There is indeed a conflict between the modes in which knowledge is produced and owned within cognitive capitalism. But this does not translate into a political conflict of the kind Gorz calls class war. Analysts often suggest that two general phenomena can undermine a productive contradiction like that of cognitive capitalism. The first is *immiseration*, in which bad conditions force a revolt. The second is *inefficiency*, in which elites tire of wasting money controlling people and not getting that last 20% out of knowledge workers made sullen by mediocre treatment. Neither of these function in the case of knowledge economies, where the knowledge worker masses are still middle class on a world scale, and where a sense of professional duty produces good enough efficiency in nearly all cases (and threats of layoffs and closure where it does not).

If we use a harsher language than is ever tolerated in US discussions, we can see within the Bush and the Obama Administrations the shadow of the ancient regime, signs of a sun king return of the Three Estates (for examples of this ideology as it bears on US executives, see Newfield 2007).

First Estate: international-level political and corporate executives enjoy a very limited accountability to the national population at large. This power rests largely on concentrations of wealth that have both intensified over the past several decades, and expanded beyond a tiny group of moguls and great families to include traders, bankers and executives who make tens or even hundreds of millions of dollars per year. Its lower reaches begin with the top 0.1% of US earners, with incomes above $1,600,000 in 2007, is better represented by 'the almost 15,000 families with incomes of $9.5 million or more a year' (Uchitelle 2007b)[18] and is skewed toward global corporations and the financial sector.[18] Its colleges are largely 'Ivy League Plus' – Harvard, Yale et al., plus Stanford, MIT, perhaps Duke, and just a few others, all private.

Second Estate: this is the enabling high-tech clergy, and it provides the highly developed legal, managerial and financial skills that enable successful business and investment in highly profitable, largely oligarchic sectors such as information technology, communications, banking, and pharmaceuticals. Medical and engineering knowledge are also important, though more indirectly. Their incomes place them in the top 1% (starting at $350,000 a year in 2007) (Ip 2009). They speak technical languages of law, management and finance that are largely indecipherable even to highly educated non-specialists, and maintain an invisible empire of ownership structures and lucrative transactions whose existence makes itself known only through occasional disasters like the 2008 financial meltdown.

Third Estate: the new Third Estate is characterised by the increasing insecurity and political helplessness of the top as well as the bottom of the rest of the population (for the UK variant on the inequality boom, see Joseph Roundtree Foundation 2007). Nearly 80% of US society has not had a raise in inflation-adjusted dollars since the 1970s, and their share of both net worth and financial wealth in the US has steadily declined (Domhoff 2009). The 19% that follows the top 1% has done the best in this group, but it too has largely seen its stable pension plans converted into mutual funds that lost a quarter of their value in the fall of 2008, has seen its health care costs mushroom, and has seen its ranks thinned through waves of mass layoffs over the past 20 years (for an accessible overview of the fate of working America, see Greenhouse 2008). Its children are taking on increasing debt to go to college in order to obtain an increasingly shaky claim on stability and affluence.[19] This estate includes blue-collar workers in construction, agriculture and hospitality, but also the vast majority of brainworkers whose jobs require college degrees, additional specialised knowledge and complicated experiential 'know-how' – nurses, social workers, accountants, urban planners, architects and college professors with doctorates in anthropology or the history of art. Though the top of this estate enjoys vastly better life chances than the bottom – I do not at all want to minimise the difference between life at the 10% income level and life at the 90% – working conditions for all of this majority group are less secure than they were 20 years ago, its productivity is less appreciated and its own condition significantly less upwardly mobile (Sawhill and Morton 2007). In knowledge companies and universities alike, a growing majority is unlikely to enjoy security, regular wage increases, or respect for its labour and output. It lacks the financial independence – even the basic sense that if fired there will be another job.

The analogy with France's pre-revolutionary estates is obviously inexact, but its type of social stratification is both intensifying and hardening in most wealthy nations. It represents a near total defeat of golden-age visions of majoritarian rule, mass prosperity, general equality and the cultural progress made possible by the reduction of scarcity. Scarcity is back, for all but that top 1% whose accumulations of lunatic, utterly unspendable amounts of personal wealth are themselves a tribute to the fear of scarcity – of life as it is lived by even the best educated little people in the increasingly defenseless world that these elites have helped create. What Barbara Ehrenreich called the middle class's 'fear of falling' now defines the life of the vast majority of knowledge workers. Knowledge management is there to draw a line around them, and between the second and third estates – between the proprietary knowledge creators, who enjoy the remnants of golden-age security, and those who are merely very well educated, highly trained, very overworked, and who do excellent labour whose effects cannot be captured by the firm but that spill over to less visible members of society, like students, or to society at large.

To conclude with only the briefest gesture towards next steps, we should imagine a two-track strategy. The first is the exposure of the leveraging and the hidden subsidies through which the Third Estate and its institutions support the other two – in many cases, the ways by which public universities support private industry, to their increasing detriment. This kind of budgetary transparency is essential for improving the quality and the equity of budgetary decisions.

And yet unless it is handled carefully, it will create an internal civil war within research universities, where wealthier and better-connected disciplines will not want to give up advantages in an economic downturn when they, too, like all competitive knowledge workers, have worked far harder than they imagined they would in order to get where they are.

The second strategy is to re-imagine and articulate the broad social and cultural missions that will flow from the other nine-tenths of knowledge workers, the non-technical brainworkers (in the traditional sense) whose ideas about diversity, equality, justice, technology for use, sustainable development and so many other issues are essential to the *indirect* modes through which knowledge and education create social value beyond that which economics can easily measure. The university is the obvious place for this re-articulation to begin, and it needs to assume a post-Kantian parity of the faculties that will allow the knowledge lost via the subordination of non-proprietary knowledge workers to make itself felt again.

Acknowledgement

Research for this paper was partially funded by US National Science Foundation Cooperative Agreement SES 05-31184.

Notes

1. For an extended discussion of the culture wars and budget wars on the American university, see my *Unmaking the public university: The forty-year assault on the middle class* (2008), especially Parts 1 and 2.
2. For the history of this now-mainstream corporate strategy, see Uchitelle (2007a).
3. For discussion of these issues as they bear on budget analyses of the crisis of the country's leading public university system, the University of California, see Newfield (2009a, 2009b). See also the statement made by Jane Wellman, Executive Director of the Delta Cost Project, in Congressional testimony (2007).
4. See Negri and Vercellone (2008, 41; an earlier example: 'La valeur d'échange de la connaissance est donc entièrement liée à la capacité pratique de limiter sa diffusion libre, c'est-à-dire de limiter avec des moyens juridiques (brevets, droits d'auteur, licences contrats) ou monopolistes, la possibilité de copier, d'imiter, de "réinventer, d'apprendre des connaissances des autres"'. See also Rullani (2000).
5. 'L'impression qui se dégage de tout cela, c'est que dans et sous le capitalisme une économie différente se forme qui est forcée par des artifices à fonctionner comme la continuation du capitalisme, sans que ses lois de fonctionnement propres soient élucidées ni compatibles avec celles du capitalisme. Si, comme vous le suggérez parfois, le capitalisme cognitif est la solution que cherche le capitalisme industriel à sa crise de suraccumulation, cette solution me semble créer plus de problèmes qu'elle n'en résout, tout en les masquant temporairement. Envisager les choses sous l'angle de la régulation nous détourne, à mon avis, du problème de fond, qui est l'incompatibilité entre l'économie capitaliste et l'économie de la connaissance. Celle-ci demande à être une économie de l'abondance, du partage, de la mise en commun de l'auto-organisation omnilatérale par concertation permanente, car c'est ainsi qu'elle est la plus féconde. Le capitalisme cherche à se l'incorporer en rendant rare ce qui est abondant et privé ce qui est public, rentable ce qui est gratuit' (Gorz 2004).
6. For a contextual argument that situates Drucker's work on the corporation as oppositional to the Keynesianism with which Galbraith sympathised, see Gilman (2006).
7. The case, originally filed in 1996, was Vizcaino v. Microsoft, US Court of Appeals for the Ninth Circuit (1999), http://www.techlawjournal.com/courts/vizcaino/19990512.htm. Microsoft settled out of court with a payment of $96 million to the permatemp plaintiffs.
8. See, for example, *TechCruch Layoff Tracker*, http://www.techcrunch.com/layoffs/.
9. For a clear inverse correlation between the size of the information technology occupation and its wages (the bigger the field, the lower the wage), see US Bureau of Labor Statistics (2007, Figure 1).
10. For example, see the summary table for an October 2007 report by the American Association of University Professors (American Association of University Professors 2007).
11. For a brief summary see Van der Werf (2007, A13). See also Bianco (2007).
12. Calculation based on author's data and data from 'Education at a glance 2009: OECD indicators' (OECD 2009).
13. The IP executive Phelps is more forthcoming about his intentions than are most of the open innovation theorists. Discussing 'inclusivity value', he says, 'Collaboration is not merely a public relations function. It enables a company to more broadly and rapidly disseminate its technologies and products into the market through the cooperative efforts of others. It provides the framework for pursuing joint product development work with other companies that can lead to greater success in the marketplace. It can facilitate entry into new markets, broaden freedom of action within a market … and provide access to needed outside technologies' (loc 586).

14. Chesbrough writes: 'Intel's approach to managing innovation has a number of obvious strengths. It is efficient, because it launches few blue-sky investigations that might lead to dead ends. The approach is also efficient because it reinvents fewer wheels, instead building on the research discoveries of others (particularly university researchers) and transferring those discoveries into the company's own development process. Intel's approach to innovation saves money as well, because Intel leverages the facilities and personnel of other institutions. Although the company often pays to fund external research projects, these grants likely do not cover the full cost of the researchers, facilities, and other overhead expenses' (Chesbrough 2006, 124).
15. A brief introduction to this Intel 'platform research' can be found at http://techresearch.intel.com/articles/Tera-Scale/1448.htm.
16. The survey data is discussed in Newfield et al. (under review). Interviews conducted by author, UC Santa Barbara, July 2008.
17. Uchitelle relies on the research of Thomas Piketty and Emmanuel Saez.
18. See Piketty and Saez (2006). One study by University of Chicago academics Steven Kaplan and Joshua Rauh concludes that in 2004 there were more than twice as many such Wall Street professionals in the top 0.5% of all earners as there were executives from non-financial companies. Mr Rauh said: 'It's hard to escape the notion' that the rising share of income going to the very richest is, in part, 'a Wall Street, financial industry-based story'. The study shows that the highest-earning hedge-fund manager earned double in 2005 what the top earner made in 2003, and the top 25 hedge-fund managers earned more in 2004 than the chief executives of all the companies in the Standard and Poor's 500-stock index, combined. It also shows profits per equity partner at the top 100 law firms doubling between 1994 and 2004, to over $1 million in 2004 dollars.
19. For example, US federal student debt increased 25% in just one year, from 2007–2008 to 2008–2009; see Chaker 2009.

References

Adams, J. 2009. Is the US losing its preeminence in higher education? National Bureau of Economic Research working paper 15233. http://www.nber.org/papers/w15233.

American Association of University Professors. 2007. October report. http://www.aaup.org/NR/rdonlyres/9218E731-A68E-4E98-A378-12251FFD3802/0/Facstatustrend7505.pdf.

Bianco, A. 2007. The dangerous wealth of the Ivy League. *Business Week*. http://www.businessweek.com/magazine/content/07_50/b4062038784589.htm.

Bureau of Labour Statistics. 2007. Chart book: Occupational employment and wages. http://www.bls.gov/oes/2007/may/figure44.pdf.

Chaker, A.M. 2009. Students borrow more than ever for college. *Wall Street Journal Online*. http://online.wsj.com/article/SB10001424052970204731804574388682129316614.html?mod=rss_com_mostcommentart.

Charle, C., and C. Soulié. 2007. *Les ravagtes de la 'modernisation' universitaire en Europe*. Paris: Éditions Syllepse.

Chesbrough, H. 2006. *Open innovation: The new imperative for creating and profiting from technology*. Boston, MA: Harvard Business School Press.

College Board. 2008. Winning the skills race and strengthening America's middle class: An action agenda for community colleges. http://www.collegeboard.com/prod_downloads/prof/community/winning_the_skills_race.pdf.

Cottet, D., J.B. Zubiri-Rey, and P. Sauvel. 2009. L'émergence du *cognitariat* face aux réformes universitaires en France. *Multitudes* 39: 56–65.

Domhoff, G.W. 2009. Wealth, income, and power. http://sociology.ucsc.edu/whorulesamerica/power/wealth.html.

Drucker, P. 1993. *Post-capitalist society*. New York: Basic Books.

Ehrenreich, Barbara, and John Ehrenreich. 1979. *Between labor and capital: The professional-managerial class*. Boston, MA: South End Press.

Florida, Richard L. 2002. *The rise of the creative class: And how it's transforming work, leisure, community and everyday life*. New York: Basic Books.

Galbraith, John K. 1967. *The new industrial state*. Boston, MA: Houghton Mifflin.

Gilman, N. 2006. The prophet of Post-Fordism: Peter Drucker and the legitimation of the corporation. In *American capitalism: Social thought and political economy in the twentieth century*, ed. N. Lichtenstein, 109–32. Philadelphia, PA: University of Pennsylvania Press.

Goldin, C., and L.F. Katz. 2008. *The race between education and technology*. Cambridge, MA: Belknap Press.

Gorz, A. 2003. *L'immatériel: Connaissance, valeur et capital*. Paris: Galilée.

Gorz, A. 2004. Économie de la connaissance, exploitation des saviors. *Multitudes* 15. http://multitudes.samizdat.net/Economie-de-la-connaissance.

Greenhouse, S. 2008. *The big squeeze: Tough times for the American worker*. New York: Knopf.

Greenwald, G. 2009. The underlying divisions in the healthcare debate. *Salon,* December 19. http://www.salon.com/opinion/greenwald/2009/12/18/corporatism/index.html.

Hartmann, E. 2009. The external quality assurance of higher education institutions: Towards a new strategy of the transationalisation of the state? Paper given at the FOREDUC conference, December, in Paris.

Ip, G. 2009. Income inequality gap widens. *Wall Street Journal,* October 12. http://online.wsj.com/public/article_print/SB119215822413557069.html.

Joseph Roundtree Foundation. 2007. New poverty and wealth maps of Britain reveal inequality to be at 40-year high. http://www.jrf.org.uk/media-centre/new-poverty-and-wealth-maps-britain-reveal-inequality-be-40-year-high.

Kerr, Clark. 1963. *The uses of the university. The Godkin lectures at Harvard University, 1963*. Cambridge, MA: Harvard University Press.

Mann, A., and T. Nunes. 2009. After the dot-com bubble: Silicon valley high-tech employment and wages in 2001 and 2008. *Bureau of Labour Statistics*. http://www.bls.gov/opub/regional_reports/200908_silicon_valley_high_tech.htm.

Munk, N. 1998. The new organization man. *Fortune* 137, no. 5: 62–6, 68, 72, 74.

National Academies. 2007. Rising above the gathering storm: Energizing and employing America for a brighter economic future. http://www.nap.edu/catalog.php?record_id=11463.

National Center for Education Statistics. 2008. Digest of education statistics. http://nces.ed.gov/programs/digest/d08/tables/dt08_186.asp.

National Science Foundation. 2006a. Science and engineering indicators. http://www.nsf.gov/statistics/seind06/c5/c5h.htm#c5hl2.

National Science Foundation. 2006b. Outputs of S&E research: Articles and patents. http://www.nsf.gov/statistics/seind06/c5/c5h.htm#c5hl3.

Negri, T., and C. Vercellone. 2008. Le rapport capital/travail dans le capitalisme cognitif. *Multitudes* 32. http://multitudes.samizdat.net/Multitudes-32-Spring-2008.

Newfield, C. 2007. Bastille conditions 1: American royalism. Middle class death trips. http://toodumbtolive.blogspot.com/2007/07/bastille-conditions-1-american-royalism.html.

Newfield, C. 2008. *Unmaking the public university: The forty-year assault on the middle class*. Cambridge, MA: Harvard University Press.

Newfield, C. 2009a. Regents commission's first speaker: Overview of the delta project. Remaking the university. http://utotherescue.blogspot.com/2009/09/regents-commissions-first-speaker.html.

Newfield, C. 2009b. Notes on the UC commission's first meeting. http://utotherescue.blogspot.com/2009/09/notes-on-uc-commissions-first-meeting.html.

Newfield, C. 2009c. Saving public higher ed: Cheaper than Christmas shopping. Remaking the University. http://utotherescue.blogspot.com/2009/12/saving-public-higher-ed-cheaper-than.html.

Newfield, C., K. Alimahomed, J. Macala, and K. Stoltzfus. Under review. Is nanotechnology changing scientific collaboration? Survey evidence from a nano-oriented campus.

Organisation for Economic Co-operation and Development (OECD). 2009. Education at a glance 2009: OECD indicators. http://www.oecd.org/document/24/0,3343,en_2649_39263238_43586328_1_1_1_37455,00.html.

Phelps, M., and D. Kline. 2009. *Burning the ships: Intellectual property and the transformation of Microsoft*. Hoboken, NJ: Wiley Publishers.

Piketty, T., and E. Saez. 2006. The evolution of top incomes: A historical and international perspective. Working paper. http://elsa.berkeley.edu/~saez/piketty-saezAEAPP06.pdf.

Poulantzas, N. 1976. The capitalist state: A reply to Millibrand and Laclau. *New Left Review* 95, January/February: 71–2.

Reich, Robert B. 1991. *The work of nations: Preparing ourselves for 21st-century capitalism.* New York: A.A. Knopf.

Rullani, E. 2000. Le capitalisme cognifit: Du déjà vue? *Multitudes* 2: 87–94.

Sawhill, I., and J.E. Morton. 2007. Economic mobility: Is the American dream alive and well? Pew charitable trusts. http://www.economicmobility.org/reports_and_research/?id=0001.

Stewart, Thomas A. 1997. *Intellectual capital: The new wealth of organizations.* New York: Doubleday/Currency.

Uchitelle, L. 2007a. *The disposable American: Layoffs and their consequences.* New York: Vintage.

Uchitelle, L. 2007b. The richest of the rich, proud of a new gilded age. *New York Times.* http://www.nytimes.com/2007/07/15/business/15gilded.html?ex=1342238400&en=96cb7bacf64440e&ei=5124&partner=permalink&exprod=permalink.

US Bureau of Labor Statistics. 2007. Chart book: Occupational employment and wages, May 2007. http://www.bls.gov/oes/2007/may/figure1.pdf.

Van der Werf, M. 2007. Rankings methodology hurts public institutions. *Chronicle of Higher Education* 58, no. 38: A13.

Wellman, J. 2007. College cost hearing: Jane Wellman. http://www.youtube.com/watch?v=lb4DZ0zlNVw.

Corporatisation, competitiveness, commercialisation: new logics in the globalising of UK higher education

Susan L. Robertson

Centre for Globalisation, Education and Societies, University of Bristol, Bristol, UK

> This paper examines the changing form and scope of higher education in the UK with a specific focus on contemporary 'globalising' developments within the sector and beyond. Situated within an analysis of transformations under way in the wider global and regional economy, and drawing on Jessop's strategic relational approach (SRA), I examine the way higher education in the UK has been restructured through the mobilisation of three key logics (corporatisation, competititiveness, commercialisation) to play a central role in the realisation of a globally-competitive education services sector and imagined 'knowledge-based economy'. The main argument of this paper is that from the early 1980s onward, successive rounds of neo-liberal political projects – shaped by these logics – were mobilised to rework the basis of capital accumulation. A central outcome was to structurally predispose UK HEIs, over time, toward new regionalising and globalising horizons of action.

Introduction

This paper examines the changing form and scope of higher education (HE) in the UK – with a specific focus on contemporary 'globalising' developments within the sector. In order to show why, how and with what consequences HE in the UK is being globalised, I look at the crucial turning point for western capitalist economies; the collapse of the Fordist settlement by the late 1960s and its role in post-war 'nation-building'; the search for a new solution to the problem of ongoing capital accumulation – including the contribution of higher education to this; the opening up of economies around the globe as a result of decisive neo-liberal interventions, including New Public Management's emphasis on corporatisation that reworked the boundaries around the higher education–state–economy–civil society relation; the advance of labour flexibility and 'competitiveness' as a rationale for this ongoing transformation; and the suturing of competitiveness and commercialisation into these social relations through the emergence of a new economic imaginary – the development of a knowledge-based economy. I will be arguing that this ongoing reorganisation has structurally and strategically transformed the sector, and its insertion into and alignment with the economy continues to be regarded as *key* to the development of a competitive nation. Indeed, as the government currently responds to the financial crisis and recession, HE policy in the UK is reinforcing this model of corporatisation–competitiveness–commercialisation, rather than its questioning (Mendelson 2009; BIS 2009). The paper begins by outlining the main theoretical anchor shaping my analysis before turning to the substantive arguments.

Analysing the globalisation of higher education – an approach

Contemporary studies of UK higher education by HE researchers tend to focus upon organisations and their transformation as a result of the implementation of New Public Management (Hood 1991). Such approaches, whilst important and useful, are not particularly helpful in understanding how these social processes are tied to changes in the nature of contemporary capitalism and changing national and world orders. When higher education studies do focus on the global, there is a tendency to privilege phenomena and outcomes that are the self-evidently 'out-there' global rather than the many ways in which the global is *also* transforming the 'in-here' within national territories. As Sassen observes, entry into global space 'is predicated on – and in turn further strengthens – particular forms of denationalisation'. And as she shows, both processes, 'the self-evidently global and denationalising dynamics destabilise existing meanings and systems' (Sassen 2006, 2). What is crucial, therefore, is that analyses take a relational view of 'horizons of action' to reveal the (uneven) inward and outward flows of projects and programmes, and their institutional materialisation, which in turn transforms the higher education landscape.

One response to the theoretical and empirical challenges posed by a relational view of globalisation is to draw upon a 'critical theory' (see Cox 1996) and strategic relational approach (SRA) (Jessop 2002, 2005) to examine UK higher education. Critical theory orients our analysis through its insistence that to understand projects, power and change, we need to place the objects for analysis within accounts of transformations and struggles taking place at multiple scales in the wider cultural political economy.

The question, however, of how particular kinds of social structures and social relations emerge requires more than the insistence that ideas, structures and material capabilities matter. We also need a theory of social change. This means making clear the relationship between actors and society, and thus between agency and the structure.

Jessop's SRA is particularly useful for this purpose. He highlights the co-constitution of subjects and objects, is concerned with the structural properties and dynamics that result from material interactions, is attentive to the 'ecological dominance' of capitalism whilst at the same time highlighting the contingent and tendential nature of structural constraints, and gives an important role to the cultural dimensions of social life (reflexivity, semiosis).

A key move in SRA is Jessop's innovative approach to *structure and agency*, as *selectively and strategically formed*. In his words:

> ... structures are thereby treated analytically as strategically selective in their form, content and operation; and actions are likewise treated as structurally constrained, more or less context sensitive, and structuring. To treat structures as *strategically selective* involves examining how a given structure may privilege some actors, some identities, some strategies, some spatial and temporal horizons, some actions over others. Likewise, to treat actions as *structurally constrained* requires exploring the ways, if any, in which actors (individual and/or collective) take account of this different privileging through strategic context analysis when undertaking a course of action. ... In short, the SRA is

concerned with the relations between structurally inscribed strategic selectivities and (differentially reflexive) structurally-oriented strategic calculation. (Jessop 2005, 48)

Second, particular importance is given to structures and actors having distinctive *spatio-temporal selectivities*. For example, the state's neo-liberal policies in higher education have enabled the advance of particular actors in the sector; those who can mobilise social, political and economic resources enabling them to strategically and selectively act *beyond* (e.g., non-protectionists, globalising universities setting up branch campuses) and *below* (e.g., regional development agencies) those boundaries which had defined the national state's historic governance of higher education in the post-war period.

Third, Jessop emphasises the *relational* dimension of structure and strategy. That is, particular structures have meaning *in relation to* specific agents in particular contexts or 'fields' pursuing specific strategies. For instance, the importance of the state's policy on increases in university fees has particular meanings to those families seeking to access higher education, each with differential access to resources, calculations around risk, and so on.

Finally, Jessop pays particular attention to the *semiotic* in social action, and the constitutive role of 'imaginaries' in economic and political life, such as ways of thinking about and representing societies, their economies and polities, as in the 'green-economy', 'knowledge-based economy', 'learning society', and so on. He argues:

> Imagined economies are discursively constituted and materially reproduced on many sites and scales, in different spatio-temporal contexts, and over various spatio-temporal horizons. They extend from one-off transactions through stable economic organizations, networks, and clusters to 'macro-economic' regimes. (Jessop 2004, 4)

However, complex stable social orders are difficult to reproduce over the long term, not only because capitalism itself is crisis prone, but because societies are never able to perfectly reproduce themselves. In other words, social systems are characterised by contingency and variety, repetition and routine.

The state plays an important part in trying to manage crises in social formations. Ruptures in the economy, the advance of new political projects, the emergence of new social projects, and so on, break existing path dependencies and power relations, and open up spaces for contestation and new alternatives. As we shall see in this paper, from the 1980s onward in the UK, higher education faced successive waves of policies that structurally and selectively altered the patterning of the higher education sector. In sum, Jessop's strategic relational approach helps us 'see' higher education in the UK at any moment as the outcome of a particular patterning of strategically-selected social relations constituted through economic and political imaginaries, with actors having differential capacities to strategically engage in, and re-organise, structures and strategies over different spatio-temporal horizons.

The strategic selectivities of New Public Management

In order to understand the changing relation between higher education, the state and the economy, we need to look back briefly to the crucial turning point for economies around the world; the late 1960s, the crisis of capitalism, and the collapse of the post-war Keynesian Welfare National State settlement (Peck and Yeung 2003; Jessop

2000). This crisis opened the space for the emergence of those social forces – in particular neo-liberals – who had advanced a critique of Keynesianism. These were voices silenced in the post-war settlement characterised by a strong national state, redistribution, and a negotiated settlement with the labour movements. Neo-liberals attacked the state as over-centralised, inefficient, ineffective, and over-bureaucratised. Crucial also was the search for a new economic development model for the west; one that might underpin a new long wave of accumulation (Harvey 2005). While free market ideologies might result in the creation of new markets, the west also faced a declining share in the production of goods following the spectacular success of the Asian Tiger economies. They began to turn to the services sectors, the high-value-added end of value creation, and to how to create new niche markets along the value chain, as the basis for value creation.

Within higher education in the UK in the 1980s, as with other public service sectors, it unleashed the beginnings of a revolution that strategically set into place new structural selectivities (Marginson and Considine 2000, 3). A key instrument in Thatcher's political project was the reinvention of government and its institutions guided by what Hood (1991) called New Public Management (NPM). HEIs were accused of harbouring 'dead wood', lacking in public accountability, and 'managerial weaknesses' (Land 2006, 106). This 'discourse of derision' (Ball 1990) culminated in the Jarratt Report (1985) which recommended reforming the institutional and financial management of higher education institutions, along the lines of the corporate sector (Silver 2003, 227). HEIs were charged with having to generate greater operating efficiencies, be more accountable, significantly expand student numbers, ensure quality, and subordinate their disciplinary (or 'tribal') interests to the overall health of the university. The first Research Assessment Exercise (RAE), introduced in 1986, placed institutions in competition with each other for 'research active' academic labour, and for a place in national league tables. However as Silver notes:

> ... the system, as it took shape, did not eliminate institutional autonomy or diversity. It directed, and in many respects seriously diminished, the former, but in the latter case it did make serious inroads into the pattern of diversity without basically undermining the diversity based on historical characteristics. (Silver 2003, 227)

During this period important other changes were under way over the institutional make-up of the sector. Notable was that in 1983, a new 'private' university – the University of Buckingham – was established. This was the first break in the UK with the governance model that had dominated university funding in the post-war period. However, it was not until early 1992, following the Conservative Minister for Education's (Kenneth Baker) decision to double overnight the proportion of young people going to 'university' by re-labeling the former polytechnics, that the overall funding environment for higher education changed in more dramatic ways. Alan Ryan (2005, 93) notes that two pressures followed from this:

> ... one came from the Treasury ... to reduce the unit of resource down to the level that reflected the price at which the cheapest supplier of a course would supply it. The other came from HEIs themselves, which were ready to expand their intakes at a very low cost. The post-1992 universities had done this throughout the 1980s, and over a decade had reduced their funding per student to some 75% of what it had been in 1980. The 'old' universities had contrived to hold the line, and were no worse off at the end of the 1980s than at the beginning. Between 1990 and 2002, however, the combined sector lost 35% of the unit of resource it had enjoyed in 1990.

Growing numbers of enrolled students in universities, along with annual 1% efficiency cuts in real terms imposed by the Conservatives (and continued under Labour who were elected in 1997), resulted in pressure on HEIs to defer programmes, such as building maintenance. Established under the Conservative government in 1996 and delivered under Labour in 1997, the National Committee of Inquiry into Higher Education, chaired by Ron Dearing, was charged with reviewing the state of higher education in the face of a gathering funding crisis and expanding student numbers coming into higher education (from 1 in 17 attending university in the early 1970s to 1 in 3 in the early 1990s). Dearing's Report, *Higher education in the learning society*, was consistent with the key tenets of New Public Management – or 'new managerialism' – with its emphasis on a compliance culture for university staff, national frameworks for degree work and academic standards, and measurable student learning and research outcomes (Trowler 1998, 26). The legitimating discourse was '*access*' and '*lifelong learning*'.

Dearing's greatest break with the past was the establishment of student fees equal to around 25% of the average cost of a degree course, to be paid up-front, and a system of maintenance loans available to students. However, there was no loan to cover the cost of fees. Whilst Dearing was keen that fee income be directed back to universities, Ryan (2005, 91) notes that the Treasury cut funding for HE by almost exactly the sums raised by the tuition fees. Under pressure to find new sources of funds, universities strategically calculated their own futures and the likely moves that would secure this future. For those HEIs willing to chart new waters, this meant looking beyond the borders of the national state to new kinds of activities, including the establishment of branch campuses, franchising programmes, increasing the enrolment of international students, and developing networks and other kinds of alliances that would enhance access to resources.

Competition, the knowledge-driven economy, and commercialisation

The election of New Labour in 1997 marked an important turning point for higher education in the UK, not so much in the overall direction of policy, but in widening, extending and deepening the globalising of the higher education sector. Labour's arrival was accompanied by a powerful new mantra: 'education, education, education'. Its shadow chorus line was 'competition, competition, competition'.

Labour's 'competitiveness' strategy articulated with projects being advanced by a broad array of actors, including domestic economies, key international agencies, and regionalising coalitions. As Cammack remarked, this was a: 'universal project aimed at maximising the level of competitiveness throughout the global capitalist economy ... promoted principally by and through the international organisations' (2009, 3). However, as will become clear in this section, national governments were also active in advancing this new competitiveness project and economic development model.

Within months New Labour had released the White Paper *Our competitive future: Building the knowledge driven economy* (DTI 1998). This agenda for change, to be realised over the next decade, placed *competition* at its heart: 'the sharpest spur to improve productivity and the best guarantee of reward for talent and innovation' (DTI 1998, 8). Universities were now cast as central engines in building this new knowledge driven economy, whilst competition was represented as including new funding streams to promote the commercialisation of university research (ibid., 6) and funds for regional development agencies to promote collaborative strategies building on 'regional know-how' linking universities to their regional economies (ibid., 7).

These initiatives were under-girded by a fundamental commitment to open markets, including the removal of barriers to international trade (ibid., 8), to innovation and entrepreneurship. This agenda was reinforced in a raft of policies that ensued: *The future of higher education* (DfES 2003); the Lambert *Review of business–university collaboration* (2003); the Sainsbury Review of Science and Innovation *The race to the top* (2007); and the Department of Business, Innovation and Skills (BIS) *Higher ambitions* (2009), where it has continued to argue:

> As a developed country we are operating at the knowledge frontier. We no longer have the choice in this globalised world to compete on low wages and low skills. We compete on knowledge – its creation, its acquisition, and its transformation into commercially successful uses. (BIS 2009, 3)

This vision for HE articulated with those unfolding at the level of Europe, and amongst the international agencies. Within Europe this included developments such as: the Bologna Process (1999) (a radical restructuring of the architecture of higher education degrees to enable greater mobility across Europe and the visibility of a European higher education sector to the global market); the launch of the Lisbon Agenda (2000), committed to developing a globally-competitive, knowledge-based economy in Europe; and the creation of the European Research Area (2000). These initiatives were to increase access to HE, enable researcher mobility, increase investment in research and development, and create a visible higher education sector that could also be marketed globally (Robertson 2006, 2009).

Amongst the international agencies, the Organisation for Economic Co-operation and Development (OECD) continued to advance its knowledge-based economy and competitiveness projects, arguing that: 'higher education drives and is driven by globalisation. It trains the highly skilled workers and contributes to the research base and capacity for innovation that determine competitiveness in the knowledge-based global economy' (Vincent-Lancrin and Kärkkäinen 2009, 13). Meanwhile the OECD, World Bank and WTO all argued that trade in education services could be deployed to help low-income countries build their higher education capacities (Robertson, Bonal, and Dale 2002; Robertson 2009). This, of course, meant that the developed economies could see new opportunities for the expansion of higher education markets, aided by a discourse of trade rather than aid. Within the UK, Labour's agenda aligned itself with this emerging set of structures and their strategic and spatio-temporal selectivities oriented to advancing 'a knowledge-based economy'.

Within the UK, transformations of higher education have taken two main forms: teaching/access, and research/innovation. These are both shaped by competitiveness and commercialisation rationales or logics.

In relation to policy directed at *teaching and access*, a higher education (following Dearing) continued to be promoted as a prerequisite and foundation for a knowledge-based economy. The government continued to promote the view that investment in a university education improved an individual's access to the global employment market, and ensured social mobility. In 1997, 921,000 students were enrolled in higher education; by 2009 it was 1.1 million.

To fund this expansion, and faced with budget constraints, universities turned to enrolling foreign fee-paying students, primarily from Asia. This was formalised by the government in a series of policy initiatives: the *Prime Minister's Initiative for*

International Education (PMI1) launched in 1999; a conscious branding effort (Education UK); and a later follow-up *Prime Minister's Initiative for International Education* (PMI2) (2003). The latest OECD (2009, 309) figures show high numbers of full-fee-paying international students in the UK as part of the overall composition of students. In the UK, non-EU international student income now contributes 8% (£1.5 billion) (Universities UK 2008, 2) of overall income (Universities UK 2009, 2), whilst EU student fees contribute 2%. Globally, the expansion in numbers of students enrolled in HE outside of their country of citizenship since 1975 has been phenomenal. The UK (15%) lags only behind Australia (20%) in terms of international student enrolments. The *Atlas of Student Mobility* (2009) reports on the distribution of international students globally. Despite the small percentage of international students in US universities in relation to the total student population enrolled, the US nevertheless has the largest share of international students (20%, though declining). This is followed by the UK (12% and declining), France (8%), Germany (8%), Australia (7%), and China (7%) (increasing by 20% per year, and an increasingly popular destination for US students). What total growth of international students there is in the UK is the result of an overall increase in the number of global international students worldwide (Lasanowski 2009, 10). And while acquisition of English continues to be a major point of attraction to the UK for international students, the drift to teaching English in other countries (Continental Europe, Singapore, Malaysia, Gulf States) is eroding the advantage the UK held in this regard (Lasanowski 2009, 11).

A second round of policy, the Government's PMI2 launched in 2003, sought to turn around the UK's stalling position in share of the higher education market. This five-year strategy, to 'build positive relationships with people around the world, share ideas and knowledge, and further our capacity for innovation and creativity' (British Council 2009), in reality is aimed at increasing the number of international students in the HE sector (100,000 new non-EU students by 2011 in universities [70,000] and further education [30,000]). PMI2 aims to:

(i) promote the benefits of a UK education to international students;
(ii) ensure international students have a positive UK experience;
(iii) help the UK and international education providers to build strategic alliances and partnerships, and demonstrate the value of the UK as a partner in education policy and delivery; and
(iv) diversify and consolidate markets.

The majority of the UK's international students come from a small number of countries. In 1998–1999, five countries provided 36% of all international students. By 2003–2004, this proportion had increased to 47%. China, India and Nigeria now dominate as source countries with significant year on year growth, whilst numbers of students from Malaysia, Japan and Hong Kong have declined. PMI2 is therefore aimed at diversifying the number of priority countries with which the UK HE sector engages. The new official target countries include Australia, Bangladesh, Brazil, Canada, China, Ghana, Hong Kong, India, Japan, Korea, Malaysia, Mexico, Nigeria, Pakistan, Russia, Saudi Arabia, Singapore, Sri Lanka, Taiwan, Thailand, Turkey, United Arab Emirates, USA, and Vietnam.

A further objective in recruiting international students to the UK was to boost the 'talent' available to the labour market following the student's graduation. The rise of China and India, as the new markets, rising superpowers, and the dominant labour-power behind key regional innovations (cf. Silicon Valley, Silicon Bangalore) have attracted policy-makers' attention (Saxenian 2006). India and China have also been singled out for partnership funding by the UK under the PMI2 scheme. The aim of these initiatives is to foster science and technology links between the UK and China; and between the UK and India.

Expanding the offer to fee-paying students was also enabled by the development of branch campuses. Branch campuses refer to 'off-shore' activity where the unit is operated by the source institution (though it can be in a joint venture with a host institution), but where the student is awarded the degree of the source institution. Becker notes that since 2006 there has been a 43% increase in international branch campuses, with more host and source countries involved. The US dominates these developments (Becker lists 78 US universities [48% of total share], compared with 14 for Australia and 13 for the UK – out of a total of 162). The US's share is shaped by its longer experience in establishing branch campuses (since the 1970s), and because 'world class' US universities are targeted (e.g., Carnegie Mellon, Johns Hopkins, Chicago, etc). The number of host countries has also increased since 2006 from 36 to 51 in 2009. Among the host countries, the United Arab Emirates is the leader (Becker 2009, 7) hosting 40 international branch campuses. These initiatives are part of the Arab region's own strategy: to develop a knowledge-based economy, and to be a provider of education services within the Arab region. Second is China with 15 campuses.

The UK is also host to branch campuses – some US-based, established in the 1970s (American Intercontinental University – 1973) and 1980s (Webster University – 1986). In 2005 the University of Chicago Booth School of Business was established in London, followed by Malaysia's Limkokwing University of Creative Technology in 2007 (also in London) offering bachelor and master degrees in communication, management, art, architecture and finance. These initiatives illustrate the complex architecture of the UK HE sector, as it is transformed from within by 'foreign' providers, and as its own institutions stretch out into space, transforming the nature of HE in other national territories. A clear pattern is emerging, worth noting. Where higher education capability is built through the establishment of branch campuses, in select cases these initiatives are then *incorporated into* (cf. Singapore, Malaysia, Hong Kong), or in the Arab region *organised around*, the idea of a 'hub'. Once established and embedded, these hubs act as regional suppliers of education services – in turn generating new spatial scales.

New Labour's HE *research and innovation* policies have sought to draw universities into a relationship with industry to enable the development of a knowledge-driven economy – with ideas, innovation, and entrepreneurship placed centre stage (DTI 1998). The challenge was, and continues to be, how to do this. The idea of the universities' third mission was championed, aided by third stream funding to ensure industry would benefit from the scientific knowledge and expertise of academics. With funding from the Office of Science and Technology (OST), universities were encouraged to launch programmes to hothouse ideas, accelerate business start-ups, and develop entrepreneurs.

To this end, the Higher Education Innovation Fund (HEIF), launched in 2001, was given further direction by the Lambert Review on university–business collaboration in 2003. New rounds of HEIF (HEIF2, HEIF3, HEIF4) were launched in 2003, 2005, and 2008 – the latter following the release of the Sainsbury Review of Science and Innovation – *The race to the top*. For universities, these new funds meant altering internal structures to take in the 'third sector' mission. Divisions were developed and expanded and projects funded concerned with the interface between industry (local and global) and the university.

A key focus in the UK's research endeavour has also been on how to count it as a share of the world research output, and how to determine the underlying basis of what is counted, so as to cast a favourable light on the UK and its 'global' institutions. Feeding into this is the Research Assessment Exercise (RAE) (see Lucas 2006), with the RAE privileging the 'international' in what counts as quality research. The RAE has deepened divisions within and between the different kinds of higher education providers around teaching and research through the establishment of league tables ranking departments and institutions.

Since 2003, global league tables, the Shanghai Jiao Tong and the Times Higher QS, in particular, have provided policy-makers and universities with a language and set of tools to advance the idea of a 'global' university. The Shanghai Jiao Tong privileges a particular form of knowledge production and its circulation: disciplines such as science, mathematics and technology, Nobel Prize holders, the presence of international students, and citations. More aggressive players in the higher education sector in the UK, such as the University of Manchester, set out to recruit Nobel award holders (Joseph Stigliz and Robert Putnam), while others, such as the University of Warwick, have responded in inventive ways, such as setting out to shape global debates, for instance with their Warwick Commissions.

There is considerable concern in Europe over the use of the Shanghai Jiao Tong for it significantly privileges US universities, with only two UK universities in the top 10 (Oxford and Cambridge) in 2008. Nevertheless, governments and individual institutions have used these 'technologies' to advance their own projects and interests: leveraging funding, branding their institutions, departments and star performers, as a means of marketing, recruiting staff and students, disciplining staff, and so on. For instance the UK announced that in 2007–2008 it has a 12% share of scientific citations (BIS 2009).

The global circuit of capital and shifting geo-strategic interests

What are the implications and challenges of these developments for the UK and the HE sector now that it is embedded in the global circuit of capital and shifting geo-strategic interests? Five stand out, which I will comment on briefly: the financial implications for the UK higher education sector with the rise of new sites of regional capability and demographic decline; emerging regional hubs are likely to select high status institutions, and demand high levels of investment in science and technology infrastructures; new challenges to academic autonomy as institutional fabrics stretch out into territories with different political and cultural traditions; new global suppliers of HE challenging the regulations around HE provision and accreditation within the UK; and the risks for some UK HE providers of their dependence on international students.

In relation to *new regional sites of capability*, Malaysia, Singapore and Mainland China, all net importers of education services, have more recently positioned themselves as regional education hubs. There is now clear movement of students from west to east beginning to take place that will have direct and indirect long-term effects on the UK academic, and wider, labour market.

UK HEIs could increase their presence in these regions through branch campuses, though increasingly the Gulf States (following Singapore's example) are seeking *high status universities*. In other words, 'brand' is becoming more and more important, as more universities enter the field. Indicators of brand, such as world global rankings, are likely to play an increasingly important role in the future. Pragmatically, for the UK this means not only understanding the politics of different ranking systems, but ensuring the current financial crisis does not jeopardise its overall performance in the various rankings amid the limits this might place on institutions' strategic intentions globally.

A related issue concerns the costs of establishing infrastructures to deliver more than just cheap business courses abroad. If demands to build knowledge economies materialise in these regions, they will require broader-based knowledge rather than low-risk cheap and quick activity. Indeed Becker notes that, 'international branch campuses can be a potentially dangerous distraction from the core business of the providing institution' (2009, 18), particularly around research. Balancing these demands in an already volatile financial environment will place new pressures on universities.

There continue to be major *establishment, servicing and other political issues* for universities in setting up global initiatives, such as branch campuses. One concerns the question of academic freedom as institutional fabrics of universities stretch out into global space (Olds 2005). For instance, the University of Warwick staff in the UK voted against establishing a branch campus in Singapore, citing 'academic freedom' issues. The plans were abandoned. Similarly, the political and cultural environment in the Gulf States creates issues for universities who depend on their high-profile academic staff to service them but whose staff do not necessarily see themselves as having a long-term commitment in the region (Becker 2009, 16).

Within the UK, new important developments within the UK HE sector are evident, particularly around changes in *state regulations* that have enabled new (for profit) providers to offer accredited courses. In 2007 BPP Holdings plc (BPP), Europe's leading provider of professional education, announced its subsidiary, BPP College of Professional Studies (BPP College), was granted degree-awarding powers by the UK Privy Council. This is the first for-profit private sector company to have been awarded such powers to enter a substantial and profitable market. BPP estimates that the market size for business and law postgraduate degrees is at least £800m per annum. In July 2009, BPP was sold to Apollo Global on the London Stock Exchange. This has stimulated a flurry of interest amongst global firms such as Bridgepoint Education and Kaplan Higher Education International in entering the UK higher education sector and applying for degree awarding powers.

Finally, the UK faces important challenges as a result of its *dependence on global education markets* at a time when there is further pressure to expand market share as a result of dramatic government funding cuts to HE. If we recall that 8% of income to HE comes from non-EU international students, any decline in income from this source, or decline in 'quality' or 'desirability' which would jeopardise student choices, would have major effects on those universities highly dependent on these global markets. Reporting on data collected in 2004, Sastry (2006) notes three institutions gained significantly more than 18% of their overall revenues from non-EU international students – London School of Economics (LSE) (33.5%); London Business School (LBS) (19.3%); and the School for Oriental and African Studies (SOAS) (31.9%). After this top three, 17 other institutions received between 17.8% (Essex) and 12.7% (Portsmouth) from international students. While the top exporting institutions, like SOAS (13%) and the LSE (11%), have a more diverse portfolio of nationalities in their international students, universities like Luton, Herfordshire and Portsmouth have international student populations that are 45% Chinese.

What stands out in all this is how poor the information is on the UK higher education sector, despite its significance for understanding the direction of the sector. By way of contrast, countries like Australia collect significant amounts of data on developments within the HE to understand implications for the sector. The combination of the UK's historic imperial positioning (and as therefore the 'natural' provider of the best 'quality' graduate education), when coupled with the fracturing and fragmentation of the HE sector as a result of NPM, means the institutional structures to manage and regulate the global education market in the UK have remained relatively underdeveloped. The recent appointment in 2009 of an International Education Research Advisory Forum, chaired by the Minister for State of Higher Education, suggests that it is now recognised matters cannot stay as they are.

Final remarks: recession and the intensification of commercialisation

On 8 June 2009, following a Ministerial reshuffle, the Department for Universities, Innovation and Skills (DIUS) was closed, replaced by the Department for Business, Innovation and Skills (BIS). Universities are now located within BIS – so that reference to university knowledge is only by way of business, innovation and skill. This highly symbolic omission signals an important new chapter in HE in the UK.

By November 2009 BIS had released a series of policy frameworks for the higher and further education sectors. *Higher ambitions: The future of universities in a knowledge economy* leaves us in little doubt as to the role that higher education is expected to play in advancing global competitiveness within a context of constrained public spending. Much continues to be made of the autonomy of universities, of widening participation, driving up excellence, and removing 'artificial caps on talent' in order to realise social justice and social mobility. However, the bottom line is that universities need to contribute *more* to Britain's economic future through commercialising research findings and creating business start-up companies. In the foreword to the report, the then Minister for Business, Innovation and Skills, Peter Mandelson, states:

> This means focusing on the key subjects essential to our economic growth, and boosting the general employability skills expected of all graduates. We will enable universities to compete for funds to provide courses in subjects relevant to Britain's economic future, working in partnerships with business. Institutions unable to meet such strategic needs can expect to see their funding reduced to provide resources for those who can. (Mendelson 2009, 4)

Strong words indeed that sit uneasily with the Minister's insistence that university autonomy will be maintained and fostered! This is clearly a point of tension between government and academics. Statements like those above can be read as the government flexing its muscles in anticipation of academic resistance to even further instrumentalisation.

Whatever the forms of resistance which do emerge, these struggles will take place on a new terrain; one that has emerged from the transformation of the sector and the strategic calculations of actors. At the heart of this new order is a globally-competitive university, seen to be the engine for, and at the service of, a knowledge-based service economy. This, in turn, embeds HE in the UK more deeply into the global economy, including its ruptures and ongoing contradictions.

One question at this point is the social and economic consequences for national economies of a globally-competitive, globally-mobile, higher education services sector? Does a globalised higher education sector, as has now emerged in the UK, risk directly contributing to, and being entangled within, the kinds of 'melt-down' we have witnessed in the finance sector over 2008–2009, and more recently in economies such as Dubai, one of the favoured sites for developing university branch campuses? These are serious questions indeed, demanding urgent public debate.

References

Atlas of Student Mobility. 2009. Global destinations for international students at the post secondary (tertiary) level, 2008. http://www.atlas.iienetwork.org/?p=48027.
Ball, S. 1990. *Politics and policy-making in education:* London/New York: Routledge.
Becker, R. 2009. *International branch campuses: Markets and strategies.* London: OBHE.
British Council. 2009. *The Prime Minister's initiative for international education.* http://www.britishcouncil.org/eumd-pmi2.htm.
Business, Innovation and Skills (BIS). 2009. *Higher ambitions: The future of universities in a knowledge economy.* London: BIS.
Cammack, P. 2009. *All power to global capital, papers in the politics of global competitivism,* No. 10. Manchester: Institute for Global Studies, Manchester Metropolitan University.
Cox, R. 1996. *Approaches to world order.* Cambridge: Cambridge University Press.
Department for Education and Skills (DfES). 2003. *The future of higher education.* London: DfES.
Department for Trade and Industry. 1998. *Our competitive future: Building the knowledge-driven economy.* London: HMSO.
Harvey, D. 2005. *A brief history of neo-liberalism.* Oxford: Oxford University Press.
HM Government. 2009. *New industry, new jobs.* London: HMSO.
Hood, C. 1991. A public management for all seasons? *Public Administration* 69, no. 1: 3–19.
Jarratt Report. 1985. *Report of the Steering Committee for Efficiency Studies in Universities.* London: Committee of Vice-Chancellors and Principals (CVCP).
Jessop, B. 2000. The changing governance of welfare: Recent trends in its primary functions, scale and models of coordination, *Social Policy and Administration* 33, no. 4: 346–59.
Jessop, B. 2002. *The future of the capitalist state.* Cambridge: Polity.
Jessop, B. 2004. Critical semiotic analysis and cultural political economy. *Critical Discourse Studies* 1, no. 2: 159–74.
Jessop, B. 2005. Critical realism and the strategic relational approach. *New Formations* 56, 40–53.
Lambert Review. 2003. *Review of business–university collaboration.* London: HMSO.
Land, R. 2006. Paradigms lost: Academic practice and exteriorising technologies. *E–Learning* 3, no. 1: 100–10.
Lasanowski, V. 2009. *International student mobility: Status report 2009.* London: OBHE.
Lucas, L. 2006. *The research game in academic life.* Basingstoke: Open University Press.
Mandelson, P. 2009. Higher education and modern life. Speech given by the Minister for the Department for Business, Innovation and Skills, July, at Birkbeck University.
Marchak, P. 1991. *The integrated circus: The New Right and the restructuring of global markets.* Montreal: McGill University Press.

Marginson, M., and M. Considine. 2000. *The enterprise university: Power, governance and reinvention in Australia*. Cambridge: Cambridge University Press.

National Committee of Inquiry into Higher Education. 1997. *Higher education in the learning society*. DfEE: London.

Olds, K. 2005. Articulating agendas and traveling principles in the layering of new strands of academic freedom in contemporary Singapore. In *Where translation is a vehicle, imitation its motor, and fashion sits at the wheel: How ideas, objects and practices travel in the global economy*, ed. B. Czarniawska and G. Sevón, 167–89. Malmö: Liber AB.

Organisation for Economic Co-operation and Development (OECD). 2008. *Education at a glance*. Paris: OECD.

Organisation for Economic Co-operation and Development (OECD). 2009. *Education at a glance*. Paris: OECD.

Peck, J., and H. Yeung. 2003. *Remaking the global economy*. London: Sage.

Robertson, S. 2006. The politics of constructing (a competitive) Europe(an) through internationalising higher education: Strategies, structures, subjects. *Perspectives in Education* 24, no. 4: 29–44.

Robertson, S. 2009. Metaphoric imaginings: Re-/visions on the idea of a university. In *Rethinking the university after Bologna*, ed. R. Barnett, J-C Guedon, J. Masschelein, M. Simons, S. Robertson, and N. Standaert, 20–30. Antwerp: Universitair Centrum Sint-Ignatius Antwerpen.

Robertson, S., X. Bonal, and R. Dale. 2002. GATS and the education service industry: The politics of scale and global reterritorialisation. *Comparative Education Review* 46, no. 4: 472–96.

Robertson, S., M. Novelli, R. Dale, L. Tikly, H. Dachi, and N. Alphonce. 2007. *Globalisation, education and development*. London: DfID.

Ryan, A. 2005. New Labour and higher education. *Oxford Review of Education* 31, no. 1: 87–100.

Sainsbury Review of Science and Innovation. 2007. *The race to the top*. London: DIUS.

Sassen, S. 2006. *Territory, authority, rights*. Princeton, NJ: Princeton University Press.

Sastry, T. 2009. *How exposed are English universities to reductions in demand from international students?* Oxford: Higher Education Policy Institute.

Saxenian, A 2006. *The new Argonauts: Regional advantage in a global economy*. Cambridge, MA: Harvard University Press.

Silver, H. 2003. *Higher education and opinion-making in twentieth century England*. London: Routledge.

Universities UK. 2008. *Higher education in facts and figures*. London: Universities UK. http://universitiesuk.ac.uk/Publications/Documents/Facts08.pdf (accessed April 26, 2009).

Universities UK. 2009. *Higher education in facts and figures*. London: Universities UK. http://universitiesuk.ac.uk/Publications/Documents/Facts09.pdf (accessed April 26, 2010).

Vincent-Lancrin, S., and K. Kärkkäinen. 2009. *Higher education to 2030: Globalisation, Vol. 2*. Paris: OECD.

Current internationalisation: the case of France

Annie Vinokur

UMR EconomiX, Université de Paris X, Paris, France

> This paper argues that higher education has a long history of globalising, though the form of these processes has been different. Two are identified; first, a normative order based on common frameworks; second, the expansion of formal exchanges of inputs and outputs from higher education. Different countries, however, are positioned differently in this. Through an analysis of France's higher education sector, the paper argues that unlike most English speaking and South Asian countries in the recent past, France seems much less interested in increasing its share of the international market of HE teaching services than in developing a competitive R-D university–industry sector. This implies the de-construction of the inherited system, and a reallocation of resources toward a new top-tier of public establishments strongly linked with private economic interests. For that purpose a radical reform of the HE sector was needed. To implement such a reform, one that is strongly opposed by a large part of the academic community, the government has relied on the external resources of international norms and rules of governance. In this field, France appears both as a norm-maker and a norm-taker.

Introduction

Knowledge, ideas, students and academics did not wait for the neo-liberal creed and policies to cross national frontiers. Higher learning went global long before capital did. So, at the present time, the 'internationalisation' of a country in the field of higher education (HE) can refer to two different, recent, processes:

- One is the participation of the country in the production/transfer/implementation of policies and norms common to several national higher education systems.
- The other is the expansion of its international formal exchange of the inputs and outputs of HE: information, students, teachers and researchers, patents, royalties, consultant services, offshore branches, joint ventures, contracts, networks, etc.

The two are strongly linked, as the abundant production of new international norms is officially justified by the necessity to construct a world market for HE related services, while their widespread diffusion is backed by the competition between nations to enlarge their share of this 'market'. The architecture of the world's system of higher education is therefore undergoing an unprecedented upheaval, all the more difficult to analyse as the current global recession will certainly have an important impact on its restructuring. So the 'internationalisation' of a country's HE proceeds from its internal and external strategies in this rapidly evolving landscape.

In this turmoil, the case of France appears as a *'cas d'école'*: in 1961, the OECD praised France and the USSR for their public, centrally planned and state financed education systems (OECD 1962), and urged the developing countries to take them as models. Now, after a long resistance to the – opposite – neo-liberal doctrine in education spread by the same OECD since the 1980s, France (along with the Russian Federation) is one of the last countries to join its trans-national fan club. It is therefore a spin-round case of transition.

France started a decade ago a string of reforms of its HE which is not yet achieved as far as its legal framework is concerned, and is only beginning to be fully implemented. It is therefore too early to assess the potential impact of the ongoing reform on its competitiveness.

However, at this stage, we can risk the following thesis:

(a) Unlike most English speaking and South Asian countries in the recent past, France seems much less interested in increasing its share of the international market of HE teaching services than in developing a competitive R-D university–industry sector. This implies the de-construction of the inherited system, and a reallocation of resources toward a new top-tier of public establishments strongly linked with private economic interests.
(b) For that purpose a radical reform of the HE sector was needed. To implement such a reform, strongly opposed by a large part of the academic community, the government needed to rely on the external resources of international norms and rules of governance. In this field, France appears both as a norm-maker and a norm-taker.

France on the international market of HE services

Latecomers in the game, the HE systems of most EU continental members have missed (so far) a step in the short history of the marketisation of HE services: that of international students as commodities. This can be a handicap or an opportunity.

The changing landscape of international HE services

HE has long been part and parcel of imperial and cold war strategies, in order to develop cultural, diplomatic and economic spheres of influence, train the elites of the subordinated countries, drain foreign brains in fields that were in shortage at home, and so on. Those strategies were state led and mostly state financed by the imperial powers, whether through the use of scholarships to attract foreign students or the creation of HE establishments in the beneficiary country.

The beginning of the 1980s was a turning point, when the New Public Management (NPM) strategies advanced by the UK and US governments reduced drastically the public resources allocated to their HE sector (see Robertson, this issue). Forced to look for extra-budgetary funds, and free to do it, the universities raised the students' fees. The result was a shift of internationally mobile students to those universities, from continental Europe, where fees in public universities were nominal. This paradoxical effect can be explained by the fact that the UK and US universities, competing for foreign students, could then provide better working conditions and amenities; but also by the specificity of the demand for HE services: (i) its price elasticity can be positive if the client – in the absence of objective indicators of quality – believes that the more expensive the better; and (ii) it is less a consumer good than an investment, largely driven by the earning prospects, i.e., by the prestige of the university's 'brand' on the labour markets. So the UK and US universities could adopt a price discrimination strategy, foreign students paying a higher price and thus subsidising the domestic students (and sometimes research).

This phase seems to be coming to an end, for reasons beyond the current economic depression: (i) the NPM was adopted by a growing number of countries; (ii) exportation of HE services through the attraction of mobile students proved a welcome bonanza for the balances of payments, so that 'higher education hubs' blossomed, especially in Asia; (iii) the emerging countries resented the brain drain of their outgoing students (Vinokur 2006) and engaged in the construction of their own full-fledged HE systems. Finally, there is the international extension both of the LMD norms and of English as a common teaching language (recommended by the OECD and the consulting agencies as the best means to attract mobile students and retain the domestic students), and the development of the ranking industry. The normalisation of the service moved the competition – dangerously for the providers – from quality to price[1] (Varghese 2008).

Acknowledging the change, the universities and governments of the North switched to the exportation of HE services to immobile foreign students through franchising, joint diplomas, etc. Those, having proven disappointing for both sending and host countries, are giving way now to offshore campuses and foreign-backed institutions. In a radical turn from the imperial and cold war period, the decision power shifts from the exporting to the host countries' governments, which tend to initiate, finance and control the operations, and to contract directly and individually with universities of the North (Soulas 2008). More recently, the global recession has spurred the development of trans-national online provision of HE services.[2]

France on the market of student mobility[3]

France is consistently the third host country (after the US and UK) for international students. Its share was 10% of a 1.5 million worldwide mobility in 1999, and 11% of 1.9 million in 2006, as the relative attraction of the US had fallen in a global market declining since 2004. The proportion of foreign students in France has steadily grown from 7.1% in 1999 to 11.7% in 2006. Except from a recent steep rise of Chinese students and the more modest but steady contributions of Germany and Italy, the 10 top home countries belong to the ex-colonial sphere of influence (mainly the Maghreb); 38% of all African international students choose France.[4]

Eighty per cent of the incoming international students go to university; literature and social sciences coming first, followed by sciences and economics and management. Thirty-six per cent of doctoral students in France are international students. France is, after Spain, the second host country of Erasmus students, and second behind the UK for the inflow of doctoral candidates of EU origin.

On the other side of the mobility scale, in 2006 France ranked sixth in the world for the number of expatriate students, and second in the OECD countries, with about 77,000 students abroad (less than a third of the inward flow). Among them 30% (23,000) are Erasmus. The UK, Belgium, the US and Germany together host 70% of the outgoing flow, but new destinations have recently grown: Scandinavia, Australia and Japan.

So France is well inserted and positioned in terms of overall share in the international movements of students, but in a somehow outdated manner, if considered qualitatively from an economic viewpoint. It has maintained its previous non-commercial policy, devoid of direct economic objectives (but not of economic costs[5]), attracting mainly international students from its traditional sphere of influence and in cultural fields of learning. However it is a privileged destination for researchers of European origins. So, since 2003, new qualitative orientations have been given to this policy, alongside the EU ambition to promote the Union as a 'knowledge economy': (i) to improve the quality of the services offered; (ii) to give precedence to foreign students of graduate level and researchers in science, technology, finance and management; and (iii) to attract brilliant students from scientifically developed countries, emerging regions and eastern Europe. The institution that has been in charge of this policy since 2006 is Campus France (ex EduFrance[6]), a centralised public agency where individual HE establishments have no influence.

There are, in France and in Europe, many voices calling for the competitive use of growing domestic and foreign students' fees by the universities, allowing them – along the lines of the Anglo-Saxon model – to raise their place in the international rankings. Therefore, becoming attractive to the best foreign students and faculty, they could enter the virtuous circle of their progress toward 'world class' standing. However, both past experience and the present situation suggest that this strategy is outdated: (i) competing for paying students has led (in the US for example) to the bubble of student lending and to the spending potlatch of universities on costs unrelated to the quality of teaching, in a negative-sum game; (ii) the growing home supply of capacity in the emerging countries reduces the demand for overseas HE training; (iii) the recession reduces both the revenues of the students and their families, and the anticipated returns on investment in mobility; (iv) the convergence of contents reduces the incentives to move and switches the competition on prices; (v) for the same reason the relatively low cost – but high profit – of cross-border distant education gathers momentum; and (vi) for the northern industries it is now more economical to recruit the specialists they need directly on the global labour market, or to delocalise their activities.

For these reasons, the northern universities – looking for commercial resources – have switched from the attraction of mobile students to a classical industrial strategy; the implementation of offshore branches. The French universities are beginning to follow the movement.

The exportation of French courses and campuses

The French *grandes écoles* of engineering and management have, for some time, developed an export strategy which rests mainly on the internal and cross-border networking of small establishments, collective labelling, and international accreditations. They were helped by the Chambers of Commerce and the Ministry of Foreign Affairs (MAE).[7]

The universities had neither the need, means, nor clearance to do the same. Instead they limited their foreign activities to cooperation agreements in relation with the MAE. With the reform, they now have the licence and the incentive to engage in autonomous ventures, as offshoring is one of their very few openings for extra-budgetary resources. But they do not have the financial means necessary to invest in offshore branches, all the more as the government has largely retired from its previous strong commitment to a cultural and educational foreign policy. So they turn to the option of foreign-backed institutions, avoiding the costly experiments their international competitors have known in previous years.

The market for foreign-backed campuses is in full bloom, as the emerging countries build their own HE systems, and/or invest in HE hubs in order to train their regional flows of mobile students. They therefore want to have strong control over the foreign institutions they invite. The creation of a foreign backed institution is initiated usually by the government of the host country (sometimes by local corporations or foundations). It chooses the university (frequently on the international rankings), and the founder and the university directly negotiate the agreement. Two recent examples in France are:

- *Paris–Sorbonne–Abu Dhabi* (2005). The Emirates assume the full cost (investment, salaries, running costs). It is also said that the partner university of Paris IV-Sorbonne, which provides the curriculum and the teachers, receives annually 15% of the fees and a €1 million royalty for the exclusive use of the brand 'Sorbonne' in the Middle East, as (but at a much higher price) did the 'Louvre' museum (Soulas 2008).
- *Tunis–Dauphine* (in progress). The University of Paris IX-Dauphine is considering forming a corporation (with a third of the shares) with two Tunisian financial firms, with the backing of the Tunisian government.

The relative powers of a government and a university are unequal in such bilateral agreements. It seems that the French government does not presently intend to interfere. But the MAE, which has no control over the establishments and has been informed of some dubious cases of French exportations of HE services, could be put in an awkward situation if called to combine the protection of French interests with the necessity to keep on good relations with foreign governments. So it is now contemplating the creation of a specific accreditation procedure for the exportation of French HE services, on the model of the UK and Australia, but with the difference that the label could entail public financial support.

The French government in the internationalisation of norms and policies

The French higher education system has never known those institutions which, combining teaching and research in all disciplinary fields, answer to the standard definition of a full-fledged university. Neither has it been horizontally stratified.[8] It was instead divided into roughly three vertical compartments:

(1) The *Grandes écoles* or *Ecoles supérieures* is a rather ill-defined sector where the establishments are generally small, selective, non-research, and train the officers of the administrative and industrial armies. In the top public institutions, the students already have the status and remuneration of civil (or military) servants. The others, public or private, free or fee-paying, compete (especially in engineering and commerce) on a market mediated by the frequent rankings. Together they host about one fifth of the students.
(2) The full time research institutions include the CNRS, a large organisation combining all fields of fundamental research, and diverse specialised institutes (nuclear energy, demography, health, agronomy, education, statistics, etc), *ad hoc* government creations (often with a *grande école* attached) each time a specific political, economic or administrative problem arose.

(3) The universities, originally designed mainly for the reproduction of the organised professions (medicine, law) and of the body of teachers in literature and science. After WWII, they were called upon to accommodate, at low cost, the masses of students heading for the rapidly expanding labour market. Open to all holders of a high school *baccalauréat*, they delivered national diplomas (a necessary ingredient of the branch negotiations, at national level, between unions, employers and state). For the past few decades, they have notably increased their research activities, mainly in partnership with the CNRS.

What they had in common (except for the private *grandes écoles*) was that they were state institutions, centrally governed in partnership between the ministries and the representatives of a tenured personnel of civil servants, and fully subsidised by public money. There was no financial and management autonomy at the level of each establishment, but a strong individual and collective academic and scientific autonomy of the professors and researchers.

This 'tangled up Gulliver', as described in the Attali report (Attali 1998), had long been thought to need some reform, in terms of both its architecture and its governance. But vested interests, contradictory objectives and strong resistance held up the process. It was resumed when, in the 1990s, the deregulation of the financial markets forced countries and their immobile factors of production into competition to attract capital funds. As evidenced by the World Competitiveness Reports' criteria, this implies: (i) lower taxes on capital and profits; (ii) the reduction of public social expenditures; (iii) a cost-effective supply of patents, innovations and a surplus of a low-cost, flexible and immediately productive workforce; and (iv) the deregulation of public services to make room for for-profit firms.

This required dismantling the whole fabric of the welfare state '*à la française*', and the dynamiting of both the architecture and the governance of the HE system. Such a radical reform could not be politically thought of in France through the normal legislative procedure, and the subsidiarity principle excluded an appeal to the EU level. A roundabout strategy was therefore adopted, using the international normalisation of HE as an external resource for the internal reform. In the first step – concerning the architecture of the HE system – the French government acted as an exporter of norms; in the following steps – related to the governance of HE – it acted as an importer.

France as a norm-maker

In 1997, Jacques Attali was commissioned by the socialist Minister of Education Claude Allègre to produce a report entitled *For a European model of higher education*. There was little in it about Europe, but much about France. However, it embodied the main ideas expressed in Paris by the European Round Table of Industrialists (ERT) about the knowledge economy:

> Why does Europe get so little 'bang for the research buck'?... It has to do with the fact that Europe spends its money in the wrong way, because it lacks institutions and funding mechanisms which are truly focused on main issues for the future: how to bring multi-disciplinary teams to tackle strategic R-D problems? ... The US research universities ... are private sector organisations, with close ties to business. Corporations are involved in funding, they sit on the universities' boards, they commission consultancy and negotiate research contracts. Since these universities must seek contracts if they are to survive – from governments as well as industry – they breed a competitive spirit ... Academics in

the US research universities tend to work on medium-term contracts, so they have a vested interest not in a rigid disciplinary continuity, but in evolving their interests into successful, contract-generating programmes. (ERT 1985, 12)

So, as the *grandes écoles* were deemed to recruit the best minds and provide the best training, and as the government laboratories and the doctoral departments of the universities had the research resources, the idea was to merge them at the top into a few 'centres of excellence' with close ties to business. They would then fulfil the main objective of the Attali report: to add R-D to the *grandes écoles*. The remainder of the university would remain free and non-selective, keep on delivering national diplomas, but offer the convenience of a supermarket where students, 'using their imagination', could 'follow simultaneously unrelated courses like literature and finance, philosophy and medicine, technology and commerce' (Attali 1998). Along the principle of the European Credit Transfer and Accumulation System (ECTS) (restricted so far to the Erasmus programme), they could capitalise on those units of knowledge anywhere and at any time in their life.

This architecture would leave untouched the vertical split between the *grandes écoles* and the university for the undergraduate students, but add a horizontal – almost watertight – stratification between an HE for the elite, and an HE for the plebeians. So two questions remained: how to harmonise the levels and lengths of HE courses so that, on the one hand, the students of the *grandes écoles* could easily merge with the graduate and postgraduate levels of the new research universities, and on the other, the students of the second class universities could believe that the bridge with the *grandes écoles* was a two-way path? The answer was the two-cycle structure, which was to become the L/MD (3/5-8):

> Such a device will throw bridges between universities and grandes écoles, and allow for the integration of research and innovation in the cursus of the engineers ... Ultimately the cursus and diplomas of all establishments of higher education will become coherent. Each student will be able to switch from one establishment to another and it will be possible to compare them all.[9]

Then, only, comes the international dimension of the project:

> Ideally, France should become a natural part of the academic journey of the most brilliant students from all countries of the world ... To start with, it is necessary to harmonise the cursus of our universities and grandes écoles with those of the other universities of the European Union ... This can be, at the initiative of France, one of the great projects of the Union for the next decade.

This was in line with the idea of a European Education Space, supported by the ERT and the EU Commission, neither of them officially entitled to implement it. So they welcomed the initiative of Claude Allègre, one year after the Attali Report, to convene three of his colleague Ministers of Education (two of them rather reluctantly) in Paris for the Sorbonne Declaration (written by Allegre's cabinet, with excerpts directly borrowed from the Attali report), which started the Bologna Process.

There was, of course, an economic concern behind the initiative. France, as a major 'exporter' of education services, was interested in the construction of this market[10] and in the GATS (1995) negotiations on services. But the standardisation of a product or service is a preliminary condition for its commercialisation, as illustrated by the simultaneous creations of the General Agreement on Tariffs and Trade (GATT) and the International Organisation for Standardisation (ISO) for industrial products at the end of WWII. The standardisation of the length of the courses was the first step needed (Vinokur 2009). The establishment of international commercial norms being a high stakes power game, it is interesting to note the ready adoption by France and Europe of the US norm (undergraduate/postgraduate) in order to compete with the US on their own ground.

The Attali report – which also contained most of the reforms of governance to come – was largely ignored in French academic circles. So the LMD and the ECTS were sold to the French universities as an EU initiative, and on the sole argument that it would facilitate the mobility of students all over Europe. Who could be against student mobility?

France as a norm-taker

French universities, as a whole, embraced enthusiastically the implementation of the LMD, all the more so as they were invited to take this opportunity to freely develop their imagination in the creation of new pluri-disciplinary and professional courses. Then the Ministry would make a discretionary selection among the submissions. This, in an already under-funded university climate, resulted in fierce competition inside and between the universities, weakening the academic solidarities which had previously proved efficient against the centralised management of the HE system. The situation was ripe for the next steps.

In order to solve the dilemma inflicted on public HE systems by the requirements of internationally mobile capital funds (supra), there was in store a ready-made, all-purpose, one-best-way: the doctrine of New Public Management (NPM). It had been experimented with in HE since the 1980s in several countries, so that the literature was overflowing with evaluations, warnings, critics and even obituaries. So, when a unanimous French national assembly joined the club officially with the LOLF[11] in 2001, an American colleague could say that France had jumped onto the last wagon of a derailed train. Why did France and the Federation of Russia embrace NPM uncritically, indeed with an apparently neophyte zeal? Perhaps because some of its tools of *governance* could be used by the central executive powers to impose the politically impossible overhaul of the *structure* of their public services, and in particular their HE system.

In Russia, the 1990s had so starved financially its HE that it was *de facto* privatised. So with the economic rebound and Putin's presidency, it was believed that the government could easily recover its power over the sector and implement its project of stratification: a top tier of would-be world class corporate universities, well subsidised by public funds, with the state standing as a public–private entrepreneur of HE services on the international market; and a lower tier of 'autonomous' establishments, not entitled to state support and therefore invited to live mainly on extra-budgetary resources or close down. However, the opponents of such a scheme have obtained in the Duma that no establishment could have its status changed without the approval of its staff. In France, the ambition to restructure the HE system comes at a time of severe budgetary restrictions and after academic disenchantment over the results of the LMD process. So both governments need to circumvent their domestic oppositions, and have chosen for this purpose to adapt external rules and policies for their own use.

In France, the LOLF (first applied in 2006), which commands the presentation of the budget to the assemblies, aggregates previously dispersed administrative activities in 34 'missions' (research and higher education is one of them); each mission is divided into a number of programmes. Their annual 'performance projects' set the indicators of results, which are then detailed in quantitative terms for each operator. The cost-effectiveness of each programme and mission can be evaluated yearly, and the budget allocated sanctions the results. There was at this stage no opposition to what was presented as a long needed rationalisation of public expenditure, an improvement over the abandoned PPBS[12] methods of planning, a more transparent, accountable and democratic budgetary process. However one of the authors of the Law wrote in the journal of the managers' union: 'it is a revolution in public management as a whole, a radical change as the managers' responsibility does not lay on the obedience to rule and norm, but on the achievement of the expected results' (Leroy 2003, 23).

It was a radical shift from the traditional central management of public services (allocation of funds on objective criteria of needs + bureaucratic control of the procedures + trust) to the NPM (setting of result targets + contractual incentive financing + mistrust). It introduced in the administration the *agency* principle, first developed in corporate governance by the shareholders concentrated in pension funds, then developed at the macro level by international lenders in the treatment of indebted governments (conditionalities), and finally applied to the management of public services everywhere. The *principal*, having no decision power inside the *agent* organisation but a financial lever, sets the objectives, commits an 'independent' agency for the auditing, and sanctions the results through contractual performance financing. This method of control 'at arm's length' is a much more flexible and efficient steering tool than the traditional bureaucratic hierarchical management. As Christopher Hood (2006) once ironically said, it is but Soviet planning plus the contractual financial lever.

However, this tool can also be used by a government to restructure a public sector if the operators are in competition exclusively or mainly for public money. This is not apparently in line with the NPM creed, which, in order both to reduce public expenditure and to force the operators to answer to the needs of all the stakeholders–customers, emphasises opening the public providers to all sources of extra-budgetary funding. In France there is no tradition of foundations or charitable giving in HE, and orders from the firms (research, lifelong learning, and so on) are a marginal source of funds. So if the main concern had been budgetary and market-oriented, the reform would have allowed the universities to increase the students' fees, a major source of funds in the countries in competition with France. The fact that the fees (in fact not fees but a registration tax) are (so far) maintained at a very low level in the universities (around 200 euro per year), giving them no elbow room, can, of course, be explained by the fear of a students' uproar. But it can also be referred to a 'starve the beast' strategy in an already under-funded segment of the sector. Having to compete for rare public funds, the establishments are much more in the hands of the government.

This hypothesis can be backed by the analysis of the objectives stated in the first (2007) university and research performance project, which does not concern the *grandes écoles*, whether public or private. The repeated reference is to the international 'visibility' and 'attractivity' of the French offer of HE services. The main indicators of performance are:

- Some of the criteria used by the Shanghai Jiao Tong dominant international ranking, in which the French establishments are rated low[13] (number and impact of publications in internationally prestigious reviews, number of Nobel distinctions and of patents, percentage of foreign students from OECD countries[14] and of foreign (European) teachers and researchers).

- The size of the establishments (a major determinant of the ranking in the international prize lists), and indicators of their territorial pooling with industries in order 'to compete with the large university centres like Munich, Oxford and Barcelona'. A parallel indicator is the threshold of student attendance for the closing of cursus and departments.
- The ratio of extra-budgetary resources from commercial activities and research contracts with the private sector. However the target for 2010, set very near the prevailing ratio, was not supposed to change the overall funding structure.
- The ratio of contractual public resources to the total public endowments. The target was to raise the contractual part from about 20% to 40%.

Two agencies were simultaneously created:

- AERES[15] (2007) is an independent administrative authority, in charge of the evaluation and ranking of all HE public establishments and research units, and of the evaluation procedures of their personnel. Its members are appointed by government decree. AERES replaces the several previous evaluation committees on which elected representatives of the personnel sat. It is also in charge of the evaluation of courses and diplomas, and intends to apply for European Quality Assurance Register (EQAR) inscription in 2010 in order to become an internationally recognised accreditation agency. Such a centralised, concentrated, multipurpose institution does not seem to exist in any other country.
- ANR[16] (2005–2007), a public administrative institution, with a governing board also appointed by decree with no elected representatives from the research institutions, is a funding agency for public and private research projects. It provides funding based on calls for proposals and peer review selection processes, for research projects having a maximum duration of four years. Projects are selected based on their scientific quality, as well as on their economic relevance for industries. The main originality of ANR, compared to similar foreign institutions, is that it is now the main institution in the French research policy as: (i) the amount distributed for short-duration R-D oriented projects tends to overtake the recurrent endowments for laboratories' fundamental research; and (ii) it involves the recruitment of researchers exclusively on short contracts.

Once the institutional frame was established, it was necessary to change the governance of the universities so that they would act as efficient *agents* of the *principal*. The agency principle implies that the agent should be free to manage its resources so as to obtain the prescribed results, i.e., considering the opposition of academics, that the presidents of the universities be given the powers of CEOs. The LRU[17] (2007) gives their 'autonomy' to the universities. The elected presidents concentrate both general policy functions and full decision power over the recruitment, promotion, allocation and performance-pay of staff. It is unique in the international landscape that the academics and their collegiate councils have only a restricted advisory function in all academic matters. Finally a recent decree (summer 2009) set on the permanent tenure of the professors and researchers. Furthermore, as the government does not fully trust the post-LRU presidencies of the universities, the NPM new bureaucracy has been somehow added to the old one, and the presidents of some establishments recently promoted to autonomy complain that they feel less free from administrative control to allocate their resources than before.

At this stage, the new model of French university differs from its foreign competitors in the international rankings by the following combination of features:

- Lower public expenditure per student.
- Prohibition of student fees.
- Prohibition of entrance selection.
- National diplomas and the lack of an internationally recognised accreditation system.
- A higher proportion of short term contractual public financing of research.
- A more concentrated governance of the establishments and a lower level of academic and scientific autonomy.

But as it is clear that these conditions ruled out any chance for a standard university to climb in the rankings, the government established in 2007 a number of special institutions exempted from those constraints. Among them are the following examples: the 'Scientific Research Foundations', public-private partnerships of private legal status, financed on public and tax-exempt private funds. This allowed, for instance, the new Paris School of Economics (PSE) to deliver master and PhD diplomas to highly selected graduate students, and to merge into a single institution a number of research units chosen from universities, research institutes and *grandes écoles*, with the result that, 'according to the rankings used by international bibliometric classifications, the cumulated scores of PSE researchers put PSE in first place in Europe, and amongst the top five in the World'.[18]

This is the dual architecture designed for the French HE by the Attali report. It proves (if this was necessary) that New Public Management, far from being a withdrawal of the state, can be a powerful tool for its forceful reinvestment of the public sphere. The empirical question now remains as to whether the ongoing reform is adapted to its first declared objective: to enlarge the share of French HE on the international markets.

Concluding remarks

The promotion of international movements of ideas, students, researchers, and so on seems now, in the dominant discourse, to be reduced to a competition between national champions with, in the function of umpires, the self-proclaimed producers of world rankings. In its recent recipe book *The challenge of establishing world-class universities* (Salmi 2009), the World Bank compares the good governance of a university to that of a football team. All users of the rankings know very well and even readily admit that their criteria are narrow and strongly biased, and that the results have little to do with the intrinsic unknown 'quality' of the competitors. They justify this resignation of intelligence on the circular premise that students, employers and foreign governments rely heavily on international rankings in their decisions. Whether or not this assertion may be empirically ascertained, and whatever (unknown) economic benefits may be expected from this mimetic competition, it becomes a self-fulfilling prophecy if widely embraced. France is no exception in this matter.

It is too early to assess the success of the French reform in promoting the appointed champions. As the above mentioned World Bank report aptly mentions, it takes more than a decree and the creaming of existing research units to establish a world class university. But the French exception here is in the use, combined with a debasing campaign, of a competitive credo and a highly centralised management through which it can inflict on the universities and research institutes an inordinately harsh treatment. NPM can be a very efficient method to exploit a stock; it is blind to its reproduction. 'Voice' having failed so far to reverse the movement, there are already some signs of 'exit'. The universities and the research institutes did attract, despite modest salaries, brilliant domestic and foreign candidates as long as they were allowed permanent tenure and scientific autonomy. The prospects of casual employment, narrowly focused research projects and a managerial direction wresting academic control from the faculty have already resulted in a drop of doctorate students and a 'thematic' brain drain from academic carriers. This could seriously hamper the international ambitions of the reform.

Notes

1. For example, last year a flow of British students moved to Holland where they could find the same curriculum, in English, and at a lower price.
2. At the very bottom of the financial crisis in 2008 the shares of the main multinational firms of online education services went up.
3. Data from Campus France (www.campusfrance.org) and Joint Research Centre, European Commission.
4. In 2007–2008, the origins of the 260,596 foreign students in France were: Africa (46.6%), Europe (24.9%), Asia and Oceania (15%), North and South America (7.6%), Middle East (5.6%). http://www.diplomatie.gouv.fr/fr/rubrique_imprim.php3?id_rubrique=4934.
5. International students in France are treated on the same footing as the domestic ones: education is free and they benefit from social security and housing subsidies. So, even if modest per student, the public cost was around €800 million in 2001 when there were 170,000 foreign students (vs. 250,000 in 2005) (Soulas 2007, 31).
6. The French Ministers of foreign affairs and education created Edufrance in 1996 to simultaneously 'sell our offer of higher education' on a market then estimated at $21 billion, and 'win the XXI century battle of intelligence' by attracting the best minds from the emerging countries. So it seems that, initially, the objective was largely to emulate the British strategy on the global student market.
7. Conférence des Grandes Ecoles 2007.
8. There is a heterogeneous post-secondary technical and professional sector (two–three years), selective, attached either to the universities or to the high schools, and therefore included in the vertical structures.
9. It also said in the report that the monopoly of the main public *grandes écoles* over the access to the top levels of the civil service would be abandoned, the students graduating from the universities being allowed to apply. This of course has never been mentioned since.
10. Cf. Note 6, supra.
11. *Loi organique relative aux lois de finances*.
12. Planning, programming, budgeting system.
13. For obvious reasons, considering the division between teaching and research units (e.g., the research production of the CNRS, rated first in Europe by Webometrics, does not enter in the Shangaï calculus) and the language 'handicap'.
14. A curious precision when industrialised countries compete mainly for the attraction of students from emerging countries.
15. *Agence d'évaluation de la recherche et de l'enseignement supérieur*.
16. *Agence nationale de la recherche*.
17. *Loi relative aux libertés et responsabilités des universités*.
18. http://www.parisschoolofeconomics.eu/spip.php?rubrique1&lang=fr.

References

Attali, Jacques. 1998. *Pour un modèle européen d'enseignement supérieur.* Rapport du Ministère de l'Education Nationale. http://www.education.gouv.fr/cid1911/pour-un-modele-europeen-d-enseignement-superieur.html.

CampusFrance. 2008. *International student mobility; key figures.* Paris: CampusFrance.

Conférence des Grandes Écoles. 2007. Les grandes écoles sur la scène internationale. Paper presented at the CRII workshop at the conference 'The perils and opportunities of the internationalisation of higher education: A critical perspective', September 25–26, 2009, University of Lausanne, Switzerland.

Hood, C. 2006. Gaming in targetworld: The target approach to managing British public services. *Public Administration Review* 66, no. 4: 515–29.

Leroy, Anne-Marie. 2003. Une révolution peut en cacher une autre. La LOLF et la gestion de la fonction publique. Cadres Plus (October). http://www.cadres-plus.net/bdd_fichiers/407-05.pdf.

Organisation for Economic Co-operation and Development (OECD). 1962. *Politiques de croissance économique et d'investissement dans l'enseignement. Conférence de Washington.* 5 vols. Paris: OECD.

Roundtable of European Industrialists (ERT). 1985. *Changing scales.* Brussels: Author. http://www.ert.be/doc/0060.pdf.

Salmi, J. 2009. *The challenge of establishing world-class universities.* Washington, DC: World Bank.

Soulas, T. 2007. *L'attraction d'étudiants étrangers par les pays développés; enjeux et approches stratégiques des Etats.* Strasbourg: Mémoire Université Robert Schuman.

Soulas, T. 2008. *L'implantation d'établissements d'enseignement supérieur à l'étranger; analyse comparée des exportations des pays développés anglophones et de la France.* Paris: Mémoire Université Paris I Panthéon-Sorbonne.

Varghese, N.V. 2008. *Globalization of higher education and cross-border mobility.* Paris: IIEP.

Vinokur, A. 2006. Brain migration revisited. *Globalisation, Societies and Education* 4, no. 1 : 7–24.

Vinokur, A. 2009. *La normalisation de l'université. (À paraître aux éditions de l'ULB).* http://netx.u-paris10.fr/foreduc/publications/normalisation_ulb.pdf.

Brazilian higher education from a post-colonial perspective

Denise Leite

Graduate Program of Education, Universidade Federal do RS, Porto Alegre, Brazil

> This article examines Brazilian higher education (HE) politics from a post-colonial perspective. The term 'post-colonial' originally referred to a historical period of colonial empires established by European nations. Nowadays, the term commonly distinguishes a field of contemporary studies of 'defamiliarisation of the imperial North' made up of successive acts of unlearning and re-learning. In the text I discuss the effects of globalisation on the Brazilian HE system, with emphasis on the outstanding role of evaluation and accreditation procedures. These are preparing the HE system for increasing internationalisation. Brazil, the new global player, is showing its potential in HE political acts of unlearning and re-learning. The epistemology could be called 'anthropophagic' because instead of copying foreign ideas there is a tendency to create new ones and re-elaborate them with a Global North anticipatory view and an accent on Global South localism.

Introduction

The main intention of this paper is to address reflections on Brazilian higher education (HE) from a post-colonial perspective.

> The use of the term 'post-colonial' originally referred to a historical period which followed the dismantling, during the late 19th and early 20th centuries, of the huge colonial empires mainly established by European nations, Britain, Portugal and France in particular. Many writers from the former colonies attempted to reclaim and re-forge their identities, writing a history from which they and their cultures had previously been excluded. (Bleakly et al. 2008, 266)

The term commonly distinguishes a field of contemporary studies where the 'others', the South (or the East, or Africa), the faraway people who live in the tropics, make their statement to the world. Since we have a Brazilian and a Latin American identity, I will address the analysis with Boaventura de Sousa Santos. For him, the important thing is the '"defamiliarization of the imperial north" made up of successive acts of unlearning in terms of knowledge-as-regulation (from order to chaos) and re-learning in terms of knowledge-as-emancipation (from colonialism to solidarity)' (Santos 1995, 508).

From a colonial point of view, Portuguese America was different from other American colonies. The difference is still visible in obvious things such as the language, the culture, and the political unity of the Brazilian territory. The difference has not been so visible in HE – Brazil was the last country of Latin America to have a university. The first Brazilian universities followed the 'Humboldtian' model and date from 1920–1934. They were established during the first years of the republic and preceded by isolated schools, based on the French model, founded in the years following 1808 when the Portuguese royal family arrived in the country.

Despite being the last country in Latin America to have its own university, Brazil now has a massified system with close to six million enrolments. In the last few decades HE reforms have brought about centralisation, diversification, evaluation and accreditation of the HE system. This last point has leveraged transformations – from internal and participative institutional evaluation processes, for example, into external procedures under national control and international convergent accreditation. This is one of the keys to the internationalisation of higher education in a globalised world. Is this condition a peril or a promise? Is it a new call from the Empire, or a golden opportunity to enter into a new power constellation? Are there visible trends and countertrends in the field of higher education in the emerging Brazilian context?

Where is Brazil, 'the new global player', now?

It all happens as though the sleeping giant were to rise again from its deep, lethargic colonial sleep, responding to republican challenges and globalising demands. Strength stored in the depths of the lands and oceans is supporting this new phase. The country is undergoing one of the best times in its history. It is a new, emerging player in the global world,[1] considered one of the emerging countries, known as BRICs (Brazil, Russia, India and China).[2] It is the ninth largest economy in the world. As to education, there is a recorded public investment of 4.6% of the GDP, which corresponds to about 117.4 billion reais (MEC/INEP 2009), 0.8% of which goes to the federal public system of higher education in which some of the country's largest and most prestigious universities are located (MEC/INEP 2009).[3]

Having a large territory, many consumers and a growing economy involves the country with the processes of globalisation. As the advertising for the University of Texas says, this means to think, work and learn globally. Globalisation, however, is not a homogeneous, uniform phenomenon, even if it reaches out to all of the developed world and parts of the world acknowledged as being on the margins, or in the Global South. Many – or almost all of these countries – move their economies at different 'tempos' and in different spaces, under the aegis of a capitalism that has managed to impose neo-liberal premises based on the Washington consensus. As was recognised by Schumpeter (1946, 198), 'the first thing to be noticed about the capitalist process is its evolutionary character'.

New relations and economic and mercantile interests are created and organised under the hegemonic force of neo-liberalism, an immense being whose mythological head appears to reside in at least three different places, and without a single address, namely, the World Bank, the International Monetary Fund and the World Trade Organisation. The command and tentacles of this being reach – with greater or lesser intensity – to the world population, of whom almost 2.8 billion people today live on less than $2 a day (World Bank 2001).[4] When it moves, this voluminous being produces huge waves, quasi-tsunamis, that have almost devastated Wall Street, wrecked the economies of politically and economically stable countries and caused a large, and not yet sufficiently estimated, proportion of the world population to become even poorer.

Emerging economies scramble along in its wake where they see niches of opportunities for their growth and internationalisation. Attentive admirers of the steps of this powerful being also find inside the emerging countries new opportunities to make money, and they turn their binoculars and sextants to sail in that direction like they did in medieval times. An inverted form of dependency appears to be taking place. Northern countries look again to the Southern countries. In a global economy, 'access to the right people at the right moment has become a comparative economic advantage' (Hartmann this issue). The emerging countries are a large market, and Brazil, a new global player, is receptive to international investments.

Globalisation and capitalist hegemony

International indicators, especially the indexes of the evaluation agencies, confirm that the general economy of the country is showing signs of doing well in the global context. This perspective includes the system of higher education (HES)[5] which was not immunised against neo-liberal policies and has a broad market in education. It is strongly privatised, since 90% of the institutions are entrepreneurial or private and community owned, and/or confessional, in a 'for profit' spirit. Seventy-three per cent of the student population is enrolled in these higher education institutions (HEIs).

Hegemonic international ideas operate according to the rules of the global game and imprint their characteristics on the ensemble of both public and private HE institutions. In this case the IMF and World Bank recommendations influenced the expansion of the system via private coverage that is under strong state control. The 'market–university' relations have been intensified. These movements have reproduced the relations between the coloniser (imperial master of the market) and the colony (the HE system and the universities), and transformed the relations between the state and the universities, both public and private. Quasi-marketisation of education effectively means to *learn globally*. Knowledge, the raw material of teaching and investigation, is the raw material of the global society, 'the key factor of the international division of labour, contributing decisively to accentuate the unequal exchanges in the world system' (Santos 1995, 439).

I will argue that the inevitable university[6] movements towards the markets can be gathered into a framework of globalisation, as the bearers of a form of capitalist hegemony. Hegemony here is understood as prevailing ideas, dominant ideas which affect and influence either directly or indirectly.

The contribution of the metaphor/model contained in Figure 1 relates to the prospective vision of a future university resulting from international evaluation and accreditation, international rankings, international partnerships, and trans-frontier cooperation. It may also be the linear model produced by the Bologna Process, based on the universalist idea of the Europe of Knowledge and its repercussions on the world periphery induced by the Tuning Latin America Project (Beneitone et al. 2007) and others. I believe that accreditation procedures will be part of the construction of the Global University, a product based on the recommendations of the international accreditation networks and the national agencies that follow international evaluation criteria. The university that resulted from globalisation would be its direct and favourite child. The Global University could be an isomorphous institution without a country, a chapter that begins as a consequence of the interdependencies constructed by globalisation managed by private interests.

Figure 1. Globalisation, capitalist hegemony and the university.
Source: Leite (2002).
Note: The framework is self-explanatory. The global financial community is represented by the IMF, WB, IDB, IBRD; global trade and services, tariffs and prices, are represented by the WTO and GATT; the global values and prices, commoditisation of the world and futures market by NYSE, Dow Jones & Nasdaq, Nikkei-TO, IBEX35-Madrid, Hang Seng, Hong Kong, Euro Stoxx 50, Chicago Stock market, BOVESPA (Brazil); the global products and corporations can be represented by Ford, Daimler-Chrysler, Shell, GE, Mitsubishi, Toyota, Wal Mart, Coca-Cola, McDonalds, Pizza Hut, Microsoft, Hewlett-Packard, Compaq, IBM, Sony, Nokia, Sanofis-Aventi, Petrobras (Brazil); the economic blocs are the EU, AFTA, NAFTA, MERCOSUL; global militaristic and economic policies are represented by NATO, UNCTAD, OPED; the global social, territorial and educational policies are handled by UN, UNESCO, ILO; the global evaluations that measure the global risk indexes are represented by Price Waterhouse, Cooper & Lybrands, Moody's, Securities and Exchange Commission, Standard & Poor's, Fitch Investors, Duff and Phelps, Thomas Bank Watch, IBCA; global information is represented by CNN, BBC, GNT, AP, France-Press, SVNS, Reuters, ASF; global communication is represented by Internet, www, ITT, AT&T. In this context, the global university at the centre of the figure is a consequence, an isomorphic model, a product of globalisation.

On the other side of the metaphor one can find the traditional university model, but that traditional Humboldtian Brazilian model of the university is changing, too. It has suffered the influence of homogenising evaluations as part of the 'reforms of the Nineties'. They produced a subtle result which I call *capitalist redesigning of universities* (Leite 2003). The redesigning is a sort of institutional performance marked by the commoditisation of knowledge, science and technology, stimulated and produced by a 'new' management that aims at making operations of private commercialisation and 'for profit' operations easier. There are direct relations between HEIs and the market – inside, within and outside the campuses.

As a rule, when capitalist redesigning begins in campuses, it affects the traditional university by formatting a hybrid model, the 'Hybrid Liberal University', which superimposes market practices and capitalist survival criteria on an institution that was traditionally independent from the market. This occurred both at public HEIs and in the private ones. On adapting and returning to the markets, the traditional functions and activities of universities succumb to capitalist redesigning.

Thus, a double face can be found in the contemporary models of universities. On the one side we find traditional universities transformed into 'Hybrid Universities' under the effects of hegemonic thinking, which superimpose market criteria on strictly academic criteria, and on the other 'Global Universities' which will be strengthened in the canons of globalisation regulated by international accreditation agencies or by WTO and GATS, and by the cosmopolitan visibility of the international rankings. These two university models or their variations might be seen as forming the parameters for the partially globalised and underdeveloped world or for the emerging countries that are facing the need to be global.

But these two 'new' models may have to survive alongside a third one, the model of the 'World Class University', an institution for the developed globalised world where the resources are abundant, students and faculty can demonstrate 'excellence' and the management and governance are favourable (supportive regulatory framework, autonomy, leadership, academic freedom). As Salmi (2009, 7–9) explains, a World Class University is established by three basic strategies:

> Upgrading a small number of existing universities that have the potential to excel (picking winners); Encouraging a number of existing institutions to merge into a new university that could achieve the synergies of a world-class institution (hybrid formula); Creating new world-class universities from scratch (clean-slate approach).

According to the condition stated by Salmi, the developing and emergent world can have their World Class Universities. Brazil, in particular, has USP, UNICAMP, UFMG and UFRGS, which appear in the Shanghai Jiao Tong Ranking. And many others will probably upgrade, seeking niches of excellence in order to capture major resources and have a high level staff and students selected from amongst the best. But for a long time they will live together with the 'Global Universities' and the 'Hybrid' ones.

Higher education under the effects of globalisation

On the basis that hegemonic thought is installed, because hegemonic capitalism doesn't exist only for economic results but also for social and cultural changes, what are the main factors that are globalising Brazilian HE? At least two factors are clear:

the governmental stimulus for internationalisation and the imposition of evaluation programs of control and regulation of the HE system.

Evaluation of the HE system

It should be pointed out that Brazil has expertise in evaluation. It set up an accreditation system that was applied to graduate studies, with a view to controlling their quality, in the 1970s – that is, before the neo-liberal reforms of the 1990s. Since then, and with successive improvements, the CAPES (Coordination of Higher Education for Personnel Improvement) evaluation has been performed. The CAPES is an agency connected to MEC (Ministry of Education), and belongs to the executive power of the nation. For postgraduate programs the quality evaluation comprises a peer review evaluation and the program productivity is measured every three years by Data-CAPES. The evaluation classifies the Graduate Program at levels from '1' to '5', and gives '6' and '7' for internationalised programs, according to criteria that are well known to the participating institutions. The HEIs influence the definition of these criteria through peer committees in disciplinary and interdisciplinary areas elected by graduate program faculty. The results of the evaluation are regularly published. The quality evaluation processes from CAPES are mandatory to the acknowledged postgraduate programs and confer temporary credentials for them.

At the beginning of the 1990s, the neo-liberal evaluation model whose results were connected to financial resources, implemented by the Thatcher government in England, worried the presidents of Brazilian public universities, who feared the implementation of a similar model in Brazil. In order to forestall this, the presidents suggested an undergraduate evaluation model to MEC (Ministry of Education) that was the opposite of the English model. It was started in 1993 and called Program for Institutional Evaluation of Brazilian Universities (PAIUB). Despite its impact on the direction of participation, taking into account the desire for democratisation and the modernisation of private and public undergraduate courses offered, it failed. However, a few years later, in a government which was noted for introducing neo-liberal ideas, this was attenuated by the introduction of the National Exam of Courses (National Examination Study Diploma), called 'Provão' by students. Despite this, the democratic and participative principles of PAIUB are still remembered by the academic community. Later on, successive governments tried to introduce new evaluation procedures in order to achieve quality control of the public and private offer of undergraduate education, under the centralised responsibility of the Ministry of Education.

Since 2004, the quality evaluation system has been administered by SINAES, the national evaluation system. The system holds an annual examination of students, the ENADE exam, an evaluation of courses and internal and external institutional evaluations of institutions with peer review. Data on HE are collected through an Annual Census of Higher Education. There is also a national ranking of institutions based on the results of the evaluation processes.[7] Quality evaluation processes from SINAES are compulsory for acknowledging undergraduate courses and to confer temporary credentials on higher education institutions similar to accreditation, which is a centralised responsibility of the Ministry of Education (MEC), its agency INEP (National Institute of Studies and Research Anísio Teixeira), and of the National Council of Education. The whole process is electronic, except the peer review of the external institutional evaluation of universities. The ENADE exam is applied once a year throughout the country. Its results qualify students to obtain a partial score to enter the university and contribute to forming the final entrance evaluation university index. It is important to highlight that 'the vestibular' examination is still used at private and public institutions.

At the core of evaluation–accreditation in the SINAES and CAPES programs is teachers' productivity. Their performance is scrutinised to the last detail and recorded in the Lattes curriculum platform (CNPq) with public access via the Web. There is an exchange of data in the spheres of executive power. Information from CNPq, CAPES and MCT, for example, can be communicated to the income tax authorities, and data can be cross-matched.

Internationalisation of the higher education system[8]

Internationalisation as an exchange of ideas and knowledge has been the prerogative of universities since ancient times and it was precisely by international liberal ideas that young law school students were buoyed up to fight against domination and to influence the advent of the Republic in 1889. From 1970 until now, the strongest force operating towards internationalisation has been that brought about by globalisation. Globalisation heralded the advent of greater concern about new models of universities, the intention being that the universities should have a better adjusted response to the challenges of the society of knowledge and information, to the new economic liberalisation and to the international markets, especially those of science and technology.

At government level, international cooperation is developed or stimulated by two main agencies, CAPES and CNPq (National Council for Scientific and Technological Development). In the world context, CAPES performs an outstanding job funding international research projects. It maintains student and faculty mobility exchange. Data indicates that Brazil sent 19,619 students to courses abroad in 2008 (GUNI 2008). The exchange activity occurs via bilateral agreements and partnerships. Diplomas obtained in foreign universities have to be validated by national institutions.

International cooperation is part of the objectives of CNPq, the National Research Council, through ASCIN – Consultancy for International Cooperation, which funds the mobility of researchers, the development of research, the capacity-building of researchers in doctoral and post-doctoral programs, and participation in international agencies. Since 1931 CNPq has signed several international agreements. CNPq belongs to the Ministry of Science and Technology (MCT) and not to the Ministry of Education. Its main arm is the agency FINEP, a research funding agency. The investments in science and technology and innovation come mostly from the Sectorial Funds and were around US$861,342,979.73 in 2009, first semester (MCT 2009).

It should be emphasised that undergraduate courses in selected professional areas of knowledge at Brazilian HEIs are being accredited by international agencies. An outstanding role is played by MERCOSUL[9] Educational through the RANA (Network of National Agencies of Accreditation) and ARCU-SUR (System of Regional Accreditation of Undergraduate Courses of the State(s) that are Part of MERCOSUL and associated states) networks whose experience began with MEXA (Experimental Mechanism for the Evaluation and Accreditation of Undergraduate Courses to Recognise the University Level Diplomas in the MERCOSUL countries, Bolivia and Chile). The ARCU-SUR system provides accreditation for courses in medicine, engineering, agronomy, architecture, nursing, veterinary medicine, and odontology. Currently the courses accredited are from the professions of agronomy, veterinary medicine, architecture and pharmacy, allowing the diplomas of the graduates to be acknowledged in different countries (Dias Sobrinho 2006; Rama 2009; for in-depth detail, see the special issue of ESS 2009).

In general, internationalisation can be stimulated by bilateral/multilateral cooperation, agreements and international partnerships, by joint research or student mobility in a Global North direction. Programs such as the Tuning Project, ALPHA, and Erasmus Mundus or ALCUE, all from the EU, have an influence on the processes of the internationalisation of higher education. However, because they involve only a few institutions and professors – the interaction can be performed with the individual applicants to scholarships or restricted to MEC specialists – their influence is not so noticeable.

In the case of Tuning, a European Union initiative, joint research was developed with Latin American countries. In Brazil there is a National Tuning Center at UFBA (Beneitone et al. 2007).

The ALPHA projects were based on the free association between researchers from different European and Latin American countries and they were supposedly the precursors of Tuning.

ALFA TUNING LATIN AMERICA

The idea behind the ALFA Tuning-Latin America Project stems from a close examination of higher education at both a regional and international level. Historically speaking, Tuning has been an exclusively European initiative. More than 135 European universities have been working towards the creation of a European Area of Higher Education since 2001. At the IV Follow-Up Meeting of the Common Area of Higher Education for the European Union, Latin America and Caribbean (EULAC) that was held in October 2002, the representatives from Latin America took heed of the results of the First Phase of Tuning. In fact, they warmed to the idea of doing a similar project with Latin America.

To promote a significant level of HE Convergence on a Latin American scale for 12 thematic areas: Business Management, Architecture, Law, Education, Nursing, Physics, Geology, History, Civil Engineering, Mathematics, Medicine and Chemistry by using widely accepted definitions of learning and professional outcomes.

(http://www.oui-iohe.org/eles/en/proyecto-tuning/tuning-latinoamerica/)

Brazil is part of the ALCUE (or UEALC) Area, as a member of MERCOSUL. ALCUE/UEALC covers countries of the European Union, MERCOSUL, the Andean Community and CARICOM. The Follow Up Committee of the ALCUE in Brazil is under the responsibility of the MEC through the Secretary for Higher Education.

Its main objective is to establish reciprocity of knowledge and cooperation among higher education systems.[10]

ALCUE

The ALCUE Common Area of Higher Education is an initiative that was originally set up by European Union, Latin American, and Caribbean countries. Its fundamental aim is [to] create a higher education platform for interaction and bilateral/multilateral cooperation. The origin of the initiative stems from the *'Conferencia de la Cúpula de Río de Janeiro'* (The Third Session of the Summit of Heads of State and Governments of Latin America, the Caribbean and the European Union), which was held June 29, 1999. It was during this meeting that the Heads of State and Government pledged their 'political will' with the aim of enhancing regional cooperation. Furthermore, higher education was viewed as a key priority for future action.

(http://www.oui-iohe.org/eles/en/espacios-comunes/latinoamericano/)

Internationalisation of higher education is also favoured by international agencies such as Fulbright, the Ford Foundation and the British Council. They have been operating locally since the mid-twentieth century, granting scholarships. The work of these agencies, international organisations from the US and UK, can be seen as contributors to the process. From the Global South frequently they are seen as a kind of 'developed countries' cultural marketing agencies'.

Fulbright[11] has maintained a student mobility and educational and cultural exchange program since 1957, when the first Fulbright Commission was appointed. It gives scholarships to Brazilian and North American students. It operates in 17 Brazilian states and is coordinated from Brasília (Franco 2002). It promotes North American culture. The Ford Foundation[13] offers graduate scholarships to Brazilian students at American universities. It selects candidates according to the criterion of belonging to certain groups. In recent years it has selected women, Afro-American and indigenous people from the Centre-West, Northeast and North of Brazil. It promotes North American culture. The British Council is the UK's international organisation for cultural relations and educational opportunities. They stimulate and support good practices in education by facilitating the collaboration of British and Brazilian institutions and agencies. They offer scholarships in the UK for Brazilian students and teachers and promote English culture in Brazil.

At the level of institutions, some authors estimate that international cooperation is still of a peripheral kind, since it reaches only particular sectors of the universities, especially research functions in general and faculty and student mobility in the South–North and South–South directions. The large universities, however, maintain specialised departments to support and guide internationalisation. At UFRGS, for instance, where internationalisation is central, this office is tasked with stimulating the academic mobility of students and faculty in both directions.

Higher education politics between globalisation and national anthropophagi: a post-colonial perspective

Having summarised the perspectives of globalisation and capitalist hegemony over universities, with a specific focus on evaluation and internationalisation, the analysis now turns to a post-colonial perspective and presents some contradictory tendencies and countertendencies.

Brief notes about post-colonialism as a theory

The perspective of analysis comes from the post-colonial theoretical trend. Santos defines a post-colonial approach thus:

> I understand by post-colonialism a set of theoretical and analytic currents, firmly rooted in cultural studies, but today present in all social sciences, which have in common the primacy they grant to the theoretical and political aspects of the unequal relations

between North and South in explaining or understanding the contemporary world. (Santos 2006, 39; Editor's translation)

For Santos, such unequal relations were historically built by colonialism. He alerts us to the fact that political colonial relations could not be completely destroyed. They can be residually alive whenever social relations are framed by authoritarianism, discrimination, and social injustice.

To what extent are we still living in a post-colonial society? In Santos' (2008) opinion there is an 'epistemology of the Global South' which aims at recovering knowledge and social practices that were forgotten and erased in their condition of dominated knowledge. When reincorporated by dominant capitalist and colonial knowledge they were renamed or repositioned in the international constellation of knowledge and powers. The incredible diversity of the world obviously produces powerful and fertile knowledge, whose plurality is infinite. The 'learned ignorance' in our time consists of, 'knowing that the epistemological diversity of the world is potentially infinite and each knowledge only knows about itself to a very limited extent'. So, as Santos says, the Global South higher education system and the university as an institution do not need to become hostage to or participate in contexts of 'learned ignorance' without a severely critical approach. It would certainly be a *'douta ignorância'* (learned ignorance) to ignore the knowledge of the Global South (Santos 2008, 27; Santos and Meneses 2009).

It would be also be learned ignorance to underestimate the global capitalist forces which ideologically support the production of knowledge and the globally oriented knowledge-based economy. In this sense, in a counter-hegemonic way, the university has the task of breaking down paradigms and reconfiguring the knowledge of academe, of science and technology, with people and community knowledge, their traditions and cultures. Some dubious and contradictory trends can be seen on the horizon.

Anthropophagi or the Southern epistemology

As I showed in the first part of this text, Brazil is an emerging country which has a unique situation in the context of its peers, the BRICs, and a distinct geopolitical leadership in Latin America. What happened when global neo-liberal ideas permeated its economy, politics and education from the early 1980s onwards? The answer can be given by a simple answer that draws on a metaphor of ancient culture: the anthropophagi. Instead of copying foreign ideas there is a tendency to create new ones and re-elaborate them with an anticipatory view and an accent of Global South localism. A critical mass and part of the political class adopts the neo-liberal policies initially, and then immediately afterwards it commits anthropophagi – it digests what it finds useful, regurgitates what does not concern it, and absorbs what will do it some good. As Mario de Andrade put it in the Anthropophagic Manifesto, which opened the Modern Art Week of 1922, in which he criticised the copying of foreign ideas without consciousness (Andrade 1976), the issue is *Tupy or not tupy. Against all importers of canned consciousness*. The reference is to the Brazilian Tupi-Guarani indigenous language, and the analogy is drawn with the verb *to be*, the Shakespearean citation *to be or not to be,* with a homophonous pronunciation.

We can point to at least three tendencies in universities that show the re-elaboration and/or construction of epistemologies: the 1990s reforms, the pressures of the globalised world and the evaluation and accreditation of universities following international criteria.

Reforms of the 1990s[12]

When the evaluative process arose it was partly an anthropophagic copy of the Global North. From now on we all have to be compulsorily evaluated. The university community introduced the initial democratic and participative format – PAIUB – with great 'buy in' from teachers and their unions. Democratic governments liberalised the economy for foreign capital and introduced national examinations. Liberalisation advanced with the Lula da Silva government, which nevertheless concentrated power over public and private education in the hands of the state – a counter-hegemonic reaction. For example, private educational entrepreneurs or confessional orders or foundations are free to act on the market as any corporation would do with shares sold on the Stock Market, mergers, campus expansions, campus reductions, to buy and sell their properties – but they would need to be an institution accredited by CAPES/MEC for graduate courses, by SINAES/MEC for undergraduate courses. Both are state agencies and the educational entrepreneurs do not choose their accreditation agency; there is no alternative to the mandatory government process. In other words, the neo-liberal principle of primacy of the market over the state is open. But the primacy of the state over the university, market or quasi-market of education is maintained by HE policies of regulation, centralisation, accreditation and control over all the system, both public and private.

Evaluation and accreditation

International accreditation agencies have flourished in Latin America in recent years, such as RIACES (the Iberoamerican Network of HE), who interact with European agencies and follow the same orientations. The Global North accreditation system is being promoted by a major agency such as UNESCO, which sponsors meetings to study the accreditation process. A very small number of the Brazilian universities are cited in international rankings. Despite this the government supplies global agencies with information from its databases to form international comparative indicators and indexes. As a countertendency to the globalisation market-oriented evaluation, the country has a centralising and regulatory evaluation, an accreditation process, managed by the state and not by the market. At a national level, a counter-countertendency can be seen in the politics of asking people to give their participatory contribution through national public hearings concerning criteria and formats of evaluations.

Internationalisation

Internationalisation is encouraged by government agencies that fund student and faculty mobility – CAPES/MEC and MCT/CNPq and FINEP – but Lula's administration encourages moves in the direction of cultural and knowledge exchange with African countries and the South Cone – especially MERCOSUL countries, following diplomatic interests. The creation of four new public universities – UNILAB, UNILA, UFFS and UFOPA – is directed towards the Global South. These new federal public universities are strategically disposed across the national territory from the Amazon region to the

Foz do Iguacu region. The first, UNILAB, the Federal University of the Community of Portuguese-Language Countries, mainly seeks its clients in the Portuguese Language community countries – Angola, Brazil, Cape Verde, Guinea-Bissau, Mozambique, St Thomas and Prince, Portugal and East Timor. By creating UNILA, University of Latin American Integration, the government intention was to look for the desired Latin American integration in and around Foz do Iguacu, the three frontiers region (Paraguay, Argentina, and Brazil). The same could be said of the objectives of UFFS, Federal University of the Southern Border, and UFOPA, University of Amazon Integration.

Coda

As in musical compositions this coda points to a finalisation aiming to integrate concepts and ideas. A complex system of HE and its coverage cannot be analysed in its totality. Many issues are absent or addressed in an incomplete form.

I have raised the importance of the state in the governance of the HE system, and the importance of the state's power instead of the invisible hand of the markets, especially in the last 10 years. Economic liberalisation advanced even further with Lula da Silva, a socialist from the workers' party, whose government nevertheless concentrated power over public and private education in the hands of the state, as noted above in the example of the state regulation of courses and accreditation.

This primacy of the state over all internal sectors of the economy, including the higher education system and its universities producing the kinds of knowledge that could enable it to emerge into the ranks of the more developed countries, may be one of the secrets of continuing growth in an international crisis.

Despite looking to the capitalist redesign of universities, a second-hand product of economic liberalisation, the emergent country deals anthropologically with managing transformation and change. This may be a post-colonial attempt to break down paradigms and reconfigure knowledge, which does not occur without contradictions and conflicts. While the internationalisation of HE and universities has been encouraged for a long time by government agencies, the new global player looks for more. Instead of sending brains to the Global North, brains are taken from the Global South.

In all changes, transformations, trends and countertrends the role of evaluation and accreditation procedures is crucial. They prepare HE systems for increasing internationalisation, with international criteria, ranking performances, international indicators and indexes as the bridge for internationalisation. The countertendency of the participative contribution to the conceptions of evaluation programs may disappear or be attenuated. It may be that in the future we will be introduced to an international accreditation of the 'Global University'.

Certainly there is a promise in the air, a golden opportunity to enter into a new power constellation. But considering tendencies and countertendencies there are questions about Brazilian HE that only the future will answer. In particular its identity is under permanent construction, seeking social inclusion in order to pay its historical debt from colonial times.

Acknowledgements

I wish to thank Dr Eva Hartmann for the invitation to the Lausanne Workshop and for her kind comments on the preliminary draft text. I would like to thank Dr Boaventura Santos for the opportunity to discuss globalisation university models during a postdoctoral internship, in

2002, at CES, the University of Coimbra, Portugal. I am grateful to Hedy Hoffmann, who translated this paper into English.

Notes

1. In general economic terms, the country is entering the twenty-first century with a strong domestic economy, solid financial institutions, an active stock market (Bovespa), and trade relations with many countries in the world. The per capita GDP rose from US$3654 in 2002 to US$8676 in 2008, while the birth rate is tending to slow down – it is estimated that this will reduce to 0.24% in 2050. It has the wealth of black gold, drilling for oil in deep waters using the most sophisticated technology. It has a large, diversified industry, including an aeronautic industry; an active export list of industrialised and primary products; and a broad profile of international partners. It has international reserves of more than 200 billion dollars and it is also transferring 10 billion dollars as a loan to the World Bank. President Lula's government priority is to invest in the social sector, with a view to reducing poverty and improving conditions of health and education. The Growth Acceleration program – PAC (*Programa de Aceleração de Crescimento*) – has been increased to R$645 billion. The Family Grant (*Bolsa Família*) program is maintained. These are funds received directly by poor families for each child enrolled in school and taken off the streets. There is financing, partly *à fonds perdu*, to build one million homes for the low-income classes. The growth acceleration measures are the results of social policies that are beginning to show positive results. In 2002 the rate of poverty in the country was 42.5% of the population. In June 2009, during a full blown world economic crisis, poverty was reduced to its lowest level, that is, 0.493 points in the GINI Index, corresponding to 31.1% of the population of the big cities, which means 14.5 million people. The Gini Index measures social inequality and it is calculated by IPEA (Instituto de Pesquisa Econômica Aplicada).
2. As compared to BRICs, the country has a GDP of US$1.573 trillion, which brings it close to Russia and is higher than the GDP of India. The per capita GDP shows the increasing purchasing power of the population. It has a higher (upper middle income) economy rating than China and India (http://data.worldbank.org/about/country-classifications/country-and-lending-groups). The HDI (Human Development Index) is close to that of Russia and higher than the HDIs of India and China. Income group: economies are divided according to 2008 GNI per capita, calculated using the World Bank Atlas method. The groups are: low income, $975 or less; lower middle income, $976–$3,855; upper middle income, $3,856–$11,905; and high income, $11,906 or more. http://web.worldbank.org/WBSITE/EXTERNAL/HOMEPORTUGUESE/.
3. http://portal.mec.gov.br/index.php?option=com_jfilter&view=colunas&Itemid=187.
4. The World Development Report 2000–2001, *Attacking poverty* (World Bank 2001) concluded that major reductions in poverty were possible despite the huge scale of the problem at the start of the new century, with 2.8 billion of the world's six billion people living on less than $2. In 1995 it was affirmed that 82.5% of the total population live in countries considered poor, and the other 14.8% live in countries considered rich, because they have 78.5% of the world's revenue. http://web.worldbank.org/WBSITE/EXTERNAL/EXTDEC/EXTRESEARCH/EXTWDRS/0,,contentMDK:20313941~menuPK:607028~pagePK:478093~piPK:477627~theSitePK: 477624,00.html.
5. Brazilian HES: 2252 HEIs, 183 universities, 5,808,017 students enrolled in 2008. http://www.inep.gov.br/download/censo/2008/Sinopse_Estatistica_da_Educacao_Superior_2008_versao_preliminar.xls.
6. In this paper I will make use of the terms university and higher education in spite of the fact that they are not interchangeable words. Universities are part of the system as well as university centers, integrated schools or technological schools and institutions.
7. The regulating legislation comprehends the Federal Constitution of 1988, Art. 84 Inc. IV and VI; the LDB (Guidelines and Educational Foundations Law), Law 9394/96 and the Decree 3860/2001.
8. BRICS Students Internationalisation (2006): Brazil: 19,619; India: 123,559; China: 343,126; Russia: 34,473 (GUNI 2007).
9. Treaty of Asunción, Protocol of Ouro Preto, Decisions Nr. 18/04 and 28/04 of the Council of the Common Market; MERCOSUL/CMC/DEC. Nr 17/08 of 30/VI/08.

10. The follow up meetings were held in: Paris, France (October 2001); Fortaleza, Brazil (March 2002); Merida, Mexico (July 2002); Cordova, Spain (October 2002); Paris, France (April 2003); Belo Horizonte, Brazil (April 2004); Madrid, Spain (November 2004); Quetaro, Mexico (March 2005); Paris, France (December 2005); Alagoas, Brazil (April 2006).
11. Commission for Educational Exchange between the United States of America and Brazil. http://www.fulbright.org.br.
12. http://www.fordfound.org/regions/brazil/overview.
13. Nineties reforms – Latin American HE system reforms oriented by globalisation pressures. They correspond to the same reforms that took place in advanced countries. See Kent (1997) and for a counterpoint Mollis (2003).

References

Andrade, Oswald. 1976. *Manifesto antropófago. Revista de antropofagia. 1a e 2a. Dentições 1928–1929.* Reediçao. São Paulo: Companhia Editorial Nacional.
Beneitone, P., C. Esquenti, J. Gonzalez, M. Maleta, G. Siufi, and R. Wagenaar, eds. 2007. *Tuning America Latina. Reflections on and outlook for higher education in Latin America.* Informe final. Projecto Tuning America Latina. Deusto and Groningen: University of Deusto, University of Groningen.
Dias Sobrinho, J. 2006. Acreditación de la educacion superior en America Latina y el Caribe. In *La educacion superior en el mundo 2007. Acreditación para la garantia de la calidad ¿qué está en juego?* ed. J. Tres, 282–95. Barcelona: GUNI, Ediciones Mundi-Prensa.
Educación Superior y Sociedad (ESS). 2009. *Experiências de convergência acadêmica en paises del Mercosur. Educacion y sociedade.* Nueva Época 14, no. 1. Caracas, Venezuela: IESALC/UNESCO.
Franco, M.E.D.P. 2002. Globalização, internacionalização e cooperação institucional. In *Educação superior no Brasil,* ed. S. Soares, 281–93. Brasília: CAPES. http://www.scribd.com/doc/3046351/Educacao-superior-no-Brasil-A-Maria-Susana-Arrosa-Soares.
Kent, R. 1997. *Los temas críticos de la educación superior en América Latina. Vol. 2. Los años 90. Expansión privada y posgrado.* Chile: FLACSO, Facultad Latinoamericana de Ciencias Sociales; Mexico: Fondo de Cultura Económica.
Leite, D. 2003, Institutional evaluation, management practices and capitalist redesign of universities. In *The higher education managerial revolution?,* ed. A. Amaral, V.L. Meek, and I. Larsen, 253–73. Dordrecht, The Netherlands: Kluwer Academic Publishers.
Ministério de Ciência e Tecnologia (MCT). 2009. Arrecadaçao, dotaçao orçamentaria e execuçao financeira. http://www.mct.gov.br/index.php/content/view/27181.html#lista (accessed August 10, 2009).
Ministério de Educação/Instituto nacional de Estudios e Pesquisas Educacionais Anísio Teixeria (MEC/INEP). 2009. Educação recebeu 117 bilhões em 2007. Assessoria de Imprensa 02 fevereiro 2009. http://www.inep.gov.br/imprensa/noticias/outras/news09_08.htm (accessed April 24, 2010).
Mollis, M. 2003. *Las universidades en América Latina: Reformadas o alteradas.* Buenos Aires: Consejo Latinoamericano de Ciencias Sociales.
Rama, C. 2009. El nacimento de la acreditación internacional. *Avaliaçao* 14, no. 2: 291–311.
Salmi, J. 2009. *The challenge of establishing world-class universities.* Washington, DC: World Bank.
Santos, B. de Sousa. 1995. *Toward a new common sense: Law, science and politics in the paradigmatic transition.* New York: Routledge.
Santos, B. de Sousa. 2006. *Conocer desde el Sur: Para una cultura política emancipatoria.* Lima: Fondo Editorial de la Facultad de Ciencias Sociales, UNMSM.
Santos, B. de Sousa. 2008. A filosofia à venda, a douta ignorância e a aposta de Pascal. *Revista Crítica de Ciências Sociais* 80: 11–43.
Santos, B. de Sousa, and M.P. Meneses. 2009. *Epistemologias do Sul.* Coimbra: Almedina.
Schumpeter, J.A. 1946. *Capitalism, socialism, and democracy.* New York: Harper and Brothers.
World Bank. 2001. *World development report 2000/2001: Attacking poverty.* Washington, DC: World Bank.

Soft power and higher education: an examination of China's Confucius Institutes

Rui Yang

Comparative Education Research Centre, University of Hong Kong, Hong Kong

> China's global presence has become a significant subject. However, little attention has been directed to the role of higher education in projecting China's soft power, and little academic work has been done directly on it, despite the fact that there has been some work on related topics. Borrowing the theories of soft power and higher education internationalisation, this article aims to fill in the gap in the literature by investigating China's projection of soft power via the conduit of recently established Confucius Institutes. Aiming to facilitate a more nuanced appraisal of China's global power and influence, it looks at Chinese higher education policy in a global context from the perspective of international power relations. Incorporating findings from an empirical case study of one Confucius Institute (based at a major Australian university) as a new distinctive model of international exchange and cooperation in higher education, this article looks at how Chinese universities interact with their international peers, in a context where China wants its universities to rival the best in the world, and invests heavily in its top universities.

Introduction

Coined by Joseph S. Nye (1990), the term soft power refers to the ability to change what others do or shape what they want (Nye 2004). Stemming from the attractiveness of a nation's culture, ideals and policies and resembling Edward Carr's (1954) 'power over opinion' and Steven Lukes' (1974) 'third dimension of power', it is usually defined as culture, education, and diplomacy, providing the capacity to persuade other nations to willingly adopt the same goals. China is promoting soft power as it seeks to establish itself as a major player in world affairs. It realises the critical role of higher education in the projection of soft power, promotes international exchange and collaboration to expand its global influence, and seeks to formalise the benefits of its rich heritage by establishing Confucius Institutes (CIs), which are centres for language study linked with universities around the world, named after the Chinese philosopher who lived from 551 to 479 BCE. The network of such institutes is a significant tool China has used to expand its international influence and promote its model of governance via the promotion of Chinese language and culture. This move is arguably China's most systematically planned soft power policy.

Despite China's global presence and the significance of the subject, little attention has been directed to the role of higher education in projecting China's soft power. Little academic work has been done directly on it, although there has been some work on related topics. This article aims to fill in the gap in the literature by investigating China's projection of soft power via the conduit of CIs. Dealing with a recent development and looking at Chinese higher education policy in a global context from a perspective of international power relations, this article focuses on the rise of China's soft power, a far less studied topic compared with China's surging economic and military power (Brzezinski and Mearsheimer 2005; Gill and Huang 2006). It examines education as an excellent yet much-neglected test case of the soft power thesis. It is one of the first empirical studies of CIs as a unique model of international exchange and cooperation in higher education characterised by multiple directions of knowledge movement, penetrating visions, and attentiveness to macro trends and micro developments.

China's economic prowess and ancient civilisation entice students worldwide for training in Chinese language and culture. It is especially attractive to countries like Australia. China has replaced Japan as Australia's top trading partner. According to Michael Wesley, the executive director of the Lowy Institute, the world of the future is going to be an Asia-centred knowledge economy (Healy 2009). As a small and peripheral economy, Australia needs to place stronger emphasis on Asian neighbours. China is a strong partner that provides extraordinary opportunities for Australia (Sutter 2005). This explains why, while there seems to be an absence of national champions among the highest level institutions to have CIs on their campuses internationally (Starr 2009), six out of Australia's elite 'Group of Eight' and nine of its total of 39 universities have established CIs.

Incorporating findings from a case study of one CI based at a major Australian university, this article explores how Chinese soft power has been expressed in China's global engagement through higher education, what China is actually trying to achieve through CIs, how CIs have been operated, and what are the limits to, problems of, and concerns about China's projection of soft power in higher education, as shown by the exercise of CIs. While the empirical data of this study are mainly based on one case in Australia, this article links them closely to the general literature on this topic to shed light on China's higher education policy and on the ways in which China expands its global role.

A case study approach is used to gain an in-depth understanding of the complexities of China's soft power policy in higher education from within the individual institution in its unique settings (Hargreaves 1993). Semi-structured interviews were employed as the main method of data collection to access the 'lived experience' of participants and to elicit the meanings that participants attribute to their actions, including their thoughts, feelings, beliefs, values, and assumptive world (Marshall and Rossman 2006). The choice of Sandstone University (a pseudonym) is based on its character as one of Australia's elite category of universities situated in a capital city, attracting significant numbers of international students from the Asia-Pacific region with China as the largest single source.

China's soft power projection through CIs

The concept of soft power has been a fundamental part of military thinking in China for over 2000 years. The so-called rise of China is a misnomer: re-emergence is more accurate. Technologically and economically, China was a world leader from CE500 to 1500 (Nye 1997; de Blij 2005). Given a historical and cultural background in soft power and moral leadership and the intense competition with the west led by the US, it is logical to expect that China will increasingly project itself on the world stage by peaceful means such as culture and education. With economic strength comes political clout around the globe. China's influence on global affairs is growing. Its actions to safeguard its interests are increasingly affecting the interests of the international community as a whole (Eisenman et al. 2007; Nye 2007). Meanwhile, recent international surveys also find that China's ascendency is causing global concern (Bortin 2008; Goldirova 2008).

Despite the significance of soft power in a global information age, policy-makers in many countries continue to overlook it. For example, Richard Gardner, a former US ambassador to Spain and Italy, pointed out that the US spent 'more on preparing for war than on trying to prevent it' by a ratio of at least 16:1 in 2001 (Johnson 2004, 63). This is especially true of China's case. History suggests that, in times of significant western attention toward China, assessments of China's global role have tended toward stereotypes, exaggerations and extremes, collectively resulting in a steady pendulum swing in perceptions of China as friend or foe that neglect careful analysis of China's various attributes and weaknesses (Sutter 2003).

Today, 'winning hearts and minds' still composes an important part of the international higher education equation (Nye 2004). In the words of former US President Eisenhower (1958), 'Just as war begins in the minds of men, so does peace'. Educational exchange falls under the rubric of soft power. Connections between institutions of higher education are a steadying and civilising influence. China has been consciously promoting international exchange and collaboration in education and skilfully employing soft power to expand its global influence. One effective policy strategy has been the combination of higher education with the appeal of Confucianism to offer Beijing a definite comparative advantage in its soft power approach (Shambaugh 2005; Kurlantzick 2006). Beijing's strategies are innovative in many ways. The most systematically planned soft power policy so far is to build up CIs worldwide.

CIs have received some criticism from political and academic circles. Some suggest that CIs have a hidden agenda beyond their stated objectives. Because most CIs operate within universities, their sponsorship of language and cultural course offerings might jeopardise the academic integrity of higher education. For example, in early talks for a CI at the University of Sydney, Jocelyn Chey (2007), a professor in Chinese studies and a former Australian diplomat in China and Hong Kong, warned that there was danger in academic institutions worldwide relinquishing Chinese studies to institutes run by the government of China. That did not happen. The issue of academic interference was also raised in Sweden in 2008 when some staff at Stockholm University, host to the Nordic CI, demanded an end to the current arrangement and the separation of the Institute from the University. On the basis of an independent assessment, the Rector of the University rejected claims that the Institute had been used for Chinese political purposes. The issue, however, was taken up in the Swedish Parliament (Starr 2009).

By far, there appears to be little factual support for the accusation of improper influence over teaching and research of CIs. The CI headquarters in Beijing does not dictate the curricular design of a language or cultural program. The teaching materials provided by Beijing have been designed to facilitate pedagogical needs and are not intended for propaganda purposes. The headquarters cannot control the contents of a lecture series or the design of a festival program. As reported by Li, Mirmirani, and Ilacqua (2009, 474), the CI at the University of Rhode Island in the US sponsored a lecture series. One invited speaker was a well-known Sinologist from Yale who openly criticised Chinese public policy, while another was a former Vice President of the Republic of China based in Taiwan who publicly denounced the unification policy proposed by the People's Republic of China (PRC). For the annual Chinese New Year festivals, sponsored by the CI at Bryant University, Consulates General from both the PRC and Taiwan have attended, while officially PRC diplomats would boycott any event which has extended invitations to delegates from Taiwan.

However, perhaps due to such criticism, the Hanban officially denies its intention of soft power projection. Its director, Xu Lin (2008), emphasises that CIs are not projecting soft power, nor aim to impose Chinese values or Chinese culture on other countries. China just hopes to be truly understood by the rest of the world. CIs are designed to be an important platform to promote Chinese culture and teach Chinese language. In contrast, the soft power concept has been enthusiastically taken up by the Chinese government (Starr 2009). In October 2007, Chinese President Hu Jintao called for enhancing the soft power of Chinese culture at the Seventeenth National Congress of the Communist Party (Xinhua News Agency 2007).

Indeed, cultural institutions are hardly new, and the global promotion of Chinese culture and language should not come as a surprise. As explained by Lu Jianming (2005), Director of the Chinese Philosophy Research Centre at Peking University, language after all is a culture carrier. As a country gains economic strength, programs are often introduced enabling people in other countries to learn its language and culture. The accusation by the Canadian Security Intelligence Service that the creation of CIs can be viewed as a part of Chinese efforts for global dominance is thus meaningless (Li, Mirmirani, and Ilacqua 2009). Examples of other cultural institutions include the Alliance Française, the British Council, Goethe-Institut, Instituto Cervantes, Instituto Camões, and the Japan Foundation.

The Chinese goal, as illustrated by Liu Yandong (2008a), China's State Councillor and the chairperson of the council of the CI headquarters, is to follow the call of the times and satisfy the desire and passion of people around the world to learn Chinese and to stand as a creative endeavour in promoting friendship and cooperation between China and the rest of the world. Research supports such claims. For example, Li-Hua (2007) finds that the network of CIs could help to reduce tensions between the US and China. Many of those involved in CI programs in western countries agree, as remarked by Timothy O'Shea (2008, 29–30), Principal of the University of Edinburgh:

> CIs worldwide can become a key player in explaining China's new role, the general public and young students alike. ... CIs not only promote knowledge about China, they can also serve as a platform facilitating engagement and mutual exchange of ideas. ... As joint enterprises between Chinese and local people, CIs should not only be locations for learning, but also for social interactions and developing friendships.

Evidence from other sources suggests a need for CIs on both Chinese and foreign sides. For instance, Professor Robert Pearce, the vice-chancellor of Lampeter University, has been reported saying that:

> We have seen no evidence of the Chinese government using the university as a propaganda tool through CIs. Lampeter is a relatively quiet place. Our belief is that we need

to offer an education that gives us an international and national reputation. Our future and that of our grandchildren are going to depend on Britain trading with China. If we don't build links now, Britain has a very bleak future. (Shepherd 2007, 11)

Similarly, Ronald K. Machtley (2008, 34), a former US government official and current President of Bryant University, made the following comments: 'Each of us has our own natural and national interests, our past, our differences, yet... we are bound by the common interest to understand China through its language and culture'.

The fast growing international demand for CIs was a surprise to the Chinese government. This demand is ultimately due to China's economic growth and increasing political influence, as illustrated by Stuart N. McCutcheon (2008, 37), Vice-Chancellor of the University of Auckland:

Our graduates need to be prepared for a global job market and to make a strong contribution to a multicultural society that New Zealand has become. ... Now Chinese is essential for the new generation of New Zealanders. ... University of Auckland therefore believes that it has a national responsibility to promote the understanding of China, its language and culture and its political, economic and social life. We want to make New Zealanders China literate. ... Also, as the president of a research university, it is my responsibility to ensure that we're well-connected to China's research, science and technology infrastructure. Therefore I was asked to reinforce our university engagement with China for the long term.

Such a judgement was confirmed repeatedly by the participants in the case study, as expressed by Interview-TE-3, below:

The real purpose of the CI is to promote Chinese culture and language. We hope to let the world understand China, especially contemporary China. The Institute is a bridge between different cultures, not only to promote the Chinese, but also to let Chinese people understand others.

Interview-EP-2 explained further:

While some people consider the CI a diplomatic approach, most people welcome this. ...To my knowledge, many institutions are keen to host a CI. ... I believe CIs have a very bright future. I do not see them as China's cultural expansion. They are aiming at promoting foreigners to understand China, and Chinese language and culture, very different from the western history of modernisation, which was indeed cultural expansion.

Another participant, Interview-BM-4, who is an influential scholar in Australia with substantial links with the business world, assessed the CI he is associated with from a positive yet different perspective:

Very small but quite successful! We want not only language and culture, but also local business community and state government. ... There are a few at our University who are critical for that reason (Chinese soft power projection). I think overall, it is positive. The general trend in China's politics is towards democracy. We need mutual understanding, not just on our side, on the Chinese side as well. The Institute is making a difference, at least in our local business community.

Interview-SM-5 responded more directly when asked about the debate over the purpose of CIs:

My personal view is that this is a very good initiative, to promote Chinese culture and provide more opportunities. I have full confidence in their future development. I don't blame China for promoting soft power. I even think China should do more.

These positive views do not mean a lack of awareness that CIs could be used as a platform by the Chinese government for launching pro-Beijing initiatives. The Chinese government has predicted such a response, as commented on by Tim Wright, Professor of Chinese Studies at Sheffield University: 'The Chinese government is well aware of the danger of CIs being perceived in this way. We are given more or less a free rein to do what we want'. Meanwhile, those working at CIs have been carefully and successfully dealing with this. For example, Professor Yao Xinzhong, Director of the CI at Lampeter University, said that: 'We make it very clear that we are independent of the Chinese government. We will not compromise our views on Chinese politics because we have a CI' (Shepherd 2007, 12).

One of the participants talked about this in a subtle way:

The CI is an excellent policy. It needs some time to form certain pattern. Hanban does not have an answer to everything. We all learn by doing. ... One issue here, when China does anything, it always wants to make it big and do it quickly. This could leave others some wrong impression. (Interview-TE-3)

In contrast, Interview-CS-1 was far more critical:

I think the initiative demonstrates our inexperience in international politics. It is something that others could hold against us. It invites humiliation. Look at what we have done, millions of dollars each year. There have been many objections. It shows China is to exert its influence. China can be influential and should be so. But it is not necessary to take an initiative like this. China appears somewhat too aggressive. With a cost of huge amount of money, what do you think we can get? It has caused much suspicion. It'd be much better if we set up specific scholarships, which would exert significant influence even if we only allocate a small part of the money we have spent on CIs. ... CIs have become a government action, quite inexperienced. It makes the already peaceful situation very tricky, and consequently causes resentment and even hatred.

The operation of CIs

With a shortage of qualified Chinese teachers abroad, through its Office of Chinese Language Council International (Hanban), China establishes CIs to spread the teaching of Mandarin and Chinese culture worldwide. According to Liu Yandong (2008b, 1), the mission is to: 'serve as a bridge for information exchange and communication of minds between the CIs around the world as well as between Chinese people and those who love Chinese language and culture'. CIs differ in significant ways from the long-established agents of French and German culture. Their basic business is Chinese language teaching and promotion with a local flavour. They are incorporated into leading universities around the world as well as being linked to China not only by their Hanban connections, but also by supportive twinning arrangements with key Chinese universities. Not only will CIs immediately benefit from the prestige and convenience of becoming parts of existing campuses, the latter will also have a vested interest in supplying the institutes with staff and funds.

The 'leading group' consisted of officials seconded from various ministries chaired by a State Councillor, Chen Zhili, while the day-to-day running of the CI program is under an executive director. There are a dozen Executive Council members from relevant government departments including education, commerce, foreign affairs and media. There is also a group of 15 non-executive council members drawn from the participating Chinese and foreign universities as well as from the Beijing Municipal Education Commission. The first officially announced CI was inaugurated in Seoul in

November 2004, after a pilot project in Tashkent in the spring of 2004. The CIs have since witnessed 'a very favourable momentum of growth' (Liu 2008a, 13). By October 2009, 375 institutes had opened. Beijing originally aimed to open some 100 of them by 2010; now it has changed its plans to 500 to meet the great demand from overseas.

Classified by their funding sources, there are three kinds of CIs: those wholly financed by Beijing headquarters, those joint ventures with local foreign partners, and those wholly sponsored by local partners but licensed by the Beijing headquarters. An overwhelming majority of the CIs are a partnership between a foreign university, the Hanban and one or more Chinese university partner, falling into the second category. Their standard agreement is made for an initial period between the foreign partner and the Hanban, which then appoints a Chinese partner institution (Starr 2009). In addition to financial backing, the headquarters supplies books, audio-visual materials and multimedia courseware for facilitating teaching and enhancing library collections. The headquarters also authorises individual institutes to use its online courses. Visits by experienced language instructors from China, as a part of the structured program, are also organised and financed by the headquarters.

The Hanban is happy to see more individual features and encourages each CI to provide additional services. For instance, the CI of New Brunswick serves as a consulting and linking centre for Canadian and Chinese business communities. It also sponsors visiting and research programs. In Australia, while the University of Queensland is 'delighted to be able to complement existing CIs, focusing on China's contribution to science, engineering and technology' (Lane 2009), another university in the same city hosts a CI that concentrates on training language teachers. Other distinctive ones include Australia's only regional CI at the University of Newcastle featuring distance education, the Institute at the Royal Melbourne Institute of Technology known for its traditional Chinese medicine programs, and the CI at the University of Melbourne taking an entirely corporate line.

In light of their own situations, CIs work out their own rules and regulations to strengthen the management of their teaching and financial affairs. For example, the regulations of the CI at Oriental University of Napoli clearly spell out the rules on financial management, the duties of Chinese and foreign directors and instructors, employment and human resource management, curriculum and teaching. The CI at the University of Memphis has a four-tiered financial management system, where an application made by the Director is followed by the Dean of the School of East Asian Studies and reviewed by the Vice President before the final approval from the President, to ensure the correct use of funds (Zhou 2008, 20–1).

The CI headquarters also promotes the spill-over effect. For example, by offering programs to facilitate the travel of businessmen and tourists, the operation of the Institute at the University of Melbourne has benefited businesses and tour companies (Interview-SM-4). Indeed, it is not unusual to find that a CI offers counselling and assistance to those who are interested in summer camps and study abroad programs. These activities result in higher enrolments in other educational institutions. It is worth mentioning that sponsoring institutions in China and hosting institutions overseas often facilitate research programs beyond those covered by contractual terms. Yunnan University, for instance, has a program on Iranian studies, which is a unique endeavour among Chinese universities. Its sponsorship of the CI at Tehran University has provided ample opportunities to strengthen the program.

However, CIs are still in their preliminary stage of development. There are a number of issues in their operation.

The first issue is quality assurance, especially when a CI is built at a university with no previous Chinese language teaching unit. Under such circumstances, the institute is often asked to provide undergraduate and postgraduate for-credit courses as part of the end qualifications offered by the university. The Chinese side is aware of quality issues. Liu (2008a, 14–5) promised to take measures, including: stepping up training and nurturing a contingent of qualified faculty and administrators to increase their capacity in cross-cultural exchanges and improve their ability to teach Chinese as a foreign language; giving full play to the role of the sociologists and existing Chinese departments in universities around the world to encourage them to actively join the ranks of faculty for CIs; broadening the channels of funding and raising the efficiency in the utilisation of funds; putting in place a set of effective evaluation mechanisms and quality assurance systems for CIs and constantly improving their quality and levels; and formulating a medium-to-long-term development plan and setting up objectives, tasks and measures for future development of CIs.

However, quality remains a major concern. When asked why, Interview-EP-2 said: 'CIs are new. Nobody really knows how to do. Much more regulations are needed. Teaching too, we do not know how to teach, which textbooks are better and for what reason'.

Interview-TE-3 looked at the problems from a different perspective: 'If they are spread too broadly, there would be many administrative problems'.

The second is financial stability. The Hanban gives each university a certain amount of money to set up a CI and promises a certain amount for a few more years. The expectation is that the Institute will self-fund after the initial period. This is not realistic. The Hanban has to accept that the institutes will require funding for a substantial period of time. In addition to the financial and political support from the Chinese side, strong sponsorship from the hosting institutions and local government is also critical for the successful operation of the institutes. For example, the city of Chicago appropriated US$4.43 million in 2008 for their CI and Chinese language teaching (Zhou 2008, 20).

However, long-term funding should not be taken for granted, as illustrated by Interview-SM-5: 'Our funding sources are mainly three: the Hanban, our university and the state government. It's getting clear that state funding is unlikely to be sustainable. Funding is my biggest worry. Where to find money and for how long?'

Thirdly, relations with the Chinese partner university have proved to be uneasy. The difficulty is multi-dimensional. It has been a familiar story that those sent by the Chinese side are thought to be short of the much-needed institutional and cultural knowledge for successful teaching overseas. It is increasingly difficult to get experienced teachers of Chinese to leave their families to go abroad on a low salary. As for Chinese partner institutions, they pay the salaries of staff sent abroad yet see little benefit from this (Starr 2009). There are some other administrative problems. Sheffield University, for example, asked for more say over which teacher was appointed. Also, it is not uncommon for teachers from the Chinese partner university to arrive much later than expected by the hosting institution, often due to visa issues.

Similar issues were mentioned by the participants in the case study, although they did not see these as problems, nor did they blame the Hanban. Instead, they saw these as teething troubles, and expressed their understanding:

> A wide range yet without a ready model is necessarily problematic. It is normal and certainly not unexpected that there would be some issues regarding the collaboration between the two sides. (Interview-TE-3)

It takes time for CIs to reach maturity. Teachers from Chinese partnership institutions need time to understand local culture and society. (Interview-EP-2)

A new form of China's higher education internationalisation

Elements of universities' long historical traditions directly affect global higher education and relations among academic institutions internationally. The expansion of universities from their European and North American heartland occurred from the mid-nineteenth century onwards. Countries that escaped colonial domination have widely adopted western models, as exemplified in China (Altbach 2001). The academic world today, however, is becoming more multi-polarised. China's representation in the international scientific community has grown rapidly since its reopening to the world. Instead of being a passive recipient to be influenced by the major world powers, China is reaching out globally and investing heavily overseas. Its use of international exchange and cooperation in higher education as an exercise of soft power is unprecedented, and has gone far beyond the comfort zone of traditional theories.

China's projection of soft power in higher education has challenged both the traditional and more recent explanations of the political economy of international higher education, characterised respectively by North–South imbalances and asymmetries and a strong orientation towards international market share. The CI program demonstrates a new form of China's higher education internationalisation, featured by a much-improved balance between introducing the world into China and bringing China to the world within an altered global landscape of higher education. Most theorists have borrowed the theory of soft power to analyse China's CIs (Nye 2007; Kurlantzick 2007; Chey 2007; Gil 2008; Ding 2008; Starr 2009), but failed to link the CIs to China's global engagement and internationalisation in higher education.

The new form is a continuity of Chinese history, of which different periods have seen different forms of China's higher education internationalisation. By the close of the eighteenth century, China's higher education had evolved according to its own logic, and never deviated from its own developmental path as a result of external influences. While western higher education models had already demonstrated their strength, China's communication with the west was intentionally hindered. China was thus unable to learn anything from such advanced models in order to reform its higher education system.

Such a mentality of cultural superiority was smashed by repeated, humiliating defeats in China's modern history by western powers and Japan (Yang 2002). Since 1895, when China's first modern university was established, learning from the west has been strongly advocated as the only way to make China strong. The past three decades of China's higher education internationalisation continued to feature the importing of foreign (western) knowledge into China. Starting from the early 2000s, China's higher education internationalisation has begun to pay particular attention to exporting Chinese knowledge to the world. In 2008, those coming to China to study (223,499) historically outnumbered those leaving China to study abroad (179,800) (Su 2009).

The CI program demonstrates this shift of focus in China's internationalisation of higher education, as illustrated by one of the participants in the case study:

> CIs and their foreign host institutions themselves are a kind of cross-cultural communication. The birth of CIs and their growth in foreign universities is a process of cross-cultural understanding. Different opinions are understandable in the collaboration between different cultures and educational systems. The right way can only be more

communication. This is a familiar process in cross-cultural communication: starting from different, even opposing views, through mutual understanding, to shared values, views and cooperation. (Interview-TE-3)

Concluding observations

Few decisions of the twentieth century have had as profound an impact on the twenty-first century world as Deng Xiaoping's announcement of China's open door policy in 1978. Deng was prophetically ambitious, wanting to bridge minds by sending Chinese students to study overseas, encouraging Chinese universities to exchange and cooperate with their counterparts worldwide. Nearly three decades later, the development has taken a more balanced shape between importing the foreign and exporting the Chinese, which requires a similar mixture of vision and boldness.

From the perspective of higher education internationalisation, CIs provide Chinese and foreign universities with a platform for collaboration and exchange. The program is part of a message China sends to the world, that it has the Chinese government's keen sense of history. It reveals China's ability to plan for the long term – very much as the great master taught. As Confucius said, 'If you think in terms of a year, plant a seed; if in terms of 10 years, plant trees; if in terms of 100 years, teach the people'.

The further growth of CIs entails mutual respect, candour, sincerity and cooperation between Chinese and foreign partners (Liu 2008a, 15). The road ahead will almost certainly be bumpy. However, as Ronald K. Machtley (2008, 35) remarked:

> If we are to succeed as a world, as people, we must see more of this activity. Confucius had it right when he said 'to be capable one must study, to be intellectual, one must learn from others'. That is truly the mission of the CI.

References

Altbach, P. 2001. The American academic model in comparative perspective. In *In defence of American higher education,* ed. P. Altbach, P. Gumport, and B. Johnstone, 11–37. Baltimore, MD: Johns Hopkins University Press.
Bortin, M. 2008. China's ascendancy causing global concern, Pew study finds. *International Herald Tribune,* June 12.
Brzezinski, Z., and J. Mearsheimer. 2005. Clash of the Titans. *Foreign Policy* 146: 46–50.
Carr, E. 1954. *The twenty years' crisis.* New York: Macmillan.
Chey, J. 2007. The gentle dragon. http://yaleglobal.yale.edu/article.print?id=10034.
de Blij, H. 2005. *Why geography matters: Three challenges facing America: Climate change, the rise of China, and global terrorism.* New York: Oxford University Press.
Ding, S. 2008. *The dragon's hidden wings: How China rises with its soft power.* Lanham, MD: Lexington Books.
Eisenhower, D. 1958. Remarks at ceremony marking the 10th anniversary of the Smith-Mundt Act. http://www.presidency.ucsb.edu/ws/index.php?pid=11196.
Eisenman, J., E. Heginbotham, and D. Mitchell. 2007. *China and the developing world.* New York: M.E. Sharpe.
Gil, J. 2008. The promotion of Chinese language learning and China's soft power. *Asian Social Science* 4, no. 10: 116–22.
Gill, B., and Y. Huang. 2006. Sources and limits of Chinese 'soft power.' *Survival* 48, no. 2: 17–36.
Goldirova, R. 2008. Europeans think China biggest threat to world security. EUobserver. http://euobserver.com/9/25981?print=1.

Hargreaves, D. 1993. What happened to symbolic interactionism? In *Controversies in classroom research*, ed. M. Hammersley, 135–52. Buckingham: Open University Press.
Healy, G. 2009. Future depends on Asian languages. *The Australian*, June 10. http://www.theaustralian.news.com.au/story/0,25197,25612156-12332,00.html.
Johnson, C. 2004. *The sorrows of empire: Militarism, secrecy, and the end of the republic.* New York: Henry Holt and Company.
Kurlantzick, J. 2006. China's charm: Implications of Chinese soft power. *Policy Brief* 47: 1–8.
Kurlantzick, J. 2007. Chinese soft power in Southeast Asia (Part I). *The Globalist*, July 2. http://www.theglobalist.com/StoryId.aspx?StoryId=6240.
Lane, B. 2009. University of Queensland set to open Chinese institute. *The Australian*, April 29. http://www.theaustralian.news.au/story/0,25197,25400541-12332,00.html.
Li, H.C., S. Mirmirani, and J.A. Ilacqua. 2009. Confucius Institutes: Distributed leadership and knowledge sharing in a worldwide network. *The Learning Organisation* 16, no. 6: 469–82.
Li-Hua, R. 2007. Knowledge transfer in international educational collaboration program: The China perspective. *Journal of Technology Management* 2, no. 1: 84–97.
Liu, Y.D. 2008a. Joint participation and equal cooperation: Create a new outlook for the development of Confucius Institutes. *Confucius Institute* 1: 11–5.
Liu, Y.D. 2008b. Foreword. *Confucius Institute* 1: 1–2.
Lu, J.M. 2005. Chinese teachers spread the world to pass heritage. *China Daily*, February 1: 3.
Lukes, S. 1974. *Power: A radical view.* New York: Macmillan.
Machtley, R.K. 2008. A speech by Ronald K. Machtley. *Confucius Institute* 1: 33–5.
Marshall, C., and G. Rossman. 2006. *Designing qualitative research*. Thousand Oaks, CA: Sage.
McCutcheon, S.N. 2008. A speech by Stuart N. McCutcheon. *Confucius Institute* 1: 37.
Nye, J. 1990. *Bound to lead: The changing nature of American power.* New York: Basic Books.
Nye, J. 1997. China's re-emergence and the future of the Asia-Pacific. *Survival* 39, no.4: 65–79.
Nye, J. 2004. *Soft power: The means to success in world politics.* New York: Public Affairs.
Nye, J. 2007. The rise of China's soft power. *Peking University Newsletter* 3: 17–8.
O'Shea, T. 2008. A speech by Timothy O'Shea. *Confucius Institute* 1: 29–30.
Shambaugh, D. 2005. Return to the Middle Kingdom: China and Asia in the early twenty-first century. In *Power shift: China and Asia's new dynamics*, ed. D. Shambaugh, 23–47. Berkeley, CA: University of California Press.
Shepherd, J. 2007. Not a propaganda tool. *The Guardian*, November 6. http://www.spinwatch.org/-news-by-category-mainmenu-9/309-education/4366-not-a-propaganda-tool.
Starr, D. 2009. Chinese language education in Europe: The Confucius Institutes. *European Journal of Education* 44, no. 1: 65–82.
Su, Y. 2009. Numbers of students going abroad to study. http://learning.sohu.com/20090326/n263029186.shtml.
Sutter, R. 2003. Why does China matter? *The Washington Quarterly* 27, no. 1: 75–89.
Sutter, R. 2005. *China's rise in Asia: Promises and perils.* Lanham, MD: Rowman and Littlefield.
Xinhua News Agency. 2007. Hu calls for enhancing 'soft power' of China's culture. http://www.china.org.cn/english/congress/228142.htm
Xu, L. 2008. Confucius Institute headquarters 2009 work plan. *Confucius Institute* 1: 74–5.
Yang, R. 2002. *Third delight: Internationalisation of higher education in China.* New York: Routledge.
Zhou, J. 2008. Work report at 2008 Confucius Institute conference. *Confucius Institute* 1: 20–7.

The Bologna Process as a hegemonic tool of Normative Power Europe (NPE): the case of Chilean and Mexican higher education

Francis Espinoza Figueroa

Department of Political Sciences and International Studies, University of Birmingham, Birmingham, UK

> The scenario of Latin America in the higher education area, especially in Chile and Mexico, appears to be significantly affected by some European influences. We can see this by examining the implementation of two 'hegemonic tools': the Bologna Process and the Tuning Project. This paper argues that if we analyse the European influences as a normative power (NPE) on the construction of a common space in higher education in Chile and Mexico, the hegemonic process may, perhaps, prove to be focused on an 'alternative imperialism', based on Eurocentric discourse, which could also be called a 'post-colonialist' strategy. This article will seek to show that European influences, exercised by the EU operating as a normative power, are only the 'tip of the iceberg' of the hegemonic process. The paper is divided into five parts: following the introduction, a general overview of the Bologna Process opens the discussion of questions of American or European hegemony. After that, I analyse NPE and the 'ontological quality' of the EU as a hegemonic power. The empirical cases of European influences, on Chilean and Mexican HE, are analysed in detail in order to show the most significant impacts on their public and university policies. Finally, I offer a view of the Bologna Process as a 'European hegemonic instrument' of NPE.

Introduction

The internationalisation of higher education has been a fashionable issue since concepts such as globalisation, Europeanisation and 'Bologna-isation' appeared on the international arena. The Bologna Process represents one of the main models for internationalising HE. In fact, its external dimension promotes a worldwide degree of attraction focused on 'the objective of increasing the international competitiveness of the European System of higher education' (Zgaga 2006, 5).

On the one hand, this issue implies structural changes for re-engineering curricula and teaching–learning processes in higher education (HE) in order to produce 'human resources' for the market. This implies the need to bring about deep shifts in undergraduate teaching and learning processes to synchronise with the modernisation of postgraduate standards throughout the world.

On the other hand, it also involves political decision-making at nation state levels, which seek to adapt foreign models within different realities or cultures. These foreign models normally represent hegemonic powers (hegemonies) which pursue practical goals such as the expansion of HE markets (Brunner and Uribe 2007). In addition, these powers implement hegemonic strategies for exerting 'symbolic domination' through language such as practices of persuasion and consensus. In this way, hegemonies maintain their power through their capacity to dominate others, persuading subordinates to accept, adopt and internalise their own values and norms.

In recent decades, the EU has formed many ties with countries in Latin America. These have brought many new economic and knowledge-based developments, with some advantages to the Latin American participants. One of the most visible effects of this 'political dialogue' between the EU and LAC (Latin America and the Caribbean) is the strengthened co-operation in higher education through the Bologna Process. This co-operation has sought to facilitate the sharing of knowledge, the transfer of technologies and the mobility of students, academics, researchers and administrators, focusing on training, employment and scientific knowledge.

In practical terms, the effects of the Bologna Process on Chilean and Mexican higher education can be observed in the processes of the strengthening of the roles of state and HE institutions. Specifically, this is seen in the design of public policies and the planning of institutional policies through formal mechanisms such as the development of specific policies and the execution of institutional adjustments.

The Bologna Process as a Trojan horse

As a preliminary approach to this issue, we might suggest that 'higher education' as a hegemonic 'social structure' could have two variants: European (as a political discursive logic) or American hegemony (as a political economic logic) – or even possibly both (EU and US hegemonies) operating in the field of higher education in Latin America. If we take this latter assumption, it would allow for a complex analysis of how hegemonic forces might be at present operating in post-modern contexts or post-industrial societies.

If we analyze the European influences as Normative Power Europe (NPE; Manners 2001), for example, on the construction of a common space in higher education in Latin America, the hegemonic process can be seen more clearly if viewed through the prism of an 'alternative imperialism', based solely on Eurocentric discourse, a 'post-colonialist' strategy. It would be based on what post-structuralist scholars like Gayatri Chakravorty Spivak (1999) have seen as the EU's linguistic means of exerting power. It would be, 'part of "Eurocentric strategies of narrativising history, so that Europe can congratulate itself for progress", [a progress] which in contemporary terms invokes the <<culture of capitalism>>' (Manners 2004, 2).

However, if we study the changes that are happening in higher education from a capitalist perspective, other conclusions could appear; for example, the strong presence of the US in the structural dynamic of the Bologna Process and the emergence of an international higher education orientated towards market demands. In this case, we may analyse the Bologna Process as a political structure which combines the processes of commodification and socialisation (Cafruny and Ryner 2007). Thus higher education, previously seen as a mainly cultural process, begins to be treated much more as a commodity, a consumer item. This is done through standardisation processes and contents which introduce neo-liberal strategies, following the globalisation process and replacing the *state welfare* policies with the concepts of *market*. In addition, the World Bank and the consortia associated with banking are also involved in the processes of making loans to educational institutions and governments to improve higher education levels or to make them more affordable to the governments concerned.

Within this approach, Jessop, Fairclough, and Wodak (2008) analyse the impact of the knowledge-based economy (KBE) on higher education. In that sense, Susan Robertson, for example, uses the umbrella of cultural political economy of Education (CPE/E) to bring to the 'table' the discussion of the role that cultural and semiotic aspects play within this hegemonic dynamic for constructing: 'a new kind of global economy whose neo-liberal tenets are being constitutionalised in a complex architecture of policies, funding programmes, agreements, protocols, indexes and registers that operate at multiple scales' (Robertson 2009, 7).

Even though it is difficult to find scholars working in the area of European influences on HE outside Europe, one could argue that Eurocentric approaches seek to show the EU as a more egalitarian and participatory model, centred in several concepts and values, including 'progressive competitiveness', 'productivity pacts', 'associative democracy' and 'social cohesion'. These terms could complement the background of what Ian Manners has named Normative Power Europe (NPE). Therefore, the main purpose of this article is an analysis of European hegemony in terms of NPE.

For the latter purpose, I prefer to see the model of the Bologna Process as a 'Trojan horse' that purports to bring a vaguely European influence yet, *in fact*, makes a more fundamental change than that might imply. The Bologna Process can be seen, then, as the most influential tool that Europe has been using to spread the norms, ideas and languages of the countries of the European Community. This process of 'Bologna-isation' is also characterised by the presence of European influences through a 'package of instruments' such as the establishment of agreements and programmes.

One may ask whether the EU is itself exercising hegemony through its foreign policies as applied in Latin America. It may be working in parallel with a global hegemony, but using a different method of exercising hegemony. This method might be described as a centripetal process, rather than as the more usual centrifugal process. This would fit with Agnew's view that 'EU influence works largely through existing institutions by creating and imposing common standards' (Agnew 2005, 23). In this case, we can consider the EU as a normative power, which would represent 'a good contemporary example of a form of hegemony without empire, if only within one-world regimes' (Agnew 2005, 23).

Normative Power Europe and the 'ontological quality' of the EU
The conception of NPE is set out most clearly by Ian Manners:

> The EU as a normative power has an ontological quality to it – that the EU can be *conceptualized* as a changer of norms in the international system; a positivist quantity to it – that the EU *acts* to change norms in the international system; and a normative quality to it – that the EU *should* act to extend its norms into the international system. (Manners 2002, 252)

Within the scholarship of Normative Power Europe (NPE), it is possible to identify clearly three significant generations. The *first generation* introduces the concept of NPE and offers an ontological contribution to the discussion because it shows us NPE as an instrument of analysis of the nature of the EU. Its existence prevails as a substantial element of the phenomenon of EU hegemony as a superpower. Within the 'first generation' of NPE, spearheaded by Ian Manners, the understanding of the EU as 'diffuser of universal values' implies the construction of a discourse based on the Enlightenment. For this reason, the need to 'quantify' or 'measure' the impact of Europe overseas emerges through positivist discourses which underline the role of the 'European authority' through its military and economic capabilities. Due to the fact that the EU cannot sometimes demonstrate its own structural capabilities, it is necessary to argue that Europe exerts a kind of pedagogic 'soft power', endeavouring to 'teach' foreign powers how to conduct themselves in world politics through several models which are characterised by the absence of physical force in the imposition of norms or rules. Andy Storey suggests that Manners proposed NPE to emphasise the presence of the EU in the international arena through its capability of influencing opinions and norms globally (Storey 2005, 2).

It is also possible to observe an *'intermediate generation'* which is predicated on three main themes, namely: analysing NPE in official documents and treaties; looking for NPE in the ways that the EU conducts itself internationally, through its policies in foreign affairs; and studying NPE as a vehicle of transferring policies from the EU as a 'norm-maker' to others as 'norm-takers'. According to Ian Manners, the EU as a normative power has followed a historical evolution through the creation of declarations, policies, treaties and agreements. In practical terms, the EU implements 'normative' strategies which have as their target purely 'civilian' objectives. The literature of normative power focuses on gaining influence over people's opinions and, consequently, their actions, because, as Ian Manners argues, the EU constitutes a different kind of power which is neither military nor purely economic. This is a power that is able to exert influence through ideas and opinions; in Manners' words, it is a power that is able to shape conceptions of those views and discourses (*'Weltanschauung'*) which are considered to be the 'norm' in social and consensual realities of human existence.

The *second generation*, led by Thomas Diez (see Diez 2005), contributes epistemologically to the discussion of NPE due to the fact that it provides determined 'lenses' or approaches to a view of a reality called 'Normative Power Europe'. This is a reality which defines the EU as the catalyst of changes in the international arena. In addition, the second generation introduces phenomenological elements because it contributes to the position of Europe within the ethical space of 'goodness' and its categories of understanding of 'identity' and 'others'. In fact, the ethical considerations of NPE define the kind of power that the EU exerts. The so-called force 'for good' develops a discourse based on the 'goodness' of Europe, and, as a result of this 'goodness', the EU constructs its own identity as well as others'.

The *third generation* contributes again ontologically, because it re-creates a new 'reality' of NPE called 'epistemic violence', through which an 'ontology of language' opens the door to the analysis of the language of NPE itself, and its implications beyond. This 'generation', led by Michel Merlinger (see 2007) – more post-structuralist and critical – refreshes the concept of NPE, opening the door for reflective analyses of the normative discourse itself. They de-construct the metanarrative of NPE through providing evidence of the 'epistemic violence' that involves NPE *per se*.

Furthermore, as part of this third generation, this paper seeks to make a hermeneutical contribution in that it interprets NPE as an 'ontological violence', not an epistemic one, in its thinking that language is 'the house of being' (Heidegger 1977/ 1947, 193). Language itself is central in the exertion of hegemony or a 'tyranny of ideas'. This paper criticises, first, those discursive constructions offered by the language of NPE itself. Secondly, it uses further constructions which reveal the hegemonic process exerted by the EU exporting its models overseas, as in the case of the Bologna Process. Thirdly, this argument undertakes a more critical analysis in which to study post-colonial strategies which possess an orientation and impact on the discourses and 'vocabularies' of others.

The 'triumphal' arrival of the European ideas in Chilean HE

In terms of Chilean *public policies*, European ideas have had a significant impact on three main aspects: the mechanism of allocating public financial resources (MECESUP); a new culture of planning and assessing projects for higher education; and, in an indirect way, the National Accreditation System, which has come under European influence. Taking into account *university policies*, European ideas have had a strong impact on the design of curricular architecture and the processes of curricular re-engineering in the 25 traditional universities. In addition, the impact is visible on the construction of a National Academic Credit System (STC – Chile) and processes of internationalisation of HE institutions.

The European ideas of the Bologna Process arrived in Chile officially in 2002 when the Council of Chancellors of Chilean Rectors (CRUCH) met European partners in Louvain, Belgium to discuss curricula and a credits system in European and Chilean universities. As a result of the meeting, events, declarations and projects were set in motion by the incorporation of European ideas within Chilean institutional and public policies.

Following the Louvain Meeting, the Chilean traditional universities signed the 'Valparaíso Declaration', in which they agreed to follow the Bologna Process. During the same year, they worked with European experts in a seminar in Santiago (Chile), analysing changes and advances in the Bologna Protocol. The Declaration of Valparaíso constitutes one of the most significant events, not only because it represented the formalisation of a political dialogue between Chile and the EU. This political dialogue also helped to construct the 'European dream' of a common space for higher education among participating countries.

The next significant event after the Valparaíso Declaration occurred in 2004, when the Chilean Government inserted the ALFA Latin America Tuning programme (for an account of this programme, see Beneitone et al. 2007) into the Programme to Improve Quality and Equity in Higher Education (MECESUP 2) projects,[1] which launched the Bologna Process officially in Chilean universities. The Chilean Government prepared, together with the World Bank, a second stage, MECESUP 2 'Tertiary Education for the Knowledge Society',[2] which is intended to be permanent, and thus to ensure continuity: it is targeted towards academic and curricular renewal, and to exploring the possibility of creating a new resource allocation instrument based on performance agreements. It also ensures international recognition for the postgraduate doctorate being offered in Chile.

Chile was one of the national centres of the ALFA Tuning Project in Latin America, and its main purpose was to strengthen the development of projects for the curricular innovation of Chilean higher education, through the support of MECESUP projects. According to Brunner (2008), Ricardo Lagos' government (2000–2006) decided to place the ALFA project in MECESUP 2 because it needed both to strengthen the MECESUP projects financially and also to justify the presence of accountability strategies through a parallel with what European universities were doing in terms of higher education. However, Roxana Pey, a civil servant and coordinator of the National Tuning Centre in Chile, argues that democratic Chilean governments located this 'centre' firmly within the MECESUP projects because it would ease the operationalisation of the projects and make it easier to develop a methodology for implementing structural changes in university curricula. It is thus argued here that European influences have 'coloured' and 'informed' the criteria by which university projects are evaluated.

In addition, through one of the major mechanisms for allocating financial development resources, MECESUP 2, it is possible to observe the development of a new culture for planning and assessing HE projects. Bologna has contributed some planning models and ideas which would support the concept of privatism argued for by Bernasconi and Brunner. The final stage of privatism is a kind of privatisation which associates the awarding of state resources with a process characterised by an emphasis on continually planning and seeking to improve the quality of educational standards. In this award process, the state conducts itself like the manager of a private business, ensuring that higher education institutions are operated in ways that achieve high degrees of efficiency, efficacy and solvency (Bernasconi 1999; Brunner and Uribe 2007). In Chile, a planning and evaluation culture within higher education emerged alongside these processes, establishing a 'mutually beneficial relationship' between Chile and the European Union.

In the next declarations, Arica (July 2005) and Santiago (August 2006), the vice-chancellors of CRUCH universities decided to constitute a network of high status institutions, which would together promote territorial harmony, student exchanges and wider collaboration in research and postgraduate studies. In addition, they made a formal decision to implement a discrete system of academic credits for the 25 traditional universities.

European ideas targeting the core of Mexican higher education

European ideas arrived in Mexico mainly through two significant actors: the Secretary of Public Education and the Consortium of Mexican Universities (CUMEX). The Bologna Process has brought about a group effort which is seeking to construct languages and mechanisms for a reciprocal understanding of systems of higher education. These are facilitating the processes of recognition of trans-national and trans-regional university curricula. This has led to them being conceived as:

> ... a space of reflection for actors who are involved with higher education. They are seeking consensus to advance in the development of qualifications which will be easily comparable and understandable both in Latin America and in Europe. (Beneitone et al. 2006, 13)

Taking into account the design and implementation of *public policies*, the Mexican government has recognised the European model as an appropriate model, even an ideal one, for internationalising Mexican higher education, specifically through 'collaboration with the European Union' (Gácel-Ávila 2005, 269). As a result, the government is implementing networks, a consortia of collaboration and academic exchanges, and student mobility between national institutions and Mexican and foreign institutions.

Another *public policy* implemented as a result of the impact of European ideas is the placing of the National Tuning Centre (see Beneitone et al., op cit) within the Secretariat of Public Education. This decision allowed government to be the vehicle of diffusion for the Bologna Process, to achieve extensive propaganda and diffusion across the whole of the Mexican higher education system. In addition, this decision has launched the implementation of strategic decisions for improving, updating and extending the international frontiers of Mexican higher education.

Furthermore, it is possible to discern an indirect impact on the accreditation and evaluation process of higher education through the National Centre of Evaluation for Higher Education (CENEVAL). It has promoted the establishment of schemes for the effective planning and continuous improvement of quality assurance within the majority of public institutions, as well as the implementation of a new institutional culture, focused on achieving good results.

European ideas have had an impact on three significant *university policies*: the internationalisation process of Mexican HE institutions; the design of curricular architecture; and the implementation of the Tuning methodology. However, it is impossible to observe a single model for making institutional adjustment in Mexican HE institutions, and even for the implementation of the Bologna Process within Mexican universities and institutes.

Mexican universities were active participants in the project of Tuning Latin America to create strategic alliances as a means of integrating Mexico into the hemispheric process of meeting worldwide challenges. These strategies were focused on the mobility of students and academics, international networks or linkages, partnerships, shared projects, and international programmes and research activities. The short-term effects of this internationalisation process have had an impact on students, academic staff and the content and design of educational programmes. Long-term, the impact will be visible in the quality of education, the profile of graduates and in the national and international positioning of institutions. In fact, the mobility between professors and students, and the research agendas of Mexican and Bologna universities, give clear evidence of international academic collaboration, bringing recognition and acceptance to the Mexican universities. They have established interest groups and demonstrated a spirit of leadership in organising academic networks.

In addition, the Bologna Process has impacted on processes of curricular re-engineering in the CUMEX's universities and Mexican technological institutes. These institutions are working on making their educational programmes more up-to-date and flexible, incorporating educational paradigms that focus on students' learning, and schemes for individual and group evaluations. Therefore, institutions are seeking efficient mechanisms for the mutual recognition of credits and implicit equality of status between courses. In addition, as part of its participation in the Tuning Project, Mexico HE institutions are working actively in a project called '6x4 UEALC, A university dialogue' (see Knight 2006), through which experts are analysing six professional careers.[3] These analyses are focused on four areas: strategies to describe and evaluate competency-based learning; a region-wide academic credit system; a common reference framework for integrating the evaluation of competencies into quality assurance and accreditation systems; and a list of key competencies for research and innovation and related training strategies. The overall goal was to improve the quality of higher education in Latin America and to facilitate greater collaboration and mobility among the higher education institutions within the region, and with the higher education sector in Europe.

The Bologna Process: a European hegemonic instrument of NPE

At this point, it is necessary to conceptualise and theorise about the impact of European ideas and language on Chilean and Mexican higher education. The degree of its impact could be regarded as a phenomenon that has the potential to influence actors and the way they operate. The concept of 'influence' infers the dominance of one actor over another. The EU has an influence over domestic, university and public policies, and operates within the role of a 'persuader'. Chile and Mexico are actors who represent the other side of the coin, the 'persuaded'. The Bologna model may not be appropriate in either Chile or Mexico, who may have felt driven to this EU model because each, for historical reasons, mistrusts US influence, but they, perceiving no other positive option, have consented to 'use' the European model for achieving their own purposes in their internal policies.

At this juncture, the importance of 'language' needs to be reassessed and clarified in the light of its impact upon scholarship itself. Language is the bearer of a vast and onerous responsibility of meanings, interpretations and – crucially – its effects upon actors and recipients: the 'persuaders' and the 'persuaded'. The subjective experience of the 'persuader' and 'persuaded' differs because of an imbalance of power and the undeniable fact that the 'persuader' holds the ability to shape, form and, therefore, define the very basis, the foundation, of meaning in language. On the other hand, the 'persuaded' experience the actions of the 'persuader' with unease because they contain an inchoate experience. This experience, as yet only in part formed, might be difficult to articulate since it is developed, in a large part, through an experience of 'rage' through the actions of the 'persuader': the 'rage' comes, in a large part, from being the subject of another's actions and intentions.

Therefore, language itself is central in the exertion of hegemony or a 'tyranny of ideas'. Language itself becomes a vehicle for hegemonic practices, as it imposes and determines ways of grasping or constructing the 'reality' or 'realities' of the world. These practices embrace processes of inclusion and exclusion, which travel in parallel, as Slavoj Zizek argues, as a 'dialectical synthesis' of opposites (Zizek 2007, 20). In simple terms, what comprises a positive discourse for one could be regarded as a 'tyranny of thoughts and words' for another.

In practical terms, the 'European Bologna language' has impacted other realities and vocabularies around the world as well as in Latin American countries, especially Chile and Mexico, through the construction of a very strong discourse focused on the creation of a higher education space. This abstract 'space' of higher education symbolises the exportation of a European model through which others will come to understand, conceive, plan and organise the functional, structural and content dynamics of the universities outside of Europe.

At the same time, the 'European Bologna language' implies a Eurocentric discourse that recognises few other contexts or any worldview outside those of Europe itself. Put simply, 'reality' is viewed solely through European eyes, and wholly without interest in or concern for pursuing an enlightened and self-critical analysis of Europe's relationship with the rest of the world. Therefore, it will be argued that the EU is focused upon its own European models, to the exclusion of the considerations of other developing parts of the world. It reveals itself as possessing an epistemological and not an ontological quality, when it offers models to reinforce pre-existent ideas, values, norms and opinions. The very question of the nature of 'goodness' arises here when applied to the concept of the 'normative power' of the Bologna Process: Is it a tyranny of ideas and language? Is the Bologna Process 'a force for good' for others outside of Europe?

Conclusions

The Bologna Process implies not only the structuring of higher education space abroad according to EU wishes but also presents a solely European model for regional integration, the exchanging of cooperative activities and strengthening of international relations. According to this paper, the Bologna Process shows two contrasting faces of the same coin, depending on which stakeholder is seeing this phenomenon.

On the one hand, the 'external dimension' of this process defined by Zgaga describes the Eurocentric point of view of the Bologna Process from a 'social dimension' focused on 'Bologna language'. In that sense, this constructivist view of the phenomenon allows us to analyse the importance of language in the construction of international relations, because, 'power relations often function through the construction in language, of hierarchical distinctions of identity/difference, sameness/otherness' (Hay 2002, 314). On the other hand, the Bologna Process is seen in Latin American eyes, especially in Chile and Mexico, as an 'internationalisation process' for higher education. In fact, it has imposed deep scientific and technological changes in the development of skills first to create knowledge, then to manage, spread and use them. Therefore, the higher education sector constitutes a strong basis from which to look more deeply at some of the structural components of power and hegemony in international relations.

The Bologna Process could mean many additional things, such as a change in the balance of power between Chilean and Mexican universities and central government, a way of designing a university government system (a new model) in Chile and Mexico, and one of the most important factors permeating the system of primary and secondary education as a consequence of the trickle-down of the ideas and structures embedded in the Bologna Process.

Finally, one could say critically that due to the fact that the EU cannot allow itself to demonstrate its own structural capabilities, it is necessary to argue that Europe exerts a kind of pedagogic 'soft power', endeavouring to 'teach' foreign powers how to conduct themselves in world politics through several models which are characterised by the absence of physical force in the imposition of norms or rules.

Notes

1. This programme of projects was created as an accreditation system in 1990.
2. It was implemented during the second half of 2005.
3. Medicine, electronic engineering, administration, maths, history and chemistry.

References

Agnew, J. 2005. *Hegemony. The new shape of global power.* Philadelphia, PA: Temple University Press.

Beneitone, P., C. Esquetini, J. González, M. Marty Maletá, G. Siufi, and R. Wagenaar. 2007. *Reflexiones y perspectivas de la educación superior en América Latina. Informe final, Proyecto Tuning-América Latina 2004–2007.* Bilbao, Spain: Universidad de Deusto.

Bernasconi, A. 1999. Second-generation reforms in Chile, international higher education. Centre of Higher Education, Boston College. http://www.bc.edu/bc_org/avp/soe/cihe/newsletter/News15/text8.html.

Brunner, J.J. 2008. El Proceso de Bolonia en el horizonte latinoamericano: Límites y posibilidades. *Revista de Educación,* Numero Extraordinario: 119–45. http://www.revistaeducacion.mec.es/re2008/re2008_06.pdf.

Brunner, J.J., and D. Uribe. 2007. *Mercados universitarios: El nuevo escenario de la educación superior.* Santiago, Chile: Ediciones Universidad Diego Portales.

Cafruny, A., and M. Ryner. 2007. Monetary union and the transatlantic and social dimensions of the crisis of the European Union. *New Political Economy* 12, no. 2: 141–65.

Diez, T. 2005. Constructing the self and changing others: Reconsidering 'Normative Power Europe'. *Millennium* 33, no. 3: 613–36.

Gácel-Ávila, J. 2005. Internationalization of higher education in Mexico. In *Higher education in Latin America: The international dimension,* ed. H. de Wit, C. Jaramillo, and J. Gácel-Ávila, 239–79. Washington, DC: The International Bank for Reconstruction and Development, and World Bank.

Hay, C. 2002. *Political analysis. A critical introduction.* London: Palgrave.

Heidegger, M. 1977/1947. *'The letter on humanism', basic writings from 'Being and time' (1927) to 'The task of thinking' (1964).* New York: Harper and Row.

Jessop, R., N. Fairclough, and R. Wodak. 2008. *Higher education and the knowledge-based economy in Europe.* Rotterdam: Sense Publishers.

Knight, J. 2006. Building a regional academic credit system in Latin America. *International Higher Education* 44: 18.

Manners, I. 2001. Normative Power Europe: The international role of the EU. Paper presented at the 7th European Community Studies Association Biennial Conference, May 31–June 2, in Madison, WI.

Manners, I. 2002. Normative Power Europe: A contradiction in terms? *Journal of Common Market Studies* 40, no. 2: 235–58.

Manners, I. 2004. Normative Power Europe reconsidered. Paper presented at the CIDEL Workshop, October 22–23, in Oslo, Norway. http://www.arena.uio.no/cidel/WorkshopOsloSecurity/Manners.pdf.

Merlinger, M. 2007. Everything is dangerous: A critique of 'Normative Power Europe'. *Security Dialogue* 38, no. 4: 435–53.

Robertson, S. 2009. Globalising higher education: The case of the UK. Paper prepared for the workshop: 'The perils and opportunities of the internationalisation of higher education: A critical perspective', September 25–26, at the Centre de recherche interdisciplinaire sur l'international (CRII), University of Lausanne, Switzerland.

Spivak, G.C. 1999. *A critique of postcolonial reason: Toward a history of the vanishing present.* Cambridge, MA: Harvard University Press.

Storey, A. 2005. Normative Power Europe? Economic partnership agreement and Africa. Paper presented at the African Studies Association of Ireland Conference, December 3, in Dublin, Ireland. http://www.pana.ie/idn/031205.html.

Zgaga, P. 2006. 'External dimension' of the Bologna Process (firstreport). Working Group of the External Dimension of the Bologna Process. http://www.bolognaoslo.com/expose/global/download.asp?id=28&fk11&thumb=.

Zizek, S. 2007. *The parallax view.* Cambridge, MA: MIT Press.

The selectivity of translation: accountability regimes in Chilean and South African higher education

Barbara Junge (formerly Dickhaus)

Globalisation and Politics Research Unit, Kassel University, Kassel, Germany

> This paper examines the translation of global educational norms of quality assurance in two countries with very different regulatory regimes in higher education: Chile and South Africa. The translation process is conceptualised here as a contested socio-political process of appropriation and creation of meaning. Drawing upon the strategic–relational concept of selectivity, the paper argues that quality assurance policies have become a hegemonic tool for re-organising higher education because a variety of – partly contradictory – meanings and interests can be attached to them: quality assurance is linked to rationales such as democratic transformation, re-establishing public governance, strengthening market governance, contributing to national competitiveness, internationalisation of higher education or positioning universities in the (global) education market. Looking at the translation of quality assurance policies with the concept of selectivity enables us to see how structure, agency, discourses and scales operate strategically-selectively in creating compromises between different interests in higher education governance.

Introduction

Researchers have identified a worldwide move away from traditional and collegial towards managerial and market forms of accountability regimes in higher education. In the last decades, external quality assurance (QA) policies like accreditations and audits – a key aspect of new accountability regimes in higher education – were developed in the US and Europe, by international organisations like the World Bank and UNESCO – and transferred to other countries around the world (Vidovich and Slee 2001; Westerheijden, Stensaker, and Rosa 2007).

QA policies have far-reaching implications for the regulatory and market structures of the higher education sector. Views of governments, universities and academics on QA in higher education therefore differ greatly, and governments partly face strong opposition from universities or academics when introducing these policies. However, QA has become a widely accepted governance tool in higher education in recent years, as Salter and Tapper note: 'the politics of governance in higher education is dominated by a discourse of quality assurance which assumes the external regulation of academic quality to be the natural state of affairs' (2000, 66).

After a transition to democracy, QA was also introduced as a key regulatory policy in the Chilean and South African higher education sectors in the 1990s – two higher education systems with very different governance structures regarding the role of the state in higher education. Even though governments there faced (partly) strong opposition, QA has become a widely accepted policy in Chile and South Africa. But how did a highly contested managerial tool for organising the higher education sector become a generally accepted regulatory policy in Chile and South Africa?

This process reflects the creation of a broad consensus on QA in higher education in two very distinct and specific national settings. A variety of meanings were attached to QA, and interests of different actors accommodated. QA therefore appears to have become a hegemonic tool for re-organising higher education, and this paper seeks to investigate how these different national compromises on QA were established.

In the first section I will sketch key issues of QA and accountability regimes in higher education. This will be followed by an outline of my theoretical framework: I will analyse the translation process from a Neo-Gramscian and strategic–relational perspective, taking the concept of 'selectivity' developed by Jessop in his strategic–relational approach (SRA) as a conceptual starting point. This serves as a framework for the analysis of the case studies in the next section. Examining the translation of accountability regimes in Chilean and South African higher education from this perspective will illustrate the role of structure, agency, discourses and scales in creating compromises on QA.

Meanings and rationales of QA in higher education

The meanings attributed to QA[1] like accreditations and audits and the rationales put forward for introducing them differ greatly and are often highly contested (Harvey and Newton 2004; Westerheijden, Stensaker, and Rosa 2007).

From a government perspective, QA encourages 'compliance to emerging or existing government policy' (Harvey and Newton 2004, 152) and facilitates public control of the sector. Governments also promote QA to strengthen 'accountability' towards students and 'the public' (e.g., to account for public money spent or to safeguard educational standards). Universities with a high reputation in terms of 'quality' often support external QA, as it presents an – internationally recognised – 'positioning device' in higher education markets. Higher education institutions (HEI) also promote QA as it facilitates internal reforms by strengthening centralised QA within universities.

On the other hand, the introduction of QA is often opposed, e.g., because it can negatively influence a university's position in the market or limit access to funding. Many academics as well as higher education researchers see QA as a new public management tool for re-organising higher education. In this view, QA is seen as disregarding the specific nature of higher education and as questioning traditional regimes of academic (self-) regulation.

Identifying a shift towards a regulatory or evaluative state, Neave (1998) and others highlight the often paradoxical role of the state in QA in higher education: it implies a prominent role of the state in organising the sector, but with a managerial tool. This is linked to what we might call the 'adaptivity' of QA policies, an important feature for this managerial tool to become hegemonic as it 'enables a terrain of dispute'[2] about the re-organisation of the higher education sector.

A strategic–relational perspective of investigating the translation of educational policies

The internationalisation and transfer of educational norms from the global to the national level has been conceptualised in a variety of different theoretical approaches. The neo-institutionalist world society approach (see Meyer and Ramirez 2000) identifies supranational forces and a *world culture* as drivers of a perceived global isomorphism of educational systems around the world. Dale (1999) in contrast emphasises the relevance of global as well as local features in this process: as globalisation's effects are not seen to be unidirectional, state 'interpretational frameworks' (Dale 1999, 441) are affected by capitalist globalisation (e.g., towards more competitiveness), but national patterns of a state's responses and of educational systems persist.

The aspects of interpretation, transfer and appropriation on different scales emphasised by Dale are reflected in the concept of 'translation', which therefore differs from concepts of policy transfer and diffusion. It is also advanced in other studies (see Westerheijden, Stensaker, and Rosa 2007) and introduced here to emphasise the contested and multidimensional characteristics of the translation process.

Jessop's SRA and his concept of selectivity provide a highly valuable framework for the analysis of translation processes, as he re-conceptualises the categories of structure, agency, discourse and scales as strategic–relational in his cultural political economy (CPE) perspective (Jessop 2008, 41–3; Moulaert and Jessop 2006).

The relationship between structure and agency is redefined, so that social structure can be studied in: 'strategic–relational terms as involving structurally inscribed strategic selectivity; and action can likewise be analysed in terms of its performance by agents with strategically calculating structural orientation' (Jessop 2008, 41). This implies that structural constraints are relational and operate selectively: they provide opportunities for some actors, and reward actions compatible with the reproduction of existing structural features like institutional arrangements and power relations, while they constrain others. Actors are reflexive and also relational as they are 'able to engage in strategic calculation about their current situation' (ibid.). They are therefore able to strategically calculate structural constraints, develop strategies accordingly and thus gain transformative power (ibid., 41–3). Furthermore, the discursive aspect of political processes is highlighted in the SRA by looking at the role of ideas, narratives, framing and discourses in constructing alliances, creating meaning and universalising interests (ibid., 48–51).

This particular understanding of the role of agency and discourses is linked to one of the sources of the SRA, the Gramscian concept of hegemony and creation of consensus by integrating different interests. According to Gramsci, some actors with a social function as organic intellectuals have a crucial role in creating consensus by universalising and legitimating ideas, norms and interests. This facilitates a focus on strategies of integrating opposing interests by linking an idea or policy to the 'common sense' or general understandings of 'how things work' or should be organised (Gramsci 1978).

Jessop also re-conceptualises scales, with reference to concepts of critical geographers (2008, 178). The politics of scale and re-scaling highlight the multiscalar characteristics of political processes as well as the 'production, reconfiguration and contestation of particular ... hierarchies among geographical scales' (Brenner 2001, 600). Thus, scales are not perceived as fixed and 'naturally given' levels of social interaction, but are strategically defined as terrains of struggles, to which relevance is assigned by actors in a specific context.

Re-conceptualising the SRA for analysing public governance in higher education

Jessop (2008) applies the SRA in a macro-level historical–materialist analysis of the capitalist state. However, he calls for a further development of 'variants of the SRA' (244), emphasising that his focus 'does not exclude other ways of developing the approach in regard to ... other fields' (244). The relevance of this approach for the field of education is illustrated in Robertson's framework of a 'cultural political economy of education' (CPE/E), which she applies to the globalisation of higher education in the UK. CPE/E looks at education as a terrain of struggles over the role of education in society (Robertson 2009), a struggle also reflected in the translation of accountability regimes in higher education.

This paper seeks to apply the theoretical framework of the SRA to the meso-level of analysis: to the field of public governance[3] in higher education. This implies an adaptation of the concept of selectivity, especially with reference to the understanding of what constitutes 'structure'. Modes of capital accumulation central to the analysis of the capitalist state are also relevant here, as changing modes of accumulation, e.g., towards a knowledge-based economy, fundamentally shape the role of universities in society and are often linked to the introduction of accountability regimes in higher education. However, the concept of structural constraints is re-conceptualised here for an analysis on the meso-level. It refers to societal power relations and their institutional reflections in the field of education as well as in (inter-)national institutional settings. Applying the concept of selectivity to this level, we can identify constraining or enabling structures in historically developed patterns of governing higher education, which shape the role of actors in the field (like universities, public agencies, Ministries of Education or private actors). Furthermore, the roles of political institutions like the national Parliament, of international actors or different scales in national policy-making, reflect meso-level structural features. Agency on the other hand is linked to strategies, which are based on strategic calculations about the context. Discursive framings of the role of the state or private actors in higher education can be seen as a crucial element in strategies of reflexive actors. Scales are also linked to agency, as the relevance of international policy transfer or the role of international actors is to be shaped by actors as part of their strategies.[4]

The selectivity of translation in the Global South: structural constraints, discursive framing, coalition building and re-scaling

The cases of Chile and South Africa reflect two very different translation processes. Both countries were among the 'first movers' of the Global South in establishing QA policies in higher education. In the early 1990s these countries underwent a fundamental transformation of their political systems towards democracy, when the dictatorial regime and Apartheid rule ended. Reforms in higher education were therefore also closely linked to struggles about the transition process. Chile and South Africa engaged in voluntary policy transfer, and referred to similar global discourses and policies of QA, even though they were mediated by partly different international organisations, networks and experts. At the same time, the two cases reflect highly different national governance structures as well as discourses on the role of government in higher education. This led to the creation of two very different national compromises regarding QA in higher education, a translation process shaped by structural, actor-related as well as discursive and scalar factors.

The case studies are based on document analysis (policy documents, academic articles, newspaper articles) and expert interviews[5] with actors in Chile and South Africa as well as with members of international organisations and networks in the field of QA.

Chile: establishing public and market governance at the same time?

After the military gained government control following the coup in 1973, the Chilean higher education sector was fundamentally restructured via measures of liberalisation and privatisation set in place since the 1980s. While only eight universities existed (two public and six private, the latter run by the Catholic Church) in the 1970s, today about 60 higher education institutions, most of them private, offer education programmes in Chile (Bernasconi and Rojas 2004). These changes established a fundamentally market-oriented system, changed power relations and created a (neo-)liberal discourse about the role of government and regulation in higher education, which form the context of current reforms.

QA was discussed among different actors in Chile since the late 1980s, and traditional forms of QA already existed before: private providers established after 1980 were subject to supervision by a public council, while traditional private (Church-run) and public universities were usually not subject to such licensing procedures. Some universities had close links to international experts and implemented self-evaluation programmes as part of internal QA since the late 1980s. While most non-traditional private universities were sceptical about QA as they thrived in the existing liberalised governance context, some prestigious – private as well as public – universities soon identified QA as a strategy to distinguish themselves in the higher education market via 'quality labels'. These prestigious and often influential universities have supported the introduction of governmental QA policies since the mid 1990s. Furthermore, an umbrella organisation of Latin American Universities, CINDA (Centro Interuniversitario de Desarrollo), had been promoting QA in Chile since the late 1980s with reference to international QA policies. CINDA can therefore be seen as the key non-governmental think tank for QA issues in Chile.

Re-establishing public governance versus re-enforcing market governance

The starting point for the national QA systems existing in Chile today was a discourse of re-regulation that emerged after the end of dictatorial rule in the early 1990s. However, there was no shared vision about crisis and dysfunction: some representatives of the central-left-wing government parties aimed at fundamental restructuring, while members of the conservative-right-wing political parties fiercely opposed reforms leading to more public governance, of which QA was seen to be part (Interview VI). Thus, opposing interests in the Chilean higher education sector and power-structures reflected in Parliament (strong opposition parties supporting a liberal approach and little state intervention) fundamentally shape the policy process and strategies applied by actors supporting the introduction of QA policies. These features form the structural constraints selectively privileging actors, strategies and discourses compatible with their reproduction.

This was strategically taken into account by actors promoting QA (public officials, representatives of universities, academics and CINDA) who sought to integrate opposing views. They engaged in strategies of re-scaling, coalition building and discursive framing to legitimise the reforms. Facing strong opposition on the national level, Chilean public officials reconfigured the terrain of struggles by referring to the international scale – discursively as well as by setting up a transnational alliance. Reference to international actors and networks therefore played a significant role in creating a QA system that was widely accepted.

Internationalisation, re-scaling and 'forum avoidance'

A crucial step was the cooperation with the World Bank for the introduction of QA in higher education, initiated in 1997 by the Chilean Ministry of Education. The cooperation with the World Bank provided for expertise and financial support and facilitated the establishment of a national commission and a pilot programme for QA. As the World Bank is generally identified with a more liberal approach in reforms, this also increased the acceptance of QA policies in the education sector (Interviews I, VIII). The pilot programme with the World Bank can also be interpreted as a strategy of 'forum avoidance': Chilean policy-makers in favour of QA avoided the struggle in parliament via first establishing the pilot programme with the World Bank, thereby creating a new status quo which was difficult to question after QA policies had been institutionalised.

The legitimising reference to the international realm and re-scaling is also reflected in the consultation of international expertise. Reference to international experiences in QA was linked to a narrative of successful reforms elsewhere, as well as to the image of careful policy design that did not simply adopt foreign concepts but created approaches suitable for the national setting of a developing country (CNAP 2007).

As anticipated, the institutionalisation of the new QA policy via a legal act in parliament proved to be a lengthy and conflictive process. Due to strong opposition by the centre-right-wing opposition, the Act for QA in higher education underwent major changes – a market for private QA agencies was established – in a drawn-out debate that took several years (Bernasconi and Rojas 2004; LeMaitre 2003; CNAP 2007).

Discursive framing: globalisation, transparency, re-regulation

On a discursive level, the call for establishing QA policies was based on defining and interpreting educational crises in an inclusive, consensual way – from a more liberal point of view, e.g., via embracing liberal notions of market failure (non-transparent markets) and taking into account the views of powerful actors in the field by linking the reforms to the prevailing 'common sense' of higher education governance. We can therefore partly identify a strategic move of actors promoting QA in Chile, shifting away from the discourse of re-regulation towards one of market transparency and successful participation in globalisation. Furthermore, massification in higher education and the need to create a 'knowledge society' were identified, linking the QA endeavour to ideas of efficiency and Chilean national competitiveness. The need to eliminate information asymmetries in the education sector (non-transparent market structures) and to establish a 'level playing field' between private and public higher education institutions was strongly promoted. QA policies were also linked to 'consumer protection' and 'value for money' arguments. Among leading universities as well as governmental actors and CINDA, the argument of globalisation, the increasing integration of Chile as a country of the Global South into global processes, and the aim to internationalise higher education were crucial for establishing a consensual view about QA policies (Bernasconi and Rojas 2004; CNAP 2007; Interviews II, III, VI). University representatives, public officials of high standing in the education sector and CINDA often played a crucial role as intellectuals in the Gramscian sense by shaping the discourses, building alliances and (discursively) integrating opposing views in the field of QA policies.

Democratisation is an important discursive reference point in Chile, while at the same time highly controversial due to the legacies and persisting support for policies established under military rule. Arguments of democratisation in the QA discourse therefore focus on democracy as market transparency and consumer protection: the transition from dictatorship to democracy is often rather seen as an opportunity structure for reforms than as a political imperative for democratic transformation (Interviews III, VI).

An important argument facilitating the introduction of external QA was a broadly shared view by different actors of the 'reality' of the Chilean higher education sector: great differences in the 'quality' of education provided by many universities (Interviews III, VI, IX). This was framed as being very particular for the liberalised higher education sector in Chile. From this perspective, a fundamental critique of QA as a managerial tool might be valid in the US and Europe, but was seen to be non-applicable to the Chilean context due to the fundamental need for re-regulation.

Thus, strategies of discursive framing, coalition building and re-scaling were facilitated in Chile as different actors' interests were partly compatible with QA: the government established a new governance mechanism, which was seen to reinforce market transparency and public governance; some universities saw QA as a 'positioning device', while CINDA promoted it with reference to global trends in accountability policies. Bernasconi (2007) therefore describes the current QA system in Chile as a 'compromise between highly divergent philosophies of regulation'.

South Africa: a new public management concept as a democratising tool?

The Apartheid government in South Africa established a highly segregated public education system. Prior to Apartheid a small number of liberal English-medium universities had been established, Afrikaans-medium universities were created later, and after 1959 the Apartheid government also set up separate universities and technikons for Blacks, Coloureds and Indians. This led to a fundamental fragmentation of the higher education system regarding public funding, teaching and research capacity, as well as access patterns to higher education. These different types of HEI[6] were subject to different forms of state control: English- and Afrikaans-medium universities enjoyed some degree of autonomy, in comparison to other universities and technikons (Hall, Symes, and Luescher 2002, 92; Luckett 2006, 172–4). This fragmentation and the dominance of state-centred governance present a powerful legacy of the Apartheid era.

After the first democratic elections in 1994, the need for 'redressing' Apartheid legacies was the key issue, and the ANC government generally enjoyed broad support and legitimacy (Cloete, Muller, and Maassen 2006). The transformation reinforced the trajectory of a strong role of the state in higher education, which now came to be seen as the key agent of change. The dominant structures and discourses in higher education are therefore characterised by public governance.[7] This and favourable domestic power structures – the ANC government held a clear majority in Parliament – constitute important structural and discursive features shaping selectivity and the terrains of contestation in the translation of QA policies. Public officials and other actors promoting new accountability regimes faced opposition that emphasised concerns about institutional legacies of discriminatory Apartheid rule and critiques of QA as a managerial tool. The strategies of discursive framing and re-scaling of actors promoting external QA reflect their strategic calculations on this context.

International influences put into perspective

In 1996 the National Commission on Higher Education (NCHE) made recommendations for a transformation of the South African higher education sector, which was to be achieved with a combination of three policies: funding, planning and quality assurance. Thus, QA was identified as one of the key tools for democratic transformation in the NCHE report (NCHE 1996, 289).

The concept of QA was brought to South Africa as a result of an intensive policy transfer since the end of Apartheid: academics, quality managers and public officials went abroad and international experts (especially from the Commonwealth and European countries) were invited to South Africa to provide expertise on QA and other educational reforms (Muller, Maassen, and Cloete 2006; Interviews V, VII). In a parallel process, these actors engaged in an international policy transfer, while national legislation was developed and institutions for QA were set up. In 1997 the Higher Education Act was created, and the Council of Higher Education (CHE), an independent public body, with a Higher Education Quality Commission (HEQC) – the national QA 'agency' – were established in 2000–2001. Since the late 1990s the Department of Education (DoE) promoted the idea of QA in workshops, an 'Accreditation Project Working Group' was set up and HEQC staff as well as 'consultants' (academics) developed an international survey of experiences with QA policies. This survey covered negative lessons as well as successful international experiences, which served as a reference point for a South African QA system (CHE 2002; Interviews I, VIII).

Thus, for establishing QA in South Africa, international meetings and global networks were important fora of exchange. However, formalised transnational alliances to overcome contestations on the national level were not established, and re-scaling had a decentralised character. Still, in some instances re-scaling was strategically employed and closely linked to discourses: actors promoting QA discursively referred to the globalisation of accountability standards in higher education, also because the South African higher education sector is well connected to international academic networks. At the same time, due to a prevailing discourse of national ownership and sovereignty, re-scaling and the influence of international actors were often discursively framed as having a limited role for the development of the South African QA system.[8] This facilitated acceptance as it demonstrated national ownership (CHE 2004; Interviews I, IV, V, VI, VIII).

A transformation imperative?

Discursively creating a context-specific meaning of QA was very important in South Africa; actors involved in this can be described as 'catalysts' and intellectuals in the Gramscian sense. Transformation was the underlying theme in the DoE's and CHE/HEQC's reasoning for QA (see also Luckett 2006, 189; CHE 2004; Interviews I, III, IV). The transformation rationale is reflected in different arguments, for example about massification. This is (discursively) linked to transformation, as student numbers increased after the barriers of access established under Apartheid had been partly deconstructed.

QA was also framed as a part of transformative public regulation. The dominant paradigm of public governance is therefore 'materialised' and discursively reinforced in discourses on QA as well as by establishing a public QA agency. The idea of transformation also refers to a widely accepted perception of dysfunction in the higher education sector: as in Chile, there was a general agreement among actors on the highly divergent 'quality' of higher education provided in different HEI due to Apartheid legacies. This was presented to be very different from the situation in Europe or the US. Framing QA as an appropriate regulatory tool for facing this problem therefore links these policies to a shared understanding ('common sense') of a very specific transformation process in a country of the Global South.

Linking QA to a powerful narrative of transformation also limits the ability to contest reforms. Critics of QA were partly perceived as withholding support for transformation (rather than as criticising a tool for re-regulating the sector) or as failing to recognise the specific need for QA in South Africa. While some of those opposing the reforms certainly feared the distributional consequences of transformation, those who questioned external QA with reference to its managerial character also felt limited in their ability to voice critical views (Interviews II, VIII, IX).

Accountability, improvement or compliance?

Some English- and Afrikaans-medium universities partly welcomed the QA initiative as a new regulatory tool, while some historically disadvantaged HEI voiced concern about possible negative results of QA due to Apartheid legacies (disadvantages stemming from discriminatory policies), linking their arguments to the idea of transformation as well. In response to this, proponents of QA underlined their awareness of these legacies and presented the South African system as improvement-oriented rather than compliance-oriented.

The critique of QA by some universities, academics and researchers is based on arguments about limitations of academic freedom and a managerial QA approach focusing on compliance: QA is seen to entail a trend towards new public management with efficiency notions prevailing. Here, the discursive link of QA to arguments of academic freedom is relevant as it links contestations of QA to struggles for academic freedom under Apartheid, which are perceived to be highly legitimate. In an effort to address this critique, the issue of academic freedom has been taken up in reports about the effects of transformation policies in the higher education sector (CHE 2004; Gouwes and Waghid 2006; Jonathan 2006; Interviews II, III, VI, VIII).

Other forms of opposition to QA in South Africa reflect different strategies and terrains of contestation. Before the public external QA policy started under the auspices of the HEQC, a university-led QA-initiative of the South African Universities

Vice-Chancellors Organisation was set up at the end of the 1990s. It was based on and framed as a 'collegial' (in contrast to a state-led or managerial) approach to QA. This initiative was not part of nor co-ordinated along with the DoE's approach, which led to criticism of the project. However, the initiative did not gain political support among the majority of universities, not least because a lack of capacity to undertake QA became evident (Interviews II, IV, X). Still, this instance is relevant as it reflects an effort to establish an alternative to public, external QA policy – and the failure to frame it successfully or to build coalitions which were able to question an emerging regulatory paradigm.

Public accountability and national sovereignty

The conflict between public QA and private providers stands for another contestation of QA in South Africa. Between the mid and late 1990s, several private, often foreign providers entered the sector and were partly seen as providing low standard educational services. As there was no adequate regulatory system in place at this time, actors often refer to this 'policy gap' when arguing for QA (CHE 2004, 48, 220; Interviews I, III). Several (international) private providers criticised the accreditation process (CHE 2004, 220) and the refusal to accredit some private providers led to the perception of a 'more punitive attitude' (van Damme 2002, 19) towards accreditation of private higher education institutions in South Africa. However, it seems that this conflict strengthened the approach of the DoE, the CHE and the HEQC towards QA and reaffirmed a positive image of the new public accountability regime in higher education. This also reflects that QA became part of the aim to 'manage the national sovereignty agenda'[9] and therefore part of a specific South African self-perception.

Conclusion

Two very different national compromises on QA were created in Chile and South Africa. This was possible as different and partly contradictory meanings were attached to it: QA came to be seen as a democratising tool, as a tool for market and public governance and as an instrument to reinforce national policy agendas of transformation, competitiveness or sovereignty. It is presented as being a 'homegrown' and at the same time international concept. Encompassing very different interests, QA has become a broadly accepted, hegemonic tool for re-organising higher education.

The strategic–relational concept of selectivity as a theoretical lens allows grasping different dimensions of this contested process of translation and consensus building. It enables us to see how structural features of governance in higher education or in the national institutional setting operate selectively and facilitate, reward or hinder some actors' ability to act. At the same time, actors' ability to act and their strategies for universalising QA by discursive framing, re-scaling and coalition building become visible.

Acknowledgements

I would like to thank Stephanie Allais, Roger Dale, Eva Hartmann, Susan Robertson and Detlef Sack for very inspiring comments on a draft version of this paper.

Notes

1. In the following, the terms 'quality assurance' or 'accountability regimes' refer to external QA mechanisms like accreditations or audits, which are seen to be different from traditional forms of academic self-regulation.
2. Many thanks to Roger Dale for this comment.
3. Public governance refers to the way in which higher education as a public service is organised and governed.
4. I would like to thank Eva Hartmann for valuable comments on the concept of re-scaling.
5. All interviews quoted here were conducted in confidentiality, and the names of interviewees are therefore withheld by mutual agreement.
6. In recent years, mergers of some universities have taken place. However, as the legacies of Apartheid persist in many ways, I will still refer to these types of HEI here (see also Luckett 2006, 172).
7. The majority of HEI are public, while there is commodification of the system to some extent due to tuition fees, competitive financing models, outsourcing, etc.
8. Spreen (2004) has identified a similar process for the transfer of outcome-based education models in South Africa.
9. I am grateful to Susan Robertson for raising this point here.

References

Bernasconi, A. 2007. Accreditation versus proliferation. *International Higher Education* 47, Spring. http://www.bc.edu/bc_org/avp/soe/cihe/newsletter/number47.

Bernasconi, A., and F. Rojas. 2004. *Informe sobre la educación superior en Chile 1980–2003*. Santiago, Chile: Estudios Nacionales.

Brenner, N. 2001. The limits to scale? Methodological reflections on scalar structuration. *Progress in Human Geography* 25, no. 4: 591–614.

Cloete, N., P. Maassen, and J. Muller. 2006. Modes of governance and the limits of policy. In *Transformations in higher education,* ed. N. Cloete, P. Maassen, R. Fehnel, T. Moja, and T. Gibbon, 289–310. Dordrecht, The Netherlands: Springer.

Comisión Nacional de Acreditación (CNAP), and Ministerio de Educación. 2007. *El modelo chileno de acreditación de la educación superior*. Santiago: Authors.

Council of Higher Education (CHE). 2002. *Aspects of programme accreditation policy and practice in selected countries and according to selected systems*. Pretoria: Council of Higher Education.

Council of Higher Education (CHE). 2004. *South African higher education in the first decade of democracy*. Pretoria: Council of Higher Education.

Dale, R. 1999. Specifying globalization effects on national policy: A focus on the mechanisms. *Journal of Education Policy* 14, no. 1: 1–17.

Gouws, A., and Y. Waghid. 2006. Editorial: Higher education quality assurance in South Africa: Accreditation in perspective. *South African Journal of Higher Education* 20, no. 6: 751–61.

Gramsci, A. 1978. *Selections from political writings*. London: Lawrence & Wishart.

Hall, M., A. Symes, and T. Luescher. 2002. *Governance in South African higher education.* Pretoria: Council of Higher Education.

Harvey, L., and J. Newton. 2004. Transforming quality evaluation. *Quality in Higher Education* 10, no. 2: 149–66.

Jessop, B. 2008. *State power*. Cambridge: Polity Press.

Jonathan, R. 2006. *Academic freedom, institutional autonomy and public accountability in higher education: A framework for analysis of the state-sector relationship in a democratic South Africa*. Pretoria: Council of Higher Education.

LeMaitre, M. 2003. *Antecedentes, situación actual y perspectivas de la evaluation y la accreditación de la educación superior en Chile*. Santiago, Chile: Estudios Nacionales.
Luckett, K. 2006. The QA of teaching and learning in higher education in South Africa. An analysis of national policy development and stakeholder response. Unpublished diss., University of Stellenbosch.
Meyer, J., and F. Ramirez. 2000. The world institutionalization of education. In *Discourse formation in comparative education*, ed. J. Schriewer, 111–32. Frankfurt am Main: Peter Lang.
Moulaert, F., and B. Jessop. 2006. *Agency, structure, institutions and discourse (ASID)*. Thematic synthesis paper, Demologos Project. http://demologos.ncl.ac.uk/wp/wp2/papers/TSP1.pdf.
National Commission on Higher Education (NCHE). 1996. *A framework for transformation*. Report. Pretoria: Author.
Neave, G. 1998. The evaluative state reconsidered. *European Journal of Education* 33, no. 3: 265–84.
Robertson, S. 2009. Globalising higher education: The case of the UK. Paper presented at 'The perils and opportunities of internationalisation of higher education: A critical perspective' workshop, September, in Université de Lausanne, Switzerland.
Salter, B., and T. Tapper. 2000. The politics of governance in higher education: The case of quality assurance. *Political Studies* 48, no. 1: 66–87.
Spreen, C. 2004. Appropriating borrowed policies: Outcomes-based education in South Africa. In *The global politics of education borrowing and lending*, ed. G. Steiner-Khamsi, 101–13. New York: Teachers College Press.
Van Damme, D. 2002. *Trends and models in international quality assurance and accreditation in higher education in relation to trade in services in education services*. Washington, DC: OECD/US Forum on trade in services. http://www.oecd.org/dataoecd/51/29/2088479.pdf.
Vidovich, L., and R. Slee. 2001. Bringing universities to account? Exploring some global and local policy tensions. *Journal of Education Policy* 16, no. 5: 431–53.
Westerheijden, D., B. Stensaker, and M. Rosa. 2007. *Quality assurance in higher education. Trends in regulation, translation and transformation*. Dordrecht, The Netherlands: Springer.

Re-orienting internationalisation in African higher education

Mala Singh

Centre for Higher Education Research and Information, The Open University, Walton Hall, Milton Keynes, UK

> In both policy and research contexts, internationalisation in African higher education is welcomed for its potential to strengthen local capacity and cautioned against for its potential to extend long-standing asymmetries of power in international partnerships. This paper examines two sets of developments which seek to re-orient internationalisation to allow for greater local control, local focus and local benefit. The one relates to a more formalised policy, planning and research approach to internationalisation and the other pertains to an intra-regional form of internationalisation under the influence of the Bologna process. The paper explores prospects for internationalisation on the continent to yield more equal North–South partnerships and to support the revitalisation agenda and its development priorities in higher education. It suggests that continuing lack of local capacity, continuing structural inequalities in partnerships, and insufficient interrogation of dominant concepts and models of internationalisation may still pose problems in moving towards an alternative internationalisation politics in African higher education.

Introduction

Internationalisation is increasingly becoming an explicit policy, planning and research theme in African higher education (Teferra and Knight 2008; Jowi and Huisman 2009). This mirrors trends in many developed and developing countries where internationalisation has been a familiar component of higher education reform discourses since the mid 1990s (Knight and de Wit 1997; Kalvermark and van der Wende 1997; Scott 1998, 2006; Teichler 2004, 2005; Kehm and Teichler 2007). Current policy understandings and approaches to internationalisation in many OECD countries are already under review, in pursuit of a broader agenda beyond academic mobility, a short-term 'selling model' (Bone 2008, 16) or an inwardly oriented regionalism (the Bologna Process). Internationalisation belongs to a suite of policy framing vocabularies which includes: knowledge societies; entrepreneurial universities; widening participation; academic mobility; cross-border education; higher education cooperation, partnerships and networks; third stream income; and regional integration. In the African context, the brain drain, past and current power asymmetries and inequalities in North–South partnerships, the relationship of internationalisation to the revitalisation of African higher education, and building local capacity are added to the equation. There are various overlaps in policy language and themes in internationalisation debates in different regional settings. However, there are also sharp differences in the politics of internationalisation in those settings, especially when considering internationalisation's role for and impact on higher education in sub-Saharan Africa as one of the poorest regions of the world.

This paper addresses some of the specific historical and political dimensions which shape the construction of the internationalisation issue in African higher education. It raises questions about the implications of internationalisation for African higher education, both in exercising agency and choice through initiating and managing internationalisation as well as being an object of the internationalisation strategies of other countries and regions.[1] I focus on two developments which seek to re-orient internationalisation in African higher education to allow for greater local control, local focus and local benefit – one relating to a more formalised policy, planning and research approach to internationalisation, and the other pertaining to internationalisation in the region under the direct and indirect influence of the Bologna Process. I examine how internationalisation risks, opportunities and challenges have been articulated by different role-players, and explore the under-addressed risk posed by the disjuncture between insufficiently interrogated global models and templates and local revitalisation needs.

Framing the internationalisation challenge

Much of the current debate in relation to African higher education focuses on developments in internationalisation of the last decade and a half. The term spans territory familiar from internationalisation debates in other regions. It covers activities which include: student and staff mobility; cross-border education in its different modalities; arrangements for the recognition and articulation of study programmes; research and teaching/training partnerships and networks; and the development of policies, structures and strategies for managing and advancing internationalisation at institutional, national systems and organisational levels. However, there are fundamental differences with countries from the Global North. African countries are, for instance, primarily 'sending' countries for mobile students and staff, and 'receiving' countries in relation to cross-border provision.[2] More crucially, the 'pre-history' of the current internationalisation on the continent has not been mainly self-initiated and self-directed forms of international cooperation in higher education but has included modes of 'internationalisation' whose colonial and post-independence legacies and their associated power imbalances remain resonant in the current debates.

According to Mamdani, 'the post-independence rush to set up universities was guided by the example of metropolitan models like Oxbridge and the Sorbonne' (1994, 1). Teferra indicates that colonial 'tutelage' in shaping the identity of African higher education extended to the replication of 'programs and curriculum, governance, [and] books' (2008, 45–55), and also to the continuing use of colonial languages of instruction. The current focus on quality as an indispensable pillar in the revitalisation of African higher education has a dark precursor in the early view that quality could not be produced or safeguarded outside of colonial/international oversight. In addition to the early and continuing influence of former colonial countries on higher education, the influences and impacts of the policies and projects of multilateral bodies like the World Bank, international aid agencies and foreign foundations on African higher education have been well documented (Samoff and Carrol 2004;

Sawyerr 2004; Teferra 2008). This history leads Mohamedbhai to conclude that African universities have been '"internationalised" right from inception' in a variety of forms (2009) and with ambivalent rationales. Mohamedbhai goes on to argue that African institutions have also aspired to an internationalised identity through 'copying' Northern conceptions and strategies for higher education, without sufficient critical interrogation of their fit to developing country or African contexts. In relation to African dependence on foreign aid, Teferra refers to the tendency locally to 'internalise' the view that 'improvement and change require external support, advice, and often personnel' (2008, 47). In this regard, African higher education has not only been a simple object of the internationalisation ideologies of others but has also developed a variety of accommodative and imitative behaviours which shift the epistemological gaze beyond the continent.

There has also been explicit resistance to the over-determining impact of colonial and post-colonial forms of internationalisation. In the 1970s, defining and establishing the African 'Development University' was an attempt to challenge and redirect the powerful post-independence international orientation. This included prioritising the role of the university in national development, with a greater emphasis on Africanisation and localisation, and the pursuit of knowledge for 'the amelioration of the conditions of the common man and woman in Africa' (Yesufu 1973, 40). It was an approach which underpinned many innovative reforms aimed at refocusing higher education on African realities and priorities. However, it fell into disrepute as a result of its overt instrumentalisation of higher education in service of African development, its lack of distance from statist and nationalist agendas, and a simplistic trade-off between local relevance and internationally benchmarked quality (Coleman 1984; Mamdani 1993, 1994). However, a discursive pattern of counter-posing the international orientation with African contextual imperatives, and an engagement with issues of power, control and autonomy in agenda and priority setting for African higher education, were already part of the politics of internationalisation.

In the last decade, a wide-ranging revitalisation project[3] has been underway in African higher education after a long period of deterioration and neglect (Sawyerr 2004) stemming from discredited World Bank orthodoxies about low rates of social and economic returns from investments in higher education. Within the framework of new orthodoxies about higher education and knowledge societies, specifically the emphasis on increasing high level human capital as part of a 'more knowledge-intensive route to development' (World Bank 2009, xxii), various reforms are underway in relation to system and institutional governance, financing, access, diversification of institutional types and modalities of provision, quality assurance, and greater levels of regional and sub-regional co-operation. Many of these trends reflect the influences of 'globalised' policy reform conceptions, which have become standard fare in rethinking higher education and its purposes and forms, irrespective of regional setting. However, the areas which they mark out are in very real need of attention in the process of rehabilitating systems and institutions which had become dysfunctional through decades of lack of investment and support by national authorities as much as by international role-players.

International partnership for African development, now qualified by an explicit emphasis on equality of partnerships and local ownership, is again firmly on the agenda of key multilateral organisations and initiatives (Paris Declaration 2005 [www.oecd.org]; Accra Agenda for Action 2008 [www.accrahlf.net]; UNESCO 2009 WCHE Communiqué). The issue of international partnerships to support

Southern development appears to be well settled as a policy norm although questions remain as to how this norm is being given effect and its impacts on strengthening African agency and producing sustained benefit. The higher education revitalisation agenda of the African Association of Universities (AAU), which includes internationalisation as a constituent theme, is supported by partnerships associated with international development aid, loans and projects of the OECD, the EU, UNESCO and the World Bank. The connection signalled between internationalisation and revitalisation in the AAU's agenda of work bears out Scott's argument that international education is 'better served by closer association with domestic reform agendas' (2006, 14). However, the range of political, economic and intellectual conduits of influence in the shaping of internationalisation in African higher education has proliferated rather than diminished, creating new political, intellectual and capacity challenges for meaningful local control over agenda and priority setting in an era where policy imposition has yielded to policy harmonisation and alignment with dominant global trends (Dale 2007, 53).

Institutionalising internationalisation

In policy discourses, in research agendas and as a multi-level suite of planning and implementation activities, the most recent wave of internationalisation is growing in 'importance and complexity' (Teferra and Knight 2008, xii) in African higher education systems and institutions. The number of African higher education institutions which participated in the 2009 International Association of Universities' Survey on Internationalisation was an increase on the last survey in 2005.[4] The AAU's focus on internationalisation in its core programme of activities for the period 2009–2013 under the theme 'Renewal and Strengthening of African Higher Education Institutions' has already been mentioned, although the internationalisation–revitalisation nexus needs more conceptual and strategic content. The lack of adequate and reliable data and context-specific analyses of many aspects of African higher education is often identified as an urgent need and a challenge to researchers and policy-makers alike, not least on the phenomenon of internationalisation. This is beginning to change with more systematic attention being accorded to the subject by scholars who include an increasing number from the continent.[5] A recently formed African Network for the Internationalisation of Education (ANIE) is likely to give greater regional visibility to the issue through its stated commitment to activities of 'research, capacity building and advocacy' (www.anienetwork.org). Attention to internationalisation is being formalised through its inclusion on continent-wide, national and institutional policy agendas, in focused research overviews and analyses, and through dedicated advocacy mechanisms.

A common starting point for many of the discussions of internationalisation in African higher education (as in other regional contexts) is the definitional question (Kehm and Teichler 2007; Teferra and Knight 2008). Although the diversity of understandings of internationalisation is referred to in many of the studies, the definition proposed by Knight is often invoked in discussion and research: internationalisation is 'the process of integrating an international, inter-cultural or global dimension into the purpose, functions or delivery of post-secondary education' (2008, 15). Knight makes a point of stressing the neutrality of the definition, hence its potential applicability to many different contexts within Africa, as to other regions and contexts. She does, however, make clear that the rationales for internationalisation span dimensions which are 'social/cultural, political, academic and economic' (2003, 27). Internationalisation is often analysed in relation to the impact of globalisation on higher education (Scott 1998; Kishun 2006; Marginson and van der Wende 2007; Teferra 2008). Less addressed in the current conjuncture, unlike in the 1970s, is the political and intellectual relationship between internationalisation and Africanisation or endogenisation (Crossman 2004).

The recent organisational activities, debates and research indicate an attempt to work towards greater definitional clarity, information gathering and sharing; to encourage a more systematic policy and planning approach to the subject within national systems and institutions; to mark out a field of scholarly study and policy research; and to grapple with the challenges of ensuring optimal benefit to African higher education from the accelerating types and volumes of internationalisation on the continent. A more substantial literature focused on disaggregating and interrogating various forms of internationalisation is still emerging. This points to an open research field in: exploring how the frequently mentioned power dynamics manifest themselves in different internationalisation projects and their impacts on local agency (Court 2004); interrogating the templates and frameworks within which the internationalisation debates have been framed; tracking and evaluating multiple simultaneous forms of internationalisation (Scott 2006, 21) driven by different interests – whether it is the 'public good' or the market, capacity development needs, elite North–South linkages, regional integration, etc; assessing the intended and unintended consequences of internationalisation for local priorities and values; and examining how internationalisation may be re-orienting understandings of the relationship between higher education and social change on the continent.

From their survey of research on internationalisation since the mid 1990s, Kehm and Teichler point out that 'internationalisation in higher education tends to be treated as *a highly normative topic with strong political undercurrents*' (2007, 262). They make special mention of the fact that 'internationalisation also reflects the existing international inequality between nations and world regions' (2007, 262). Although this is primarily a reference to the direction of mobility from developing to developed countries, the internationalisation inequalities in relation to African higher education include the factors which accelerate mobility (decaying infrastructure, limited institutional and staff capacity, overcrowded lecture rooms, no research funding, political authoritarianism) but also extend to the power relations between international partners whose institutional, national and regional capacities and resources remain grossly unequal. This is a challenge to the 'intentionally neutral' technical definition of internationalisation by Knight, given her own recognition of potential non-neutral usages: 'a definition needs to be objective enough that it can be used to describe a phenomenon which is, in fact, universal but which has different purposes and outcomes, depending on the actor or stakeholder' (2008, 15). A number of normative and political concerns have already been flagged in the emerging policy and research discourses on internationalisation in African higher education (Zeleza 2005; Teferra 2008; Obamba and Mwema 2009). However, in accepting the neutrality of the definition as a starting point, there is a danger that such concerns can easily become subsumed under the informational task of mapping the 'shape and size' of internationalisation, the technical task of gathering and analysing data about different aspects of internationalisation, or the organisational task of developing policy frameworks and implementation structures to manage internationalisation at institutional and national levels.

What are the caveats attaching to the recognition of the potential strategic and educational benefits of internationalisation on the continent? Analysts have sought to identify the risks associated with internationalisation while pointing to its benefits and opportunities. The most frequently mentioned are:

- The possibility for enhanced internationalisation to aggravate the already grave loss of intellectual and professional resources in the form of the brain drain. Jowi argues that the loss translates into 'further marginalization of Africa in global knowledge production as it depletes the already scanty capacity' (2009, 274).
- The potential for increasing the hegemony of western/Northern knowledges, cultural values and languages at the expense of indigenous knowledges (Assie-Lumumba 2006, 137), African cultural norms and identities, and local languages (Brock-Utne 2003, 44–6; Barasa 2009); the dangers of cultural homogenisation (Knight 2008, 35), curriculum homogenisation and loss of cultural identity (Jowi 2009, 274).
- The commodification of higher education (Singh 2004; Teferra 2008), relating to the treatment of higher education as a tradeable commodity within GATS.
- Continuing unequal relationships between universities in the Global North and South, 'imitative modernizations in developing countries', and easy penetration of western knowledge in African higher education curricula (Jowi 2009, 274).

Many of these concerns have been identified by African universities themselves in their responses to International Association of Universities (IAU) surveys on internationalisation (2003, 2005 and 2009). From the 2009 survey, Egron-Polak reports that the issues of the brain drain, the displacement of other priorities, and the loss of cultural identity are the three top risks identified by African universities, with commodification of education and degree mills moving to lower ranks. Despite the concerns about Northern hegemonies and unequal power relations in partnerships, the top benefit from internationalisation was identified as strengthened research and knowledge production. This trend is an indication of sometimes contradictory concerns which, on the one hand, echo the prevailing global discourses about the dominant role of knowledge in contemporary socio-economic development and the role of research in reputational hierarchies like rankings, but on the other hand reflect a strong imperative to rehabilitate and strengthen the knowledge production function in order that African higher education could re-assert control over the setting of educational and research directions and priorities as well as contribute more effectively to local development agendas.

The identified risks have already evoked responses in the form of policy statements and guidelines for minimising the risks of internationalisation. For example, the IAU, which promotes international cooperation among higher education institutions, indicates its awareness of the minimal impact of international cooperation on 'global wealth and resource distribution' (www.iau-aiu.net). Recognising the realities of asymmetries of power and control, the IAU's policy positions stress the need for 'ethical conduct', and building capacity in developing countries for 'global equity'. However, scepticism remains about the efficacy of 'soaring goodwill' and partnership 'rhetoric' in eliminating: 'entrenched power asymmetries without a broader effort to reconfigure the patterns and dynamics of resource endowments and flows between northern and southern ... partners' (Obamba and Mwema 2009, 362–3). The decisive questions relate to what it will take to change the 'structural and epistemological' conditions (Obamba and Mwema 2009, 362) which frame North–South asymmetry and what equal partnerships mean within settings permeated by inequalities of resourcing and agenda-setting capacity. What are the next steps in going beyond risk identification and normative assertions to setting up international relationships characterised by increasing symmetries of power and capacity? The translation of norm into practice requires a sustained exploration of the political, policy and material conditions for exercising greater agency and control from within African higher education, taking account of the fact that these may differ greatly due to the complex variety of institutional, national and sub-regional differences as well as differences in the agendas and approaches of external partners. The internationalisation agenda will also benefit from extending the concern about power asymmetries in North–South internationalisation to internal institutional or system asymmetries created or reinforced by internationalisation in African higher education. This will require a policy and research focus on the different local benefits of internationalisation, how they are distributed, to whom and with what impact.

Some of the baseline-setting literature on internationalisation has generated a framework for analysis which provides easily usable definitional and thematic parameters. This has shaped the ways in which accounts and analyses of internationalisation are constructed. So, for example, the analytical frameworks devised by Knight and de Wit (1995) have come to function as a global template for analyses of internationalisation in a range of regional and national settings. This is evident in the similarity of approach in publications relating to internationalisation, whether in Europe, Latin America, the Asia Pacific or Africa. The national case studies in these different regions ostensibly furnish the regional, national and local variants and specificities of internationalisation trends. However, the analytical frame of reference remains largely un-interrogated, functioning as a single, common, 'neutral' analytical model. Knight's definition of internationalisation (cited earlier) may need some qualification when invoked in relation to many current forms of internationalisation in African higher education. Given the history of internationalisation as 'imposition' (Dale 2007, 53) in Africa and continuing concerns about the power and control of internationalisation agendas, activities and benefits, the Knight definition presumes unproblematised agency and control and unqualified terms of integration in internationalisation processes.

The Bologna model in African higher education internationalisation

Debates on higher education reform in the US, Australia, Asia and Latin America indicate that higher education policy-makers and analysts are considering the Bologna Process as a model for change in higher education in their own regions and systems. This influence is being intensified as a result of a European decision to extend cooperation initiatives beyond Europe, as part of a consideration of the external dimensions of the Bologna Process. African higher education has not been exempt from the Bologna influence. The impact and influence is twofold. It is direct, for example, in the forms of: higher education institutions (mainly in Francophone and Lusophone sub-Saharan Africa) aligning their qualifications structures and curricula with the Bologna architecture; staff and student involvement in the Erasmus Mundus programme which facilitates academic mobility to Europe; and participation in special projects designed to foster European-African co-operation.[6] The influence is also indirect in the forms of: policy borrowing from the Bologna model, in respect of political and economic aspirations for continental integration; setting goals for greater levels of educational co-operation and articulation at regional and sub-regional levels; and fashioning instruments to manage and support academic mobility (e.g., qualifications recognition systems, quality assurance, etc).

In relation to Bologna emulation, the African Union (AU) adopted and started planning for a harmonisation strategy for higher education programmes in Africa in 2007. This strategy, together with accompanying measures to expand ratification of the Arusha Convention[7] and to strengthen quality assurance, is part of a continent-wide project to revitalise and reform higher education to enable it to contribute to the social and economic development of the continent. Greater levels of co-operation and co-ordination in higher education are part of a larger AU ambition for regional integration and leveraging power globally as a more unified continent.

The rationales and purposes of harmonisation are rendered in a language resonant of Bologna considerations:

> Harmonization will benefit Africa, since it will allow for greater intra-regional mobility, thereby fostering increased sharing of information, intellectual resources, and research ... On a broader level, harmonization has the potential to create a common African higher education and research space. (AU 2007, 3)

The goals of the strategy include 'bridging the gap between disparate education system[s]', strengthening higher education capacity to produce graduates with competencies suited to the social and economic development needs of the continent, and the development of effective quality assurance mechanisms and common benchmarks for excellence. Sub-regional collaborative initiatives in higher education are again[8] on the agenda, linked to the revival of the regional economic communities, viewed by the AU as the strategic mechanisms through which pan-African goals can be achieved. The AU indicates that it is open to learning from other initiatives both from the continent and beyond: the Strategy, 'will actively seek to integrate, learn from, and build on institutional, national, regional, continental, and global efforts wherever possible, rather than "reinventing the wheel"' (2007, 5).

A meeting to discuss the harmonisation strategy held under the auspices of the AAU (as the implementing agency) in Ghana in February 2009 indicates a process at the most preliminary of discussion stages, with clear cautions expressed by the AAU Secretary General about the need for a 'clear road map with objectives and target dates', the high levels of financial and human resources required for successful harmonisation, and the 'lack of capacity at all levels in Africa'. A vast gap is evident between the political ambition of the harmonisation strategy and the capacity to steer, coordinate and implement the strategy at the level of the AU itself, within the AAU as the implementing body, and in the national systems and institutions where the strategy must be given effect. Many of the sub-regional initiatives are also at a very preliminary stage, with a number of projects planned for quality assurance and credit accumulation and transfer, but which are yet to reach full operational status. A sober observation made in a research report based on data from four studies about the state of higher education in the SADC region (as one of five regional economic communities) refers to a 'profusion of areas of weakness, deterioration, neglect, and even ... a vacuum within the higher education systems of the SADC countries' (SARUA 2008, 3). This is probably valid for many of the sub-regions, again highlighting issues of political resolve and capacity challenges in relation to policy implementation, infrastructure, financing, coordination and monitoring a complex Bologna-type agreement on the continent.

As in the Bologna reforms, quality assurance features prominently in the AU's harmonisation strategy. There has been a rapid expansion of quality assurance planning and activities at institutional and national levels as well as in organisations like the AAU itself. Several higher education institutions are developing formal quality assurance policies and mechanisms, and many countries are establishing new national structures for quality assurance and accreditation (one third of African countries according to the World Bank 2009). In 2008, the AAU launched a project (supported by UNESCO and the World Bank) to support quality assurance at its member universities, strengthen the capacity of national agencies on the continent, and encourage the sharing of information on quality assurance. An African Quality Assurance Network (AfriQAN) was launched in 2009 as part of this project. The flurry of activity in developing quality assurance policies and structures cannot in itself yield the desired levels of quality improvement in the face of continuing resource and capacity constraints in institutional provision. Further, the setting up of elaborate quality assurance architectures does not automatically translate into increasing levels of quality within institutions and programmes, a concern also expressed in relation to the Bologna process.

The lack of capacity has created the space for the shaping of quality assurance and other revitalisation projects by international consultants, especially where development aid or World Bank loans are part of the reform package. It is not clear how their involvement is shaping the translation of global policy and system templates for quality and other reforms into local applications. This may represent in many instances a missed opportunity for creative local engagement with such templates or for the conceptualisation of new or alternative approaches, when viewed from the perspective of concerns about the strengthening of African agency in the shaping of the policy and intellectual environment in African higher education. Examples of where this has occurred (for instance, conceptualising quality assurance in post-1994 South Africa to take account of social justice priorities, Lange and Singh 2009) indicate a complex mix of conditions which are currently not easily replicable in many African higher education systems. These include non-dependence on external aid and its conditionalities, requisite levels of national financing, available local intellectual and management capacity, and an enabling political and policy space.

The AU harmonisation strategy is an uneasy mix of discursive commonalities with Bologna policy in how regional integration challenges and their corresponding 'solutions' in higher education are represented, and glaring discontinuities with Bologna in respect of the structural and political conditions for goal achievement. The idea of an 'African higher education and research space' is largely aspirational, with a very fragile operational base in place to give it effect. The Bologna dimension also exposes multiple tensions along different fronts. There is the trade-off between focusing on African–European linkages on the one hand and promoting a strong regional internationalisation on the other. The latter regional aspiration itself has to juggle tensions between local revitalisation demands and the use of Northern strategic models and instruments which have different political and economic premises. There are also the competing demands of urgently needed domestic/national reforms on the one hand and the imperatives of regionalisation on the other. In negotiating the complex sets of choices emerging from this situation, some of the following issues are pertinent:

- It is not yet clear whether Bologna-related internationalisation is opening up the spaces for a different power dynamic in the interactions and relationships of

African and European higher education systems, institutions and individuals. There are negative and positive prognoses associated with Bologna developments, especially their impact within Africa. Hartman, for instance, analyses Bologna as a norm-setting project of a potentially 'imperialising' European Union, where European norms for quality assurance are likely to become internationally pre-eminent through the desire of non-European countries and their agencies to be included in the European Quality Register (2008). Khelfaoui sees in Bologna 'a new paradigm of domination' closely linked to market 'liberalisation' and one which prevents African states and societies from defining 'their own public policies' (2009, 24). On the other hand, Charlier and Croche (2009) see possibilities in the Bologna Process for Africa to set its own definitions and criteria for quality, taking pressing local realities into account, and thus proactively helping to shape and be part of an international higher education space. Both positions point to questions about the spaces available and the conditions necessary within African higher education for the exercise of choice and for the mediation of 'international' norms by local understandings, priorities and perspectives. The policy language of the AU harmonisation strategy does take account of local purposes and goals[9] but without a substantial interrogation of the fit of its borrowed model for achieving those goals. Further, the take-up thus far of many of the Bologna instruments (like quality assurance) does not indicate more than a technical adaptation of globally dominant models to local settings, instead of a creative reorientation of those models to contextual imperatives.

- The different forms and modalities of Bologna impacts have produced a multi-layered internationalisation environment where the direct interactions prioritise African–European partnerships (WENR and WES 2007), whereas the indirect influence in the form of a continent-wide harmonisation strategy encourages regional internationalisation and co-operation. It may be difficult to dislodge the North–South linkages as the preferred form of internationalisation unless and until the different forms of regional internationalisation are seen to yield equivalent academic, financial and reputational advantages. This highlights the continuing reverberation of issues of power and capacity in the internationalisation debate and the ongoing tilt towards the North–South linkage. Ogachi points out that, despite an arrangement for academic mobility being in place, for example, in East Africa, first choice opportunities for students from the region have been universities in 'western countries' (2009, 338).

- Reichert (2009, 1) makes the point that one of the unintended effects of the Bologna process was its catalysing role in giving impetus to national reform agendas in ways that went beyond the Bologna 'action line'. To what extent is the harmonisation strategy likely to be a strong stimulus for national higher education reform in African countries? In his analysis of the challenges facing African higher education, Sawyerr argues for the 'primary responsibility of the state in establishing and maintaining higher education systems' and also identifies the need for 'system level policy frameworks to guide strategic choices' in every country (2004, 51). Many African countries are in the process of developing national policy frameworks and structures for higher education (SARUA 2008; World Bank 2009) but implementation is still very new and fragile. It is not clear that the harmonisation strategy, given its own preliminary status and weak institutionalisation, will be a significant influence in accelerating or strengthening domestic reform initiatives, especially if there is weak regional coordination at the top and limited national capacity for take-up from below. Conversely, the need to focus on national agendas may also constrain attention to regional forms of internationalisation.

Conclusion

The issue of internationalisation in African higher education can be interpreted and managed in a multitude of descriptively neutral and politically charged ways. It encompasses normative, ideological and pragmatic approaches which range from a focus on academic mobility data or accounts of institutional policies and structures to the ideological contours of North–South partnerships or African borrowing of dominant Northern conceptions and strategies of internationalisation. In a globalising era, where developing countries also operate in Southern power blocs, internationalisation increasingly includes South–South partnerships and influences.[10] Added to this complexity are the potentially huge differences in the types and levels of internationalisation and approaches to its management in different institutions, national systems and sub-regions of the continent. African higher education will remain the continuing target (object) of the internationalisation strategies of others but it is also seeking to re-orient these for local purposes as well as initiating its own internationalisation projects. Asymmetries of power may well be a continuing feature of North–South partnerships but institutional strategies may also be generating internal inequalities relating to how internationalisation opportunities and benefits are distributed. This range of realities and reference points makes it necessary to take into account but go beyond idealistic normative stipulations, one-dimensional descriptive accounts or paralysing pessimistic prognoses of new forms of imperial domination.

What are the prospects for internationalisation in African higher education to yield more equal North–South partnerships, to support more clearly the revitalisation agenda and its development priorities, and to facilitate the benefits of cosmopolitanism for African higher education? The two sets of developments analysed in this paper attempt to shift the odds in favour of African higher education. Continuing lack of local capacity, continuing geopolitical conditions of structural inequality, and insufficient interrogation and contextualisation of dominant concepts and models of internationalisation may still pose problems in moving towards an alternative internationalisation politics in African higher education.

Notes

1. I am applying to internationalisation an argument made by Scott (1998, 122) about the impact of globalisation on higher education institutions.
2. A counter-factual example is South Africa, which has an increasing number of African students (CHE 2009, 26–7) and staff migrating to its HEIs, and which is also a 'sending' country for cross-border education.
3. See, for example, various case studies of higher education in Africa published under the auspices of the Partnership for Higher Education in Africa, James Curry Ltd, Oxford.
4. This still only adds up to 6% of the global total (41 institutions out of a survey sample of 745). See Egron-Polak, ANIE Conference, PPT 2009, http://www.anienetwork.org.
5. See, for example, Kishun (2006); Teferra and Knight (2008); presenters at the First ANIE Annual Conference, Kenya, September 2009; and the special issue of *Higher Education Policy* on 'African Universities and Internationalisation', Vol. 22, No. 3, September 2009.

6. See, for example, the 2008 EUA project 'Access to success: Trust and exchange between Europe and Africa'. There is also a planned European Commission initiative for a Tuning Project in African Higher Education.
7. The Arusha Convention, adopted in 1981 to facilitate cross-border recognition of studies and qualifications in African higher education, has been ratified only by 20 African countries. It has not been effective as a legal, political and educational instrument for academic mobility. In the AU's renewed initiative, an expanded ratification of the Arusha Convention is envisaged, with a target of 80% of African countries signed up by 2015.
8. See Ogachi (2009) on sub-regional higher education initiatives in the post-independence 1960s.
9. See Dale's distinction between the influence of external reform models on 'policy *programmes* and *organization*' as well as on 'policy goals and values' (2007, 52).
10. See Yang's analysis of 'soft power' relating to Chinese government funding for Confucius Centres at African universities to support the study of Chinese culture and language (this issue).

References

African Union (AU). 2007. *Harmonization of higher education programmes in Africa: A strategy for the African Union.* Summary report. Addis Ababa, Ethiopia: Author.

Assie-Lumumba, N. 2006. *Higher education in Africa: Crisis, reforms and transformation. CODESRIA working paper.* Dakar, Senegal: Council for the Development of Social Science Research in Africa.

Association of African Universities (AAU). 2009. *Regional harmonization of higher education for Africa.* Report. Accra, Ghana: Author.

Barasa, S. 2009. Accomodative education language policies as a driving force in the internationalisation of higher education. PowerPoint presentation at the ANIE conference, September 3–4, in Nairobi, Kenya. http://www.anienetwork.org.

Bone, D. 2008. Internationalisation of higher education: A 10 year review. Department for Business Innovation and Skills. http://www.bis.gov.uk.

Brock-Utne, B. 2003. Formulating higher education policies in Africa: The pressure from external forces and the neo-liberal agenda. *Journal of Higher Education in Africa* 1, no. 1: 24–56.

Charlier, J-E., and S. Croche. 2009. Can the Bologna Process make the move faster towards the development of an international space for higher education where Africa would find its place? *Journal of Higher Education in Africa* 7, nos. 1–2: 41–61.

Coleman, J. 1984. The idea of the developmental university. In *Universities in national development: A report of the Nordic Association for the Study of Education in Developing Countries,* ed. A. Hetland, 85–104. Stockholm: Almquist and Wiksell International.

Council on Higher Education. 2009. *Higher education monitor.* No. 8. Pretoria: Author.

Court, D. 2004. Comments on Samoff, J. and B. Carrol, 'The promise of partnership and the continuities of dependence'. *African Studies Review* 47, no. 1: 201–7.

Crossman, P. 2004. Perceptions of 'Africanisation' or 'Endogenisation' at African universities: Issues and recommendations. In *African universities in the twenty-first century, Vol. 2, Knowledge and society,* ed. P.T. Zeleza and A. Olukoshi, 321–40. Pretoria: UNISA Press, CODESRIA.

Dale, R. 2007. Specifying globalization effects on national policy. In the *RoutledgeFalmer reader in education policy and politics,* ed. B. Lingard and J. Ozga, 48–64. London: Routledge.

De Wit, H. 1995. *Strategies for internationalization of higher education.* Amsterdam: EAIE.

Egron-Polak, E. 2009. Internationalization of higher education: Tracking global trends and regional challenges. PowerPoint presentation at the ANIE Conference, September 3–4, in Nairobi, Kenya.

Hartman, H. 2008. Bologna goes global: A new imperialism in the making? *Globalisation, Societies and Education* 6, no. 3: 205–18.
Jowi, J.O. 2009. Internationalization of higher education in Africa: Developments, emerging trends, issues and policy implications. *Higher Education Policy* 22, no. 3: 263–81.
Jowi, J.O., and J. Huisman. 2009. Special issue: African universities and internationalization. *Higher Education Policy* 22, no. 3.
Kalvermark, T., and M. van der Wende. 1997. *National policies for the internationalization of higher education in Europe.* Stockholm: Swedish National Agency for Higher Education.
Kehm, B.M., and U. Teichler. 2007. Research on internationalisation in higher education. *Journal of Studies in International Education* 11, nos. 3–4: 260–73.
Khelfaoui, H. 2009. The Bologna Process in Africa: Globalization or return to 'colonial situation'? *Journal of Higher Education in Africa* 7, nos. 1–2: 23–40.
Kishun, R. 2006. *The internationalisation of higher education in South Africa.* Durban: IEASA.
Knight, J. 2003. Internationalisation: Meaning and models. In *Internationalisation and quality in South African universities,* ed. M. Smout, 15–35. Pretoria: SAUVCA.
Knight, J. 2008. The internationalisation of higher education: Complexities and realities. In *Higher education in Africa: The international dimension,* ed. D. Teferra and J. Knight, 1–43. Accra: AAU.
Knight, J., and H. de Wit. 1997. *Internationalization of higher education in Asia Pacific countries.* Amsterdam: EAIE.
Lange, L., and M. Singh. 2009. Equity issues in quality assurance in South African higher education. In *Equity and quality assurance: A marriage of two minds,* ed. M. Martin, 37–74. Paris: UNESCO and CIEP.
Mamdani, M. 1993. University crisis and reform: Reflections on the African experience. *Review of African Political Economy* 58: 7–19.
Mamdani, M. 1994. Introduction. In *The quest for academic freedom in Africa,* ed. M. Diouf and M. Mamdani, 1–15. Dakar: CODESRIA.
Marginson, S., and M. van der Wende. 2007. *Globalisation and higher education. OECD working paper 8.* Paris: OECD.
Mohamedbhai, G. 2009. WCHE online forum discussion, 6 June. https://communities.unesco.org/wws/admin/wche_forum.
Obamba, M.O., and J.K. Mwema. 2009. Symmetry and asymmetry: New contours, paradigms and politics in African academic partnerships. *Higher Education Policy* 22, no. 3: 349–71.
Ogachi, O. 2009. Internationalization *vs.* regionalization of higher education in East Africa and the challenges of quality assurance and knowledge production. *Higher Education Policy* 22, no. 3: 331–47.
Partnership for Higher Education in Africa. 2003–2007. *Case studies of higher education in Africa.* Oxford: James Curry.
Reichert, S. 2009. The unintended effects of the Bologna reforms. *International Higher Education,* No. 57. Boston, MA: Boston College Center for International Higher Education.
Samoff, J., and B. Carrol. 2004. The promise of partnership and continuities of dependence: External support to Higher Education in Africa. *African Studies Review* 47, no. 1: 67–199.
SARUA Study Series. 2008. *Towards a common future: Higher education in the SADC region.* Johannesburg: SARUA Study Series.
Sawyerr, A. 2004. Challenges facing African universities: Selected issues. *African Studies Review* 47, no. 1: 1–59.
Scott, P. 1998. Massification, internationalization and globalization. In *The globalization of higher education,* ed. P. Scott, 108–29. Buckingham: Open University Press.
Scott, P. 2006. Internationalising higher education: A global perspective. In *The internationalisation of higher education in South Africa,* ed. R. Kishun, 13–28. Durban: IEASA.

Singh, M. 2004. Higher education in Africa, international co-operation and GATS. In *The implications of WTO/GATS for higher education in Africa,* ed. AAU, 107–18. Accra: AAU.

Teferra, D. 2008. The international dimensions of higher education in Africa: Status, challenges and prospects. In *Higher education in Africa: The international dimension,* ed. D. Teferra and J. Knight, 44–79. Boston: CIHE.

Teferra, D., and P.G. Altbach. 2003. *African higher education: An international reference handbook.* Bloomington, IN: Indiana University Press.

Teferra, D., and J. Knight. 2008. *Higher education in Africa: The international dimension.* Boston, MA: CIHE.

Teichler, U. 2004. The changing debate on internationalization of higher education. *Higher Education* 48, no. 1: 5–26.

Teichler, U. 2005. Research on higher education in Europe. *European Journal of Education* 40, no. 4: 447–69.

Wandira, A. 1977. *The African university in development.* Johannesburg: Ravan Press.

World Bank. 2009. *Accelerating catch-up: Tertiary education for growth in sub-Saharan Africa.* Washington, DC: World Bank.

World Education News and Reviews, and World Education Services. 2007. The impact of the Bologna Process beyond Europe, Part 1. *World Education News and Reviews* 20, no. 4: 1–5.

Yesufu, J.M. 1973. *Creating the African university: Emerging issues of the 1970s.* Ibadan: Oxford University Press.

Zeleza, P.T. 2005. Transnational education and African universities. *Journal of Higher Education in Africa* 3, no. 1: 1–28.

Small world: access to higher education between methodological nationalism and international organisations

Gaële Goastellec

Observervatory Science, Policy and Society, University of Lausanne, Lausanne, Switzerland

> What do the shared norms emerging in the regulation of access reveal about the higher education internationalisation process? The history of access norms brings to light two characteristics of this process: the spreading of sociotechnic tools and the emergence of moral entrepreneurs. Based on case studies carried out in France, the US, South Africa and Indonesia, the analysis reveals how a common search for equality of opportunity in access is intertwined with the international diffusion of 'university knowledge' (modes of organisations, tools, techniques), a multiform process that can take an anecdotic, accidental or all-rational form.

Traditionally, when questioning the internationalisation of access to higher education, two dimensions are put under scrutiny. First come students' influxes: the students' mobility and its corollary, the ability of higher education national systems and institutions to register foreign students as well as the geography of these students' origins are analysed. Second is the extra-national structure of access: the role played by foreign providers such as universities registering at distance or university satellite campuses (Ziguras 2003) is investigated. But besides these now two classic dimensions of analysis, another process testifies to the complexity of internationalisation: the globalisation of access norms.

When it comes to changes affecting access to higher education, internationalisation and globalisation cannot be disentangled. They are part of a dialectical relation (Marginson and Van der Wende 2006) that must be analysed as such. The globalisation of access can be subsumed as the process through which common norms emerge. These norms testify of a shared frame to interpret the world, a frame whose production tends to escape the Nation State.[1] They are intertwined with higher education internationalisation, i.e., 'the process of integrating an international, intercultural or global dimension into the purposes, functions or delivery of post-secondary education' (Knight 2003).

What are the shared norms emerging in the regulation of access to higher education and what do they reveal about the higher education internationalisation process? Based on case studies carried out by the author during the last 10 years in France, the US, South Africa and Indonesia, this paper attempts to identify the complex processes lying behind the access issue in the global arena. It is structured in two main parts. The first part presents the global norms emerging in the regulation of access; the second part identifies two characteristics of the globalisation of access norms: the spreading of sociotechnic tools, and the emergence of moral entrepreneurs.

Changing access: a history

When analysing access from a historical and international perspective, the higher education systems' comparison reveals a double trend: an obvious and well known one, the global diffusion of the massification's ideal, and a more discrete one, the move from the norm of inherited merit to the norm of equality of opportunities.

A long-distance revolution: massification

Massification has long been perceived as a desirable goal of higher education. The starting point of this process can be located in the US when in 1944 President Roosevelt signed the GI bill, providing the veterans of the Second World War with easy access to higher education. This trend became patent when the American congress, reacting to the launch of Sputnik in 1957, voted in the National Defense Education Act, entitling universities to regular federal funding. Aimed at increasing the number of American researchers, this Act was also a vote for massification, as it led to an early enlargement of access. It is thus not surprising that a typology of massification emerged as early as the 1970s in the work of the American researcher Trow (Trow 1973).

Indeed, in the US, the massification process accelerated after the 1960s. Even if it later increased at a slower pace, the total number of students still grew from 14.8 million to 17.5 million between 2000 and 2006 (Scott 2009), while the number of students worldwide rose from 13 million in 1960 to about 100 million in 2000 (Gradstein and Nikitin 2004). Although this increase is in part related to a mechanical phenomenon of demographic augmentation, it also corresponds to national policies aimed at enlarging higher education systems, as testified to by the boost in access rates: for example, European higher education systems registered on average 1% of the relevant age group at the very beginning of the twentieth century (Ringer 2004), compared with 51% at the beginning of the following century (OECD 2004). The second half of the twentieth century is thus characterised by the universal rise of mass higher education as a significant element of wider social change (Tapper and Palfreyman 2005).

Starting in the US as a political and economic issue, and tool of the Cold War through scientific competition, the rise of mass higher education is one of the main universal dynamics of the second half of the twentieth century. And whether massification is reached or not, as a worldwide trend it constitutes a decisive dynamic, leading to a revolution in access norms and more widely in higher education organisation and functions.

Norming access

When looking at changes in access to higher education, three norms can be identified that have dominated its organisation. Although they appeared successively and thus can be perceived as sequential stages, this does not mean that the later norms necessarily replace the former. They can be superimposed in a higher education system, depending on the institution considered. As a result, they should be considered as models or ideal types orienting access changes.[2]

First, there is the norm of 'inherited merit'. Higher education systems have been created by an elite (political authorities, religious leaders or colonisers) to answer particular purposes such as educating specific professions (lawyers and doctors in the first Parisian faculties, clergy and civic leaders in the first eight American colleges founded before the American revolution, etc). Built up on a highly centralised model, these systems limit access to a restricted urban population: in South Africa, the first colleges were created in the nineteenth century in the Cape Province, where most of the British migrants were concentrated. In Indonesia, it was in Jakarta that the first faculties were set up to educate the Dutch colonisers and the priyayi, the local elite. In France, their creation took place in Paris; in the US the first colleges were established on the East Coast. Access is thus principally limited to those who belong to an elite or who are identified as serving the ruling groups. The 'inherited merit' norm can thus be seen in relation with the 'elite' form of higher education described by Trow (2007) as 'shaping the mind and character of a ruling class, a preparation for elite roles' (243).

Nevertheless, higher education systems were so discreet in the national environment (as only a tiny percentage of an age group could access higher education) that they were not necessarily perceived as hampering social mobility. However that may be, access to higher education also reflected a restricted understanding of otherness: some groups, the numerically dominant (such as women mostly everywhere, non-whites in South Africa, etc), were considered as statutorily different and thus they were not entitled to the same rights as the ruling group. The 'inherited merit' norm ruling access also corresponded to the understanding of some social inequalities as legitimated, justified, or so to say, 'naturally fair'.

Things changed in the first half of the twentieth century. The norm of equality of rights affirmed itself as a consequence of changes in higher education roles and in political principles sustaining societal organisation. Modifications in the workforce induced by transformations of the national economy called for increased access to higher education, while relief in major social conflicts that were until then structuring the society (male/women, white/black) encouraged an opening of access to higher education to previously excluded groups. We thus observe the diffusion of the ideal of universal access to primary education to further areas of education. This principle was to become fundamental in the organisation of higher education, along with the meritocratic ideal. Higher education remained elitist by principle and advocated selective access. Mostly, academic performance was considered the result of 'natural intelligence'; the influence of socio-economic determinants was therefore denied.

Equality of rights was accompanied by the higher education geographic decentralisation. For example, in France, the number of universities doubled between the end of the Second World War and 1970, before this dynamic expanded to middle size towns between 1980 and 2000 (Filâtre and Grossetti 2003). In South Africa, new universities were built in the 1960s and 1970s, following the track of separated development (Waast and Gaillard 2001). In Indonesia, each province was provided with a state university between 1956 and 1963. The geographic development of the higher education sector also favoured the integration of the system through the building up of national access policies.

Hand in hand with this process of decentralisation came a diversification of the degrees proposed within universities and the creation of new kinds of institutions, usually aimed at providing non-traditional students with some higher or tertiary education (see for example community colleges in the US, IUT and BTS in France, private institutions in Indonesia). However, a shared rule consisted in dedicating non-selective institutions to the enlargement of access.

Thus, the equality of rights in access was gradually being provided legally (as former rules excluding some groups were banned) and formally through the opening of both new institutions and degrees. As a result, the former prerogatives of some ruling groups regarding access were preserved, while the demand for access of the other groups was partly answered. The result can be summarised as follows: formally equal, but apart.

The second half of the twentieth century was characterised by a further step towards the realisation of equality through the diffusion of an equality of opportunities norm. This time, it was not only about providing general access to all groups of individuals, but providing equal opportunity for every social group to access the same institutions and degrees. With this new attention paid to internal inequalities in higher education, flagship institutions, traditionally educating the elite, came under scrutiny. At the base of this ideal lay the belief that intelligence is equally spread amongst all social groups, and thus that there was no reason why some groups should benefit from greater access to the most rewarding segments of higher education. The equality of opportunity norm thus can be read as an attempt to entitle each citizen (with equivalent academic abilities) to sit in the same classroom, regardless of their social origin. This attempt corresponds to the period of the end of segregation in the US and the need to compensate for past inequalities. Equality of opportunity thus emerged from social struggles.

The focus thus shifted from higher education systems' levels of massification to the distribution of students within the higher education institutions and degrees – and, as a result, to who could (and should be able to) access the flagship institutions and formations.

This transformation of access norms underlines the changes in the role devolved to higher education systems and the increased necessity to testify to the legitimacy of the elite they produce. Access norms thus increasingly tended to escape the nation states: they appeared as a global trend that diffused across contrasting national contexts.

Spreading the changes: sociotechnic tools and moral entrepreneurs

How have these norms been diffused and what do they tell us about the internationalisation of higher education systems?

The diffusion of sociotechnic tools
Standardised examination tests

Developed in the US in the first half of the twentieth century, standardised examination tests were created to provide universities with a common tool of selecting students. Originally, the instigators of the test were looking for a way to replace an elite based on birth with an elite based on diplomas. Invented by a professor of psychology, the SAT (the Scholastic Assessment Test) was promoted by J.B. Conant, then president of the prestigious Harvard University. Spreading progressively between 1934 and 1948, it was first used by Ivy League universities, and was then adopted by public universities such as the Californian system in 1960 (see Goastellec 2003).

Dictating access to American universities, similar tests can be found today in a large number of higher education systems. For example, in Israel, the establishment in 1981 of a National Institute for Testing and Evaluation by the Israeli universities, whose aim has been to construct a Psychometric Entrance Test that would be valid for applicants to all the Israeli universities, is not without similarities to the American SAT (the NITE was to provide standardised tests accepted by all the universities). The same type of tests can also be found in South Africa, where the University of Cape Town is also developing national entrance examinations. How have these tests been diffused?

The Indonesian case underlines the importance of the international circulation of students and researchers in these technological transfers: the adoption of a national entrance examination by Indonesian public universities may not have been possible if members of the Indonesian elite had not studied in the US since the 1960s (for example, PhD students in economics at the University of Berkeley, in California). Indeed, one can link the development of admission tests in Indonesia to the encounter of graduate students in computer sciences with the SAT (Scholastic Aptitude Test). Professor Toemin A. Masoem, dean of the Universitas Indonesia (UI) department of computer science at the beginning of the twenty-first century, was trained in 1979 in the field of educational testing by the ETS (Educational Testing Service), the American Company which commercialised the SAT. Later on, he introduced the use of a similar entrance examination in Indonesia, solving the problem of the territorial management of Indonesian higher education. The UMPTN was openly patterned on the SAT. Similar to the SAT, the test was developed by a private company and first implemented by the most elite higher education institutions.

The diffusion of sociotechnic tools through technological transfer testifies to the intertwined internationalisation and globalisation of higher education systems. Based on the circulation of both individuals (students and researchers) and knowledge, they can be perceived as a way to solve both geographical and academic measurement problems in the organisation of access. Besides the practical dimension, they also carry with them certain beliefs: when J.B. Conant promoted the SAT in the 1940s, his aim was to identify pure intelligence, disconnected from culture (Conant 1940). These tests are thus vectors of the ideal of equality of rights: social backgrounds were not supposed to interplay with the measurement of individual talents. The failing of these tests to implement equality led to improvements in the organisation of access: the diffusion of alternative admission practices.

Alternative admission practices

The birth of alternative admission practices can be linked to a historical context: the necessity of correcting historical inequalities produced by social segregation in access to higher education. It is thus not surprising that these practices appeared in the US during the 1960s, particularly in selective institutions such as the University of Berkeley (see Goastellec 2004). These practices generally came in addition to admission tests. For example, at first, quotas were introduced to weight the disparity of racial access remaining after the tests. Following legal inquiries in the 1990s, holistic admission processes (that take into account all the dimensions of the individual) replaced the use of quotas (Goastellec 2008). These procedures progressively diffused into other higher education systems, partly due to the increasing international networking of flagship institutions, as well as a more important role played by the higher education ministries' associations.

For example, the adoption by the French Parisian Institute of Political Sciences of a second path of admission was visibly inspired by those used in the US.[3] As for

Indonesia, the top institutions developed a second path of admission named the 'regional excellence seed' (*Penelusuran bibit unggul daerah*), which facilitates access for students coming from ethnic minorities (non-Javanese) under the cover of geographic diversity. The selection of a national elite introduces a new diversity aimed at providing more legitimacy to a group that has historically been dominated by the Javanese. In some other countries, sometimes due to the transformation of the population composition, it is the government that implements tools to take into account ethnic minorities (for example in Ireland).

The diffusion of alternative admission practices (quotas, specific selection processes for minority students) is aimed both at correcting bias in the measure of academic competences (considering that admission tests favour students with a certain type of culture) and resolving the problem of legitimacy in higher education by improving the diversity and hence the societal representation of the elite. These processes translate the idea that access to higher education, or at least access to the most elitist institution, should offer equitable representation to the various groups composing society. Equality of opportunity is thus the ultimate ideal diffused by alternative admission processes. Developed in countries with contrasting levels of higher education massification, they testify that higher education systems are increasingly expected to be a democratic window onto a society's organisation.

Depending on the national context and higher education history and configuration, these norms are sustained by elitist higher education institutions (UC Berkeley, Sciences-Po Paris, ITBandung, University of Cape Town, etc). But they can also be implemented by national authorities through funding instruments aimed at inciting higher education institutions to widen access. These incentives mainly consist in indexing part of institutional funding on the characteristics of the students registered (socio-economic background, belonging to ethnic minorities, etc) and sometimes on the characteristics of those taken to graduation. In South Africa for example, the funding framework takes into account the proportion of disadvantaged students. In France, the delegate ministry of higher education is working on a more comprehensive funding framework.

The comparison of national processes reveals a common trend in rethinking equity funding, and the imbrications of the equity with the funding dimension. That is to say, institutions are accountable in terms of their ability to promote educational/social mobility. We thus observe a diffusion of this equity norm both through some of the flagship institutions and through national authorities (ministries, departments of education, etc).

The spreading of admission tools and practices through policy borrowing between the national flagship education institutions sustains the diffusion of access norms, in particular that of equality of opportunity. This diffusion can be an unexpected consequence of the adoption of a tool aimed at rationalising access procedures. For example, it is because the results obtained at the standardised examination tests revealed disparities between social groups that the search for admission processes correcting inequalities started. Social scientists play a decisive role in characterising inequalities produced by admission processes.

Moral entrepreneurs and the equity norm

Conceptualised by H. Becker, moral entrepreneurs are individuals or groups of individuals that either create or enforce a norm, but in every case use their influence to diffuse this norm. Usually part of a dominant group of the society, they often initiate their crusade in the political arena. They differ from political entrepreneurs not due to a lack of a political dimension in their activity but because through the norms they set, they define a moral ideal without addressing the issue of how the norm should be implemented (Becker 1973). Both social scientists and international bodies thus can be categorised as moral entrepreneurs.

Social scientists

The norm of equality of rights has long been associated with the massification of higher education and the belief that the enlargement of access would enhance individual opportunities. Social scientists have largely participated in the abandonment of this view: the analysis of access has shifted from a global quantitative approach (i.e., the measure of an individual's absolute chances to enter higher education) to a more qualitative understanding (i.e., the widening of higher education: who accesses which institutions, which degrees and with which result? What are the relative odds of the different social groups in higher education?). The necessity of measuring the performance of higher education systems regarding equity is illustrated by the development of research questioning the link between access enlargement and inequality reduction.

Since the beginning of the 1990s, research that investigates student distribution within higher education has multiplied. For example, in 1989, Brint and Karabel identified a diversion process characterised by the orientation of American working class students towards non-elite opportunities and lower status positions. Analysing the French system, other research pointed out that social specialisation according to students' social backgrounds creates 'segregated democratization' (Duru-Bellat 2005). This analysis echoes other research (Raftery and Hout 1993; Shavit and Blossfeld 1993) showing that inequalities between individuals are maintained until the advantaged class reaches a point of saturation. This hypothesis, known as maximally maintained inequality (MMI), underlines the fact that investments in education do not necessarily warrant higher outputs for an individual; it thus questions the link between investment in human capital and the distribution of individual private benefits. But research results also evolve: discussing the effect of higher education's mass expansion on inequalities, Shavit et al. showed in 2007 that all social classes benefit from the expansion of higher education; in 1993, they found that in most countries educational expansion was not associated with a reduction of educational inequalities (Shavit and Blossfeld 1993). Finally, numerous debates and polemics exist about the instruments measuring inequalities (Vinod, Wang, and Fan 2002; Breen and Jonasson 2005), as most of the statistical models fuel controversies.

Whatsoever, the focus on quantitative democratisation has been challenged by investigations on qualitative democratisation (Prost 1986), i.e. reducing social inequalities in schooling trajectories. These social differences in access to education are also analysed though conflict theory, underlying the role of the dominant groups' social strategies to reproduce their privileges through education (Weber 1971; Bourdieu 1979). More widely, research questioning qualitative democratisation sustains a complexification of the reading of inequalities, and an increased link between scientific research and higher education policies.

This research, always looking as it is for further discrete inequalities, sustains the search for a fairer higher education system. It is reinforced by the discourses of international bodies that call for the implementation of the equality of opportunities norm.

International bodies

The equality of opportunities norm has recently been the target of a normalisation process at the international level. As a norm – written documents resulting from a consensus aimed at achieving an optimal level of organisation in a specific context and applied on a voluntary basis (Borraz 2004) – equality of opportunities in access has been formalised since the end of the 1990s by international bodies such as UNESCO, the World Bank, the OECD, the European Community, etc.

This trend emerges principally from the *World declaration on higher education for the twenty-first century: Vision and action*, initiated by UNESCO and adopted by the World Conference on Higher Education in 1998. This report dedicates its third article to the question of equity of access. Two points in this article are particularly worth mentioning, as they articulate two features of the equality of opportunities principle (although they can also contradict each other):

(a) In keeping with Article 26.1 of the Universal Declaration of Human Rights, admission to higher education should be based on the merit, capacity, efforts, perseverance and devotion showed by those seeking access to it, and can take place in a lifelong scheme, at any time, with due recognition of previously acquired skills. As a consequence, no discrimination can be accepted in granting access to higher education on grounds of race, gender, language or religion, or economic, cultural or social distinctions, or physical disabilities.

(d) Access to higher education for members of some special target groups, such as indigenous peoples, cultural and linguistic minorities, disadvantaged groups, peoples living under occupation and those who suffer from disabilities, must be actively facilitated …

These two points underline both the principle of non-discrimination (or an identity-blinded selection process), associated with the idea of meritocratic selection (point 'a'), and the principle of affirmative action (point 'd') towards some categories of individuals. This second goal was developed in 2000 by the World Bank along with UNESCO in the report *Higher education in developing countries: Peril and promise*, which underlines the necessity of offering access to higher education to students 'from disadvantaged backgrounds'.

In 2006, the Commission of European Communities went even further with a communication on 'efficiency and equity in European education and training system', stating that higher education institutions: 'should be encouraged to develop comprehensive outreach and access policies, which could include the introduction of bridging programs and earmarked places'.

We can see here the reappearance – although less explicitly than in the worldwide declaration on higher education – of the necessity of taking identities into account in the organisation of access to higher education. The Commission also advocates the articulation of equity and efficiency in higher education policies by inciting national public authorities to: 'create appropriate conditions and incentives to generate higher investment from public and private sources, including, where appropriate, tuition fees combined with accompanying financial measures for the disadvantaged' (Commission of European Communities 2006).

The same year, the meeting of OECD Education Ministers in June 2006 had for its title 'Higher education. Quality, equity and efficiency' (Athens, 27–28 June). As outlined in the chair summary, one of the targets to be addressed concerned a:

More equitable education: access to higher education needs to be widened to benefit all social groups. This is a real challenge for school systems, as well as for higher education. Action is therefore needed throughout education systems to tackle the problem.

In particular, ministers reached the following points of agreement: they 'affirmed their commitment to widen higher education participation to promote social inclusion and expand lifelong learning' and 'accepted that a wider diversification of institutional profiles is needed to meet the full range of national needs and individuals' aspirations'.

We can see here emerging from these discourses the necessity to diversify not only higher education systems but also the student body. Those extracts reveal that behind the general category of 'disadvantaged' individuals, some groups are identified as 'social groups', 'linguistic minorities', 'indigenous communities', or handicapped persons. By doing so, international bodies call for the taking into account of collective identities in the organisation of higher education and in the implementation of equity policies.

These various calls for equity policies underline the increased recognition of the role played by higher education systems in the building up of democratic society or at least in the affirmation of a democratic ideal. Of course, the definition of this norm of access by international bodies does not have a constraining effect. Nevertheless, as a norm, it has a scientific, technical and democratic legitimacy.

Finally, what is at stake in the small world of access concerns the legitimacy of the higher education organisation, measured through the students' characteristics in the various degrees and institutions, but overall in the most selective sectors of higher education systems. Everything happens as if the degree of widening of higher education systems were an indicator of one society's level of democracy: the global spreading of access norms such as the norm of equality of opportunity underlines the progressive diffusion of a shared frame to interpret the world that resembles a democratic ideal.

This article has discussed global changes in access norms and related them to the actions of sociotechnic tools and moral entrepreneurs. In other words, the common search for equality of opportunity in access is sustained by the international diffusion of 'university knowledge' (modes of organisations, tools, techniques), a multiform process that can take an anecdotic, accidental or all-rational form. Starting as a technological innovation in the US, diffused and adapted by elitists' higher education institutions worldwide, this norm, now formalised by international bodies, has come a long distance. It still has a long way to go to be translated into what it calls for: the elite circulation through higher education wished by J.B. Conant more than half a century ago.

Notes

1. This definition of the globalisation of access borrows Muller's more general definition of globalisation (Muller 2000).
2. For a more detailed version of this typology see Clancy and Goastellec (2007) and Goastellec (2008).
3. In 2001, the governing body of this institution adopted conventions allowing a specific student admission (dossiers and interviews instead of the usual entrance examination) in seven high schools that are part of the Priority Education Zones (ZEP). If this second path of admission does not directly promote student access on the basis of ethno-racial or social belonging, this territorial positive discriminatory measure targets 'without naming them expressively, and, overall, without naming them exclusively, groups that, in the US, would

without doubt have been apprehended as ethnic or racial minorities' (Calvès 2005, 31). Simultaneously, it answers a socio-economic need, these areas being identified on the basis of students' socio-economic backgrounds.

References

Becker, H.S. 1973. *Outsiders: Study in the sociology of deviance.* New York: Free Press.
Borraz, O. 2004. Les normes, instruments dépolitisés de l'action publique. In *Gouverner par les instruments,* ed. P. Lascoumes and P. Le Gales, 123–61. Paris: Presses de Science Po.
Bourdieu, P. 1979. *La distinction, critique sociale du jugement.* Paris: Minuit.
Breen, R., and J.O. Jonsson. 2005. Inequality of opportunity in comparative perspective: Recent research on educational attainment and social mobility. *Annual Review of Sociology* 31: 223–43.
Brint, S., and J. Karabel. 1989. *The diverted dream: Community colleges and the promise of educational opportunity in America, 1900–1985.* Oxford: Oxford University Press.
Calvès, G. 2005. Les politiques de discrimination positive. *Pouvoirs* 111: 29–40.
Clancy, P., and G. Goastellec. 2007. Questioning access and equity in higher education: Policy and performance in a comparative perspective. *Higher Education Quarterly* 61, no. 2: 136–54.
Commission of the European Communities. 2006. Efficiency and equity in European education and training systems. Communication from the commission to the Council and to the European Parliament, Brussels, com 181 final.
Conant, J.B. 1940. Education for a classless society: The Jeffersonian tradition. *The Atlantic Monthly* (May): 593–602.
Duru-Bellat, M. 2005. Democratisation of education and reduction in inequalities of opportunities: An obvious link? Paper presented at the European Conference on Educational Research, December, in Dublin, Ireland.
Filâtre, D., and M. Grossetti. 2003. La carte scientifique française. In *La territorialisation de l'enseignement supérieur et de la recherché,* ed. M. Grossetti and P. Losego, 21–44. Paris: L'Harmattan.
Goastellec, G. 2003. Le SAT et l'accès aux études supérieures: Le recrutement des élites américaines en question. *Sociologie du Travail* 45, no. 4: 473–90.
Goastellec, G. 2004. Entre politique des quotas et égalité: L'Université de Californie à Berkeley. *Cahiers Internationaux de Sociologie* 116: 141–64.
Goastellec, G. 2008. Globalization and implementation of an equity norm in higher education. *Peabody Journal of Education* 83, no. 1: 73–85.
Gradstein, M., and D. Nikitin. 2004. *Education expansion: Evidence and interpretation.* Research working paper. Washington, DC: World Bank.
Knight, J. 2003. Updating the definition of internationalization. *International Higher Education* 33 (Fall): 2–3.
Marginson, S., and M. Van der Wende. 2006. Globalisation and higher education. Draft paper, prepared for OECD.
Ministère Éducation Nationale (MEN). 2005. *Repères et références statistiques.* Paris: DEP.
Muller, P. 2000. L'analyse cognitive des politiques publiques. Vers une sociologie de l'action publique. *Revue Française de Science Politique* 50, no. 2: 189–207.
Organisation for Economic Co-operation and Development (OECD). 2004. *Education at a glance.* Paris: OECD.
Organisation for Economic Co-operation and Development (OECD) Education Ministers. 2006. Higher education. Quality, equity and efficiency. Athens, June 27–28, meeting summary.

Prost, A. 1986. *L'enseignement s'est-il démocratisé?* Paris: PUF.
Raftery, A.E., and M. Hout. 1993. Maximally maintained inequalities: Expansion, reform and opportunity in Irish education, 1921–1975. *Sociology of Education* 66, no. 1: 41–62.
Ringer, F. 2004. Admission. In *A history of the university in Europe, Vol. III, Universities in the nineteenth and early twentieth centuries (1800–1945)*, ed. W. Rüegg, 233–68. Cambridge: Cambridge University Press.
Scott, P. 2009. Access in higher education in Europe and North America. Paper prepared for the UNESCO Forum on Higher Education in the Europe Region: Access, values, quality and competitiveness, May 21–24, in Bucharest, Romania.
Shavit, Y., and H.-P. Blossfeld. 1993. *Persistent inequalities: A comparative study of educational attainment in thirteen countries.* Boulder, CO: Westview.
Shavit, Y., R. Arum, and A. Gamoran. 2007. *Expansion, differentiation and inequality of access to higher education: A comparative study.* Stanford, CA: Stanford University Press.
Tapper, T., and D. Palfreyman. 2005. *Understanding mass higher education.* New York: RoutledgeFalmer.
Trow, M. 1973. *Problems in the transition from elite to mass higher education.* Berkeley, CA: Carnegie Commission on Higher Education.
Trow, M. 2007. Reflections on the transition from elite to universal access: Forms and phases of Higher Education in modern societies since WWII. In *International handbook of higher education,* ed. J.F.F. Forest and P. Altbach, 243–80. Dordrecht, The Netherlands: Springer.
Vinod, T., Y. Wang, and X. Fan. 2002. A new dataset on inequality in education: Gini and Theil Indices of Schooling for 140 countries, 1960–2000. World Bank report. Mimeo, World Bank.
Waast, R., and J. Gaillard. 2001. *Science in South Africa* (Country report). Stallenbosch, South Africa: Institut for Research and Development, University of Stallenbosch.
Weber, M. 1971. *Economie et société.* Paris: Plon.
World Bank. 2000. *Higher education in developing countries: Peril and promise.* Washington, DC: World Bank.
World Conference on Higher Education. 1998. World declaration on higher education for the twenty-first century: Vision and action. http://www.unesco.org/education/educprog/wche/declaration_eng.htm.
Ziguras, C. 2003. The impact of the GATS on transnational tertiary education: Comparing experiences of New Zealand, Australia, Singapore and Malaysia. *The Australian Educational Researcher* 30, no. 3: 89–109.

Singapore: bridgehead of the West or counterforce? The s[t]imulation of creative and critical thought in Singapore's higher education policies

Ingrid Hoofd

Communications and New Media Programme, National University of Singapore, Singapore

> This paper argues that the welcoming by western humanists of pedagogies of critical and creative thinking in Asian universities – as if such thinking will breed an eastern counter-voice to western neo-liberalism – is misguided. The paper will question the rise of creative and critical thinking in higher education in Asia by analysing the intersections of the neo-liberal economy, new media technologies, and such new 'thinking' in the post-colonial context of Singapore and its national university. The paper will conclude that in the new hegemonic configuration under technological acceleration, higher education becomes a nationalist *and* globalist project in which privileged Singaporean students constitute the new 'upwardly mobile' by branding themselves as 'creative Asians'.

> Beware of ends; but what would a university be without ends? (Derrida 2004, 153)

In Europe as well as Asia, higher education is undergoing rapid transformation. These transformations nonetheless do not occur in quite the same ways in the west and the east. While many European universities had to leave their classic *Bildungsideal* behind for a more pragmatic model of education, many Asian universities, especially those in the new global cities like Hong Kong, Dubai and Singapore, are perhaps surprisingly emphasising critical and creative thinking above old pedagogies of acquiring knowledge for vocational goals. Moreover, Asian universities in the new global cities have increasingly managed to purchase western academics like me in an effort to harness 'global talent' for teaching and research, resulting in the further global dissemination of western ideas about science, justice and progress. At first glance, such a transformation in the Asian educational context might be welcomed by academics teaching in the humanities, where critical and creative approaches in the form of 'questioning' have always been fundamental to the democratic ideal. As such, the rise of critical thinking in Asia may spur hopes of an 'eastern' counter-voice to western neo-liberal imperialism. However, I suggest that the straightforward welcoming of new critical and creative thinking in Asian universities by western humanists is problematic. I will question the rise of creative and critical thinking in higher education in Asia in this paper by analysing the intersections of the neo-liberal economy, new media technologies, and such new 'thinking' in the post-colonial context of Singapore and its National University (NUS), at which I teach feminist and continental philosophy.

Such an analysis opens up a range of important questions around the implications of the neo-liberalisation of education in the Asian context. This is because this change appears to diverge from an earlier colonial and post-colonial logic, in which western hegemony sought to reproduce itself by luring Asian academics and students towards its own western institutions. Gayatri Spivak has aptly sketched this old post-colonial logic in *Outside in the teaching machine*. Her chapter 'Marginality in the teaching machine' discusses how the revalidation of the west relies on a constant and precarious reproduction of marginality. She exemplifies this reproduction with how her own upward mobility was an effect of her subjugation as an 'authentic Indian voice' in western academia (Spivak 1993, 54–5). While her position as an academic 'Indian' speaking from 'the east' has provided her empowerment and income, this subjugation is nonetheless part of the discursive, economic and technological violence committed by the west on the non-west. The claim to authentic marginality is therefore paradoxically a *commitment* to an imperialist subjugation. The Asian academic becomes the agent of a new form of colonialism, as much as she has been bought by and 'buys into' the western academic–humanist mindset and its reliance on marginality.

In my case as a white western academic being 'lured' to the east, the roles seem to be reversed. But does this superficial reversal mean that global cultural hegemony – paralleling the economic rise of China and India – is shifting towards the east and away from the west, or is this reversal symptomatic of a new economic–cultural logic through which the west retains its hegemony? Does it still make sense to conceptualise current hegemony in terms of east versus west? In order to mobilise while showing the limitations of using the east as a counter-point to the west in the matter of the neo-liberalisation of education, I will engage the emergence of creative and critical thinking in NUS through 'western' philosopher Martin Heidegger from an 'eastern' locality. I am using Heidegger's ideas on thought and technology especially because what is at stake is how to *think* of an alternative to technocratic globalisation. Moreover, my engagement with Heidegger in this paper parallels my teaching of such 'dead white men' to an ostensibly non-white middle-upper class student body at NUS. This will lead me to argue that a cybernetic acceleration of thought in- and outside NUS engenders a *s(t)imulation* of politics in academia, despite (and because of) all rhetoric about the potentials of new media for emancipation. The new logic at work at the heart of higher education in Asia is hence a thoroughly ambiguous affair that should be understood in relation to emerging global elites in the west *and* east. I will call these new elites *speed-elites* because of their reliance on technological acceleration and the neo-liberal transgression of borders (Armitage and Graham 2001). Speed-elitism, rather than Eurocentrism, is the primary nexus around which contemporary disparities are organised, even though it builds on the formalisation of Eurocentric national and racial differences. In this new configuration of hegemony under technological acceleration, higher education becomes a nationalist *and* globalist project in which my Singaporean students constitute the Spivakian upwardly mobile by branding themselves as 'creative Asians'.

Technological innovation is a driving force behind most Asian universities, and it is in light of this that the call for creativity and criticality should be appreciated. This pervasive techno-drive is in Singapore intimately related to the unequal relationship between the west and Asia in which NUS operates. It would therefore be a mistake to regard Singapore's new educational policies as clear-cut counter-examples to the neo-liberalisation taking place in European academia, because the difference between east and west has itself become one of the nodes around which the simulation of thought occurs. Nonetheless, a re-reading in the Singapore context of a tension in continental philosophy could help open up this neo-liberalism. I will use Heidegger's work here to argue that a hegemonic cybernetic aesthetic is complicit in an ongoing usurpation of critical debate – like this one between Europe and Asia – in an ever more vicious global economy which all higher education today serves. 'Thinking' becomes petrified within a worldwide system of (academic) institutions, networks and their accelerated capital flows. I will illustrate this petrifaction of thought through an analysis of the Singapore Renaissance City campaign, which seeks to push critical and creative thinking in education for the advancement of the local industries. This analysis will show that NUS's arguments for 'creativity' and 'critical thinking' correspond with the modularisation of political and economic production within neo-liberalism, as well as with the ongoing de-politicisation of the workforce. But it is also in light of my *critically tracing* such thinking back to its petrifaction through the Singapore example, that thought once more emerges as singular – thus addressing the fissure between modern technology as empowering and oppressive that riddles Heidegger's work, and allowing the NUS case to unsettle western metaphysics and its current manifestation as neo-liberal acceleration, just as my Asian students unsettle my western authority in the classroom by questioning its cultural specificity.

Let me begin by briefly recalling Heidegger's argument around the relationship between forms of thinking, social change and technology. Heidegger argues in 'The question concerning technology' that technology's essence (ειδος) is never neutral, and that human activity and thought are organised within the technological realm (Heidegger 1993b, 312). The essence of modern technology for Heidegger lies in the intensification of the western *idea* of instrumentalism. This gives rise to the increasing complicity of thought in hegemony. Heidegger's critique opens up the possibility of an analysis of tools and pedagogies in terms of their involvement in the (re)production of hegemony in a society like Singapore. For Heidegger, the subject of technology is always to some extent technology's object, and modern technology simply extends this objectification.

The question is whether this aggravation of objectification is manifest in Singapore due to the massive adoption in Asian universities of digital technologies for management, research and teaching. Also, one could wonder what gives rise to the inconsistent claim in Heidegger that on the one hand τηχνη is art (ποιησις) and an *opening up* to singular thought (through revealing), and on the other hand modern technology is *totalitarian*, objectifying the subject (Heidegger 1993b, 317). Do we understand the adoption and teaching of 'western' philosophy and technology by a white person in NUS as oppressive or empowering for the Asian student and the world at large? In 'What calls for thinking?' and 'The end of philosophy and the task for thinking', Heidegger concludes that contemporary technology marks the *death* of philosophy into its logical culmination, the techno-sciences, which are indeed vigorously pursued in NUS. Every conceptualisation has ended up as a calculated digit in the cybernetic space of flows. Philosophy could become that culmination because it has itself always, like the techno-sciences, assumed the ideal of transparent communication through the belief that concepts are transcendental truths. Heidegger states that this completion of philosophy means that: 'Cybernetics transforms language into an exchange of news ... scientific truth is equated with efficiency ... [and] the operational and model-based character of representational-calculative thinking becomes dominant' (Heidegger 1993a, 434–5). We can absolutely discern the dominance of such cybernetic thinking in NUS as well as in most other Asian universities, and students have to comply with such thinking *en masse*. In 'What calls for thinking', Heidegger stresses that this thinking, whether it takes the form of rationalist philosophy or scientific empiricism, is in fact not thinking at all, but rather the setting to work of a pre-described reasoning that has suppressed the grounding gestures which 'clear' a space for thinking (αληθεια). Paradoxically however, it is also this growing gap between the suppressed (concealed) and the obvious (unconcealed) techno-scientific truth that for Heidegger *calls for a more originary thinking* – if one is willing to question those grounds that make (teaching) philosophy possible (Heidegger 1993c, 389).

Heidegger's analysis initially complicates the simplistic rhetoric of student and citizen empowerment and emancipation in higher education in Asia. As Lev Manovich also claims in 'On totalitarian interactivity', the appeal of cybernetics is precisely totalitarian because it inserts one into a system of command and control that simply renders one an object of capitalist production (Manovich 1996). Meanwhile, this objectification is falsely *experienced* as 'freedom' because its historical and aesthetic particularity is concealed from conscious apprehension – thus making it today in Heidegger's words 'most thought-provoking in our thought-provoking time that we are still not thinking' (Heidegger 1993c, 371). It is alongside this argument that I can claim that the erosion of the terms 'critical and creative thinking' in higher education marks an increase of neo-liberal objectification of the learning and working subject of techno-culture, who unlearns to *really* think outside and question its institutional possibility. Heidegger says in 'The end of philosophy' that this 'more sober-minded' (Heidegger 1993a, 449) real thinking is 'a thinking that [is] neither metaphysics nor science … [which] has withdrawn itself continually and increasingly' (Heidegger 1993a, 436). *Real* thinking is aware of the *limitations* of thinking and its enmeshment in neo-liberal acceleration. As new media were largely developed in western universities during the 'anti-eastern' Cold War period, this technological development possibly signifies a more aggressive involvement of media in the post-colonial stratification of Asian societies, their individuals, and their modes of academic exchange, in which *thought* has become petrified within the neo-liberal space of flows. The technologies of acceleration paradoxically have a *de*celerating effect on the subject's ability to 'think differently' and to create true political or economic alternatives.

This ongoing petrifaction of thought, which subjugates students, researchers and citizens in east and west differentially in a post-colonial and neo-liberal logic by targeting them *as if* they are agents of real social change, emerges from the rhetoric of the Singapore government's Renaissance City campaign. The argument for pedagogies that stimulate creative and critical thinking in higher education has proliferated as part of the ambitious goal of this campaign to expand Singapore's economic productivity. This proliferation coincides with the recent upsurge of the global and Asian interactive media industry, and interactive tools and methods are heralded as the main techniques to induce creative and critical thought in learners. Singapore's Minister for Information, Communication and the Arts (MICA), Lee Boon Yang (2007), has been making a big case for nurturing entrepreneurs as 'creative talent with good conceptual and critical thinking skills'. Lee's aim is to harness the economic global surge around the creative industries, and to 'take advantage of the worldwide demand for distinctive content, products, and services' – in other words, to make 'Singaporean' culture and products a distinct global commodity for largely western consumption (Lee 2007). For this purpose, MICA has set up Creative Industries Scholarships and launched the Creative Community Singapore (CCS) to 'help budding entrepreneurs' (MICA 2006). CCS is currently sponsoring several projects, among which is the Moulding Educational Entrepreneurs through Innovative Gaming (MEETING), which aims to 'empower' students with 'productive, creative, and critical thinking abilities' by training them to design digital games (Lee 2007). Lee fails to mention that a significant number of these games are made for military purposes, and that many trainees will end up working for the Singapore army. But even outside these explicit complicities of the creative industries in military endeavours, such training and innovation is problematic due to the way in which it is driven by a cybernetic market expansion and its usurpation of critical and creative thought.

The targeting of Singaporean citizens and students for the Renaissance City campaign emerges especially from its 'Renaissance City report: Culture and the arts in Renaissance Singapore'. This Ministry of Information and the Arts (MIA) document calls for the emergence of a 'type of Singapore person' who has certain 'Renaissance qualities' in order to 'meet the economic challenges of the new millennium' (MIA 2000, 38). Harping on an optimistic and romantic notion of, 'Renaissance Man as an individual imbued with an inquiring mind, an adventurous spirit and wide ranging abilities', the document urges the Singaporean to become an individual who:

> ... dares to be different ... [who] is able to bring a distinct value-added advantage to each activity that he engages in ... [and who] balances his passion for results and an abhorrence for idleness with the wisdom that the journey is as important as the destination. (MIA 2000, 38)

The use of the Renaissance man metaphor is emblematic here. After all, the post-colonial logic that drives Singapore's higher education has taken its cue from the west since its inception – whether it concerns ideas, tools, or now even people. In all three local universities, there has been a disproportional intake of western researchers over recent years, and the systems of assessment and ranking are an amalgamation of the older British and newer American models. Another example of the post-colonial logic that informs academic research is the collaboration between NUS and MIT (the Massachusetts Institute of Technology), which is euphemistically called the Singapore–MIT Alliance. In this alliance, MIT's research attains global status by encapsulating Asian cultural difference through its alliance with NUS. Singapore sponsors the collaboration with MIT on the agreement that NUS can make use of the prestigious name of MIT in its brochures – the American MIT enjoys after all a much higher standing than some Asian university. This means however that MIT is sustained with Singapore's money, and that this collaboration, despite buoyancy about the alliance from NUS's and MIT's researchers, appears as starkly uneven. It is arguably a neo-colonial form of exploitation through the incorporation of eastern culture into western academic practice.

The MIA document, in warding off possible perceptions of neo-colonial exploitation, emphasises that this social contract does not mean that the Singaporean becomes 'a mere actor in a vast nameless play, but a co-writer of the Singapore Story' (MIA 2000, 39). But one may wonder what input the Singaporean has as a 'co-writer' when such an interpellation is fostered by a government that writes this document without the input of almost all of its citizens. What space is there for the Singaporean to be 'different' when his role is being circumscribed in such extremely meritocratic and European-masculine terms? What room is there for thought to make a difference, when not just creative thinking, but even the very notion of philosophical wisdom itself is submerged in the constant call for innovation, entrepreneurship and productivity? In terms of the Singapore student effectively becoming an instrument for the need for innovation of the neo-liberal knowledge economy, the attempt to exorcise fears of the Singaporean becoming a 'mere actor' rings increasingly false. More such rhetorical slippages emerge later on in the document, when it claims that the Renaissance Singaporean will allow Singapore to be '*plugged into* the global networks [of] communications, finance and commerce' (MIA 2000, 40, italics mine), and when it underlines that 'being Singaporean is more than being an economic *machine*' (MIA 2000, 42, my italics). These slippages aptly describe the usurpation of thought and the Asian graduate within the cybernetic machinery, and signify the moments at which the rhetoric of freedom and difference becomes part of the larger economic imperative. Telling here is also that the document pushes for 'Singapore' to become a reputable brand name for 'technologically advanced, aesthetically designed, and creatively packaged products and services' (MIA 2000, 40), making Singapore's difference from the west a mere marketing label, just as the east more generally functions as a hallucination of alterity vis-à-vis the west.

While the Singapore government is making a major effort to restructure its higher education for the demands of the global neo-liberal economy, several pundits misguidedly claim that governmental incentives towards creative and critical thinking through interactive tools will breed more alternative political views and more 'out-of-the-box' thinking. This would, these analysts argue, challenge and subvert local authoritarianism, and eventually democratise Singapore. In a recent piece in *The Chronicle of Higher Education* tendentiously titled 'A Pandora's Box in Singapore', Martha Ann Overland suggests for instance that the promotion of creative and critical thinking in higher education in Singapore, which encourages students to 'push boundaries and ask difficult questions', is a 'liability' for a 'deeply conservative society governed by a powerful single political party that permits little criticism' (Overland 2007). Likewise, participants on a listserv for creative industries herald the expansion of these industries into China and Southeast Asia as a form of democratisation. In 'Picnic creative China', Amsterdam-based researcher Qilan Zhao asks whether there 'is a role for creativity' in a country like China, that is known for its 'cheap imitations and piracy', and argues that the Internet has allowed 'average people to become national heroes'. Online enterprise and activism will, according to Qilan, 'challenge [Chinese government] authority' (Qilan 2007).

At the core of this paternalistic argument dwells the erroneous idea that creativity and critical thought are inherently resistant, and that this type of thought and knowledge *as such* can turn the political status quo on its head. But this emancipatory connotation of 'creativity' and 'criticality' is brought about by the deluded western humanist conception of the term 'creative'. This conception allows proponents of the creative industries to claim that 'original thinking' is being fostered, when in actual fact the opposite is the case. Let me mobilise here my critical tracing à la Heidegger from an 'eastern' locality. Originally, the verb 'to create', from the Latin *creare*, simply meant 'to make', and bore nothing of the contemporary western connotations of originality, genius and imagination – in fact, neither ancient Greek nor Latin had any word corresponding with the current English usage of creativity. The word 'creative', as pointing to a distinctly inventive and rational quality of a person, only entered the English language around 1680 at the height of the Enlightenment, and marked the western shift from God as the entity facilitating 'creation out of nothing' to the human, as if *he* is an agent–genius (Partridge 1990). Most eastern languages do not have a term to capture the idea of human creativity in the western sense of originality – rather, to be creative in Chinese cultures means instead skilfully *copying* the master or masterpiece as closely as possible, something my Chinese students are incredibly apt at doing, and which opens them up to accusations of plagiarism. Authors of the problematic western rendition of creativity and criticality, like Overland and Qilan, tend to take a condescending stance towards culture and politics in the supposedly 'un-free', 'imitative' and 'conservative' Asian countries like Singapore and China. To argue that creativity will contest the 'conservative' Singapore government, is then not only a naïve analysis that problematically celebrates western values as inherently superior (as the Singapore government, in an ostensibly self-defeating post-colonial argument, also does in its idealisation of Renaissance Man), but also forgets that creative or critical thinking *never* takes place in a economical, institutional or political vacuum. Again, the creative industries and their modes of thought are more likely to be involved in the reproduction of neo-liberalism and its crisis-management through assimilating the student body in global acceleration, than in the effective contestation of such structures. It is not surprising that a Chinese scholar like Qilan gets invited to the Netherlands to research 'the democratising effects of creativity and new media' and speak 'on behalf of the oppressed Chinese people', because his rhetoric serves the self-gratifying image of western cultural superiority, which in turn facilitates post-colonial forms of economic exploitation.

So in light of the *simulation of thought* which gives rise to this western misconception of 'creating' to circulate, the current proliferation of critical and creative pedagogies and tools in Singapore marks the *disappearance* of subversive thought and action under neo-liberalisation. The emphasis on pedagogies for creative and critical thinking dissimulates the increasing complicity of contemporary academic thought in acceleration. A case in point here would also be the fact that the term 'critical' increasingly pops up in NUS's policies and pedagogies, and that the term is fast losing all its political traction. This erosion of the term 'critical' shows itself in NUS's Centre for Development of Teaching and Learning (CDTL) modules on how to induce critical thinking. In these courses, now all kinds of problem-solving techniques go under the 'critical' heading. This includes ways to guide students to get to the 'correct' explanations of empirical questions and to pose 'truths' (CDTL 2007). But such fostering of thought exhibits a very limited notion of questioning – rather, it appears that thought here is *managed*, under the guise of the students' freedom to explore. This management seeks to establish culturally specific and economically productive grounds, frameworks and axioms as universal. *Real* critical thought, in the tradition of Heidegger, should be a problem-generating or *complicating* exercise that opens up to the *ambiguities* of justice and truth, rather than a problem-*solving* one that views justice as a by-product of economical and technological progress towards a *scientific* truth. But the problem-generating evocation of the term for obvious reasons does not go down well with Singapore's academic and governmental decision-makers, who understand their responsibility in terms of enhancing graduate employability. At this junction of these two incompatible definitions of critical thought emerges a strong relationship between the urgent moral demands of the new global economy for breeding a creative class in Asia's global cities, and the incessant *speeding up* of this economy through the new communication technologies. The push for creative and critical thinking, in Singapore and other Asian countries, could be read as a *symptom* of capitalism's excess production through speed. The Renaissance City campaign shows how Singaporean culture and creativity have become assets for networked circulation, production and innovation, and its citizen-students mere targets of such rhetoric and its cybernetic acceleration.

The disappearance of *true* critical thought therefore points directly to the reformulation of the mandate of the contemporary university, whether this entails the European move to pragmatism or the Asian shift towards creative and critical thinking. In 'Theory after theory, institutional questions', Bill Readings argues that the university today is marked by the notion of excellence in the service of technocratic capitalism. He notes that, 'Excellence is non-referential, a unit of value entirely internal to the system, which marks nothing more than the moment of technology's self-reflection' (Readings 1997, 23). This idea of excellence is still tied to previous ideals of the university as one of culture and reason (or indeed: *thinking*). But excellence is not tied to any particular type of content, and thus is extremely useful for the capitalist logic of 'production and processing of information' since it allows for 'diversity without threatening the unity of the system' (Readings 2001, 23). The demand for excellence by nurturing a cosmopolitan and cultured student-citizen who can 'think critically' returns forcefully in former NUS president Shih Choon Fong's 'Focus, collaborate, thrive', a speech given at the University of Melbourne. Shih calls upon the humanities to 'prepar[e] citizens and societies for a new tomorrow that is driven by science and technology' and the 'tectonic changes' that have transformed the world (Shih 2007, 4). Shih mentions the 'shifting centres of gravity' due to the rise of India and China, and the 'increased cultural complexity' that this shift has brought about (Shih 2007, 2). NUS should according to Shih have a 'functional mission and a civilising mission … the civilising mission relates to character development of the global citizen' (Shih 2007, 5). Our 'duty' as educators is to 'engage in the broad social, humanistic, and philosophical issues of our times' (Shih 2007, 8). This call to philosophy returns in the inaugural address of Tan Chorn Chuan, who is the new NUS president. Tan urged teachers to help 'students to become thinking individuals with questioning minds' so that graduates will be 'effective in diverse cultural settings' and 'equip[ped] … to make a difference in a globalised world full of opportunities' (Tan 2008, 8–11).

Shih's and Tan's demands for the humanities make sense foremost for those whom 'space and time have shrunk' (Shih 2007, 3); those who will travel to foreign places and communicate with other (read: mostly western) cultures after graduation, like corporate knowledge workers, politicians and academics. As much as NUS prides itself in being a 'global knowledge enterprise', it is logical that it is a prime example of the way contemporary higher education is wrapped up in the post-colonial stipulations of global capital, as NUS's aim of catering for the global demands of 'distinctive cultural content' shows. This binding of cultural production to the logic of speed has therefore become its main feature. Cultural differences as content, *especially* when it claims to be critically engaging western or Chinese authority, no longer makes a difference to neo-liberal acceleration. But this means that the Heideggerian critique can in this context also be set to work *against* itself and Readings' pessimistic interpretation. For how then may we understand the *possibility* of a critique like this one in a contemporary Asian university marked by the cyberneticisation of thought and the death of western philosophy? While there is after all an obvious purchase in NUS to my being white, and while western humanist philosophies of power, dissent and dialogue have become the central concepts around which my teaching revolves, some of my students have obliquely remarked how the assumption of the western moral superiority of *questioning* technocratic neo-liberalism grounds my teachings.

My students have also observed how the rationale behind my teaching is not 'directly' applicable knowledge and skills, but essentially a sort of 'building character'. They realise that this may be useful for their post-academic international careers as Singapore's politicians or entrepreneurs. As much as these responses unsettle my teaching *by being true to* its basic tenet of questioning, it is my hope that the students' Asian counter-signing of the critical philosophies of 'dead white men' at least opens up a space of inquiry beyond the post-colonial logic.

So if we instead take Heidegger's and my distinction between true and false critical thinking and creativity, as I showed with the eastern challenge to the western definition of creativity and critique, as *itself a symptom* of the capitalist petrifaction of thought, we can see that Heidegger *himself* already simulates thought through an apocalyptic rhetoric of completion, thereby reviving thought *as if* it is singular. This (paper's) *productive interplay* between urgency and duration of thought that the injustice of speed-elitism demands, is a present-day manifestation of the humanist inconsistency between, on the one hand, the necessity of the apocalyptic argument to make possible a universal claim *about* neo-liberalism, and, on the other hand, the impossibility of completing this claim due to its enmeshment *with* neo-liberalism. 'Real' critical thought seems at this injunction just as complicit in acceleration as the watered-down version of critical and creative thought in the Singaporean policy papers and NUS pedagogies. But my intention here is not to fabricate a thinking *outside* of contemporary arrangements of neo-liberal power – quite the contrary; I suggest that the proliferation of 'creative and critical thinking' marks the *deficit and promise* of western humanism and its implosion into neo-liberalism for Asia – a humanism that I also, by being loyal to NUS's imperative to 'think critically', perform. On the one hand then, the emphasis on critical thinking and new media in education will lead to a widening of income gaps due to its exclusionary entrepreneurial techno-logic. This stratification will evoke the 'old' humanist promise of justice as it slips away from us beyond the horizon of neo-liberalism. No mere creative or critical engagement with new media will be capable of simply reversing this, as these techniques are the essential ingredients of neo-liberal acceleration. The push for creativity and critical thinking will foremost promote the speed-elite's ascendance in the years to come. Yet on the other hand, the future *outcomes* of the s(t)imulation of thinking cannot be known beforehand, since thought works through the technological and hence cannot fully predict the (effects of) the technological. Such is the ambiguous potential opened up by critically mobilising 'Asia' as a counter-point to the 'west': *not* a reversal of the Spivakian scheme, but a speed-elitist expropriation of 'dead white men' by the Singaporean upwardly mobile steeped in a thoroughly post-colonial logic.

By delving into the problematic creative and critical thinking in NUS, I have revealed the grounds which clear the space for thinking (Heidegger's αληθεια) within the Asian knowledge economy. *Thought* (and hence also my thinking) here functions within a neo-liberal system of information exchange, turning 'thinking researchers and students' into instruments of production within this post-colonial framework. It is perhaps of interest here to note that the economist Joseph Schumpeter (1962) claimed that capitalism compulsively needs to foster innovation through 'creative destruction' – a term that points towards the violent side of the subjugation of students and researchers as cybernetic instruments. The current completion of western philosophy in technological mastery marks the increasing post-colonial objectification of the Singaporean student body in the face of the Renaissance City campaign's demand for creative and critical thinking. But the best students in my classes also become upwardly mobile through scoring marks by learning to question their relative positions of privilege. My teaching does then precisely what the NUS presidents would want me to do: to provide students with the ability of creative and critical thinking, with the 'development of character', that the new speed-elite needs for its entrepreneurial, ambassadorial and research-oriented endeavours and international connections. And this paper, written by a white woman in NUS and simulating the Renaissance ideal through its critical gesture, is itself an *effect* of Singapore's call for creativity and criticality. This situation marks my western privilege, but also hands the promising torch of questioning (neo-liberalism) to the future elites: my Singaporean students.

References

Armitage, J., and P. Graham. 2001. Dromoeconomics: Towards a political economy of speed. *Parallax* 7, no. 1: 111–23.
Centre for Development of Teaching and Learning. 2007. Academic inquiry and critical thinking. Handout for Knowledge, Thinking and Inquiry Seminar. http://www.cdtl.nus.edu.sg/pdp/pdp-kti.htm.
Creative Community Singapore. 2007. Meeting. https://app.creativecommunity.sg/Learning-Briefs/MEETING/tabid/184/Default.aspx.
Derrida, J. 2004. The principle of reason: The university in the eyes of its pupils. In *Eyes of the university,* 129–55. Stanford, CA: Stanford University Press.
Heidegger, M. 1993a. The end of philosophy and the task of thinking. In *Basic writings: From 'Being and time' (1927) to 'The task of thinking' (1964),* ed. D. Farrell Krell, 427–49. New York: HarperCollins.
Heidegger, M. 1993b. The question concerning technology. In *Basic writings: From 'Being and time' (1927) to 'The task of thinking' (1964),* ed. D. Farrell Krell, 307–42. New York: HarperCollins.
Heidegger, M. 1993c. What calls for thinking? In *Basic writings: From 'Being and time' (1927) to 'The task of thinking' (1964),* ed. D. Farrell Krell, 365–92. New York: Harper-Collins.
Lee, B.Y. 2007. Speech by Dr Lee Boon Yang, Minister for Information, Communications and the Arts, at the 2007 Creative Industries Scholarships Award Ceremony. http://www.mica.gov.sg/pressroom/press_070828.htm.
Manovich, L. 1996. On totalitarian interactivity. http://www.manovich.net/TEXT/totalitarian.html.
Ministry of Information and the Arts. 2000. *Renaissance city report: Culture and the arts in Renaissance Singapore.* Singapore: Ministry of Information and the Arts.
Ministry of Information, Communications and the Arts. 2006. Creative industries. http://www.mica.gov.sg/mica_business/b_creative.html.
Overland, M.A. 2007. A Pandora's Box in Singapore. *The Chronicle of Higher Education* 53, no. 42: A38.
Partridge, E. 1990. *Origins. An etymological dictionary of Modern English.* London: Routledge.
Qilan, Z. 2007. Picnic Creative China. http://mastersofmedia.hum.uva.nl/2007/10/03/picnic-creative-china/.
Readings, B. 1997. Theory after theory. Institutional questions. In *The politics of research,* ed. A.E. Kaplan and G. Levine, 21–33. New Brunswick, NJ: Rutgers University Press.
Schumpeter, J. 1962. The process of creative destruction. In *Capitalism, socialism and democracy,* 81–6. New York: Harper Torchbooks.
Shih, C.F. 2007. Focus, collaborate, thrive. Speech at the Education, Science, and the Future of Australia Public Seminar Series, University of Melbourne. http://www.nus.edu.sg/president/speeches/2007/unimelb_1.htm.
Spivak, G.C. 1993. Marginality in the teaching machine. In *Outside in the teaching machine,* 53–76. London: Routledge.
Tan, C.C. 2008. Continuity and transformation. State of the University Address, National University of Singapore. http://www.nus.edu.sg/soua/2008/SoUA_10_Oct_08.pdf.

The United Nations Educational, Scientific and Cultural Organisation: pawn or global player?

Eva Hartmann

Institute for Political and International Studies, University of Lausanne, Lausanne, Switzerland

> This contribution aims at exploring the significance of the new generation of UNESCO conventions for the recognition of higher education qualifications. It discusses three possible scenarios and links them to the empirical findings of a study that compares the enabling conditions of the first generation of recognition conventions established in the 1970s and 1980s with the ones establishing the second generation today. Taking an interdisciplinary approach, the paper argues that the changes illustrate a more general shift in the architecture of the global order and highlights a new role of UNESCO.

Introduction

In October 2009, the General Assembly of the United Nations Educational, Scientific and Cultural Organisation (UNESCO) gave the green light to amending the first-generation regional convention on the recognition of higher education qualifications for the African states and for the Asia-Pacific states (UNESCO 2009). This reform project was initiated 10 years after the start of the Bologna Process, which has made a success story out of the reform of the UNESCO recognition convention for the European region, the Lisbon Convention.

This contribution explores the significance of this new generation of UNESCO recognition conventions for the role of UNESCO in a global context by distinguishing three possible scenarios. Does this development represent a major step forward in the promotion of global solidarity, as a *first* scenario would suggest? The international higher education community had already emphasised the linkages between mobility and solidarity in 1998, on the occasion of the first World Conference of Higher Education, where it called upon UNESCO to:

> ... promote international academic mobility as a means to advance knowledge and knowledge-sharing in order to bring about and promote solidarity as a main element of the global knowledge society of tomorrow. (UNESCO 1998, Nos. III.11)

A *second* scenario sees the decision rather in the context of an emerging global labour market, with the UNESCO recognition regime complementing the regulation of free movement of service providers in the framework of the General Agreement on

Trade in Services (GATS). This scenario emphasises the need for experts providing services in a foreign country to have their qualifications recognised.

A *third* scenario points to the role of UNESCO as an important standard-setting organisation in the emerging trade in educational services. The second generation recognition conventions promote external quality control of higher education institutions, which in turn makes it possible to treat domestic and foreign higher education institutions alike. In the framework of liberalisation, such non-discriminatory measures risk aggravating competition between universities with very different infrastructures and resources. Atilio Boron, the former Executive Secretary of the Latin American Council of Social Sciences (CLACSO), points out the possible negative effect for higher education institutions in the South:

> All the 'barriers' to the free flow of 'educational services' will be removed ... and LAC [Latin American and Carribean] universities will have to fairly 'compete' in the provision of higher education with some of the richest and strongest universities of the North. (Boron 2003, 120)

In this contribution I ask which of these three scenarios captures best the significance of a strengthened recognition regime in a global context. To analyse the broader context, I draw on the concept of hegemony as developed by Antonio Gramsci and further developed by Nicos Poulantzas and Bob Jessop, which I will outline in the first part. A second part develops a historical perspective and compares the enabling conditions of the first generation of recognition regimes with the second, with a view to situating UNESCO in this broader framework. The paper takes an interdisciplinary approach and argues that the changes which can be observed in this sector illustrate a more general shift in the architecture of the global order. Accordingly the paper aims at contributing to the discipline of international relations by examining a policy sector that has so far been neglected in that field of study. It also seeks to broaden the perspective of critical higher education studies beyond methodological nationalism by embedding the case study in a broader political framework.

The selectivity of hegemony

Antonio Gramsci's theory of hegemony highlights the importance of ideas and norms in the organisation of societies, notably in capitalist societies that build on a division between mental and manual labour (Gramsci 1978). Accordingly this approach reintegrates a more Hegelian tradition into historical materialism, and highlights the ideational dimension of power. Hegemony goes hand-in-hand with the establishment of a specific production and accumulation regime and, in more general terms, promotes a specific lifestyle as well as ways of thinking, behaving and consuming. Education plays a crucial role in socialising young people into this way of living.

Gramsci's theory provides a useful way of analysing the role of intellectuals, understood here in a broad sense (Gramsci 1978). We could also call the intellectuals that Gramsci has in mind 'knowledge workers'. The majority of them work in the industry even though they have a university degree. Gramsci assigns a pivotal role to intellectuals with close ties to the emerging social forces in the struggle for the new accumulation regime, which is accompanied by a fundamental change in societal relations. He calls this group of 'norm entrepreneurs' organic intellectuals. Their task is twofold: (a) to endow the emerging social forces with a certain homogeneity and cohesion and make them aware of their function in the social and political fields as well as the economic field; and (b) to articulate an ethico-political project that is capable of gaining the support of subaltern forces by including some of their concerns. Accordingly, intellectuals establish a system of alliances, characterised by an ideational hierarchy. It is the relative autonomy of these intellectuals that underpins their role in integrating the interests of allies in the articulation of the politico-ethical project claiming a hegemonic status. Hence a hegemonic order cannot be reduced to the interests of one single group. It is rather the result of a social compromise, structured by the principle of *divide et impera*. The nature of this compromise may vary according to the power position of both the different allies and the subalterns. Accordingly, the concept of hegemony as developed by Gramsci is Janus-faced. Hegemony is instrumental to underpinning a system of dominance and exploitation. But it can also be part of revolutionary strategies of the subalterns promoting a different society and challenging existing exploitation, marginalisation and silencing. The main question is who is privileged and legitimated by the hegemonic compromise, and whose experience of exploitation and subjecthood is marginalised or cannot even be spoken (Spivak 1998)?

Poulantzas develops the Gramscian perspective further in his theory of the capitalist state by giving more weight to the institutional dimension of the hegemonic order. With the increasing complexity of capitalism, the state with its institutional arrangements has taken over the role of the intellectuals (Poulantzas 1978). Crucial for Poulantzas' notion of the state is the assumption that capitalist societies are characterised not only by the distinction between the dominant and the subordinated class but also by different fractions within the capitalist class.[1] The different interests, views and perspectives of the fractions crystallise in the different departments, agencies, branches and apparatuses of the state. The state itself is the form of mediation between these different material condensations of social forces. To fulfil this organisational function as a mediator, the state needs relative autonomy. At the same time the state has no centre; it is rather a precarious balance of conflicting and contradictory interests, a structured terrain, a site of contestation and strategic interventions (Poulantzas 1978, 154–62).

Drawing on this perspective, we can understand higher education institutions as an institutionalised mode of establishing alliances between different intellectuals. The recognition of foreign higher education qualifications is crucial for establishing cross-border alliances.

Neo-Gramscian scholars have made a major contribution by introducing Gramsci's concept of hegemony into the field of international relations (IR) (Cox 1987). Cox characterises global hegemony as having three main elements that – reciprocally combined – constitute a historical structure. The first element includes ideas, understood as intersubjective meanings as well as collective images of world order. A post-colonial perspective developed in this vein underlines the ideational dimension of the North–South relation (Spivak 1998). The second element entails material capabilities that refer to accumulated resources; last but not least, there are institutions which amalgamate the previous two elements (Cox 1996, 100).

Drawing on Poulantzas, we can place the emphasis on the heterogeneity of international politics with the different international organisations and regimes as a specific material condensation of social forces. This accentuation raises the question as to whether the international condensation of conflicting interests has enough autonomy to be able to play a mediating role with a view to ensuring the general interest of capital, including a certain compromise between capital and labour.

Jessop's concept of strategic selectivity helps to better operationalise these questions for empirical research (Jessop 2008). Jessop points out how political strategies forge the institutional capacity of the state. The institutional capacity of the state, with its selectivity, in turn has an impact on the strategic choices made by the actors and consequently on the formation of strategies. Applied to an analysis of international politics, the concept of strategic selectivity sees international organisations as the result of political strategies whose underpinning by social forces needs to be examined. The selectivity built into the organisations in turn privileges some social forces over others, which in turn is reflected in the way actors make choices.

Drawing on this perspective we can understand UNESCO to be a nodal point in the global constellation of conflicting forces, structured by a specific selectivity. We can then ask what condensation of the social forces characterised this UN organisation in the Cold War period, and compare these findings with the condensation of social forces that characterises UNESCO today. To what extent has the change weakened or strengthened the organisation's autonomy and hence its capacity to mediate between conflicting interests?

Internationalisation in the 1970s

Since its establishment in 1945, UNESCO has promoted the international exchange of persons active in the fields of education and science (UNESCO 1945, Art I.2c). However, this idea only took the concrete form of a first generation of conventions on the recognition of qualifications covering different regions in the 1970s: one convention for Latin America and the Caribbean (adopted in 1975), one for the Arab States (1978), one for Europe as a region (1979), one for Africa (1981), one for Asia and the Pacific (1983), and one for the Arab and European states bordering on the Mediterranean (1976). The geographical restriction is remarkable, and distinguishes these conventions from all other UNESCO conventions which are international in scope. The restriction is anything but self-evident. In the 1960s it was still a matter of controversy, which sheds light on the condensation of power within UNESCO at that time. The General Assembly preferred an international convention, while the more exclusive UNESCO Executive Board was more inclined towards a regional scope from the beginning, which prevailed in the end (UNESCO 1965, 9; UNESCO 1968, 15 [C/Resol. 1.262]).

Latin America, the Arab states, and Europe underpinned the regional version, though for very different reasons. In the Arab countries and Latin America, a regional orientation has become a major strategy aiming at strengthening their position in a global architecture and challenging the existing hegemonic order. Export-substituting industrialisation was at that time a key strategy, advocated by well-known scholars like Raúl Prebisch (Dosch and Faust 2000). Prebisch was also the first secretary general of the United Nations Conference on Trade and Development (UNCTAD) in the 1960s, and was centrally involved in the political project calling for a New Economic Order (Murphy 1984). Countries of the South, united in the Group of 77, endeavoured through this project to change the terms of the international trade architecture. A major success was the UN Declaration for the Establishment of a New International Economic Order, adopted by the United Nations General Assembly in 1974 (UN 1974). At the same time, a New Information Order was declared in the framework of UNESCO with a view to challenging the emerging global information order increasingly dominated by big mass media enterprises and capital-intensive new technologies (Sewell 1975; Wells 1987).[2]

The interest of the European region in a regional scope was different, though also related to regionalisation. A regional recognition convention was welcomed as a way of coordinating higher education policies and improving recognition of higher education qualifications in an intergovernmental framework, without delegating competences to the supranational framework of the European Community (EC) (Hartmann 2008a). A second motive for the European region was linked to the Cold War. A UNESCO convention for the European region had the advantage of including the Soviet Union, and became an element in the general endeavour to ease tension (UNESCO 1972). The drafting and promulgating of the European UNESCO recognition convention became part of the Helsinki process initiated by the Conference for Security and Co-operation in Europe (CSCE) (CSCE 1975, 52). As a consequence, the US and Canada also became involved in the UNESCO convention project and, together with the pan-European countries, signed the European UNESCO convention in December 1979.[3]

The low ratification and accession rate of the recognition conventions for the Asia-Pacific region and for the African region indicates that the regional scope was not in the interest of most countries in these regions.[4] However, they did not have enough say within UNESCO to get their interests realised. Hence, UNESCO, characterised by a specific condensation of social forces, became a platform for mediation between Europe and Latin America and the Arab States, as well as between east and west.

However, this mediating role became much more difficult in the mid 1980s due to the decision of the US and the UK to withdraw from UNESCO with a view to demonstrating their dissatisfaction with the organisation's policy. The withdrawal of these two rich members resulted in a one-third cut in UNESCO's budget, and marginalised this organisation in the global architecture of international organisations (Hüfner 1998, 36; Wells 1987).

The post-Cold War era

With the intensification of the international market and increasing migration in the 1980s, the recognition issue gained in importance. However, UNESCO's recognition conventions turned out to be declarations of intent rather than effective instruments for facilitating recognition. Due to their rather general wording, the recognition conventions left much room for interpretation to the bodies in the host countries assessing and recognising foreign qualifications. In addition, countries of the South feared that they would be excluded from recognition arrangements developed in Europe and the US. In a UNESCO report, they pointed out critically that:

> The most highly industrialised countries tend to establish their own systems of co-operation in education and research. On the other hand, the developing countries have greater difficulty in setting up, on a regional or international basis, the type of co-operation machinery which can consolidate their educational and scientific institutions. In actual fact, it is a vicious circle: those States which stand in greatest need of co-operation in these educational domains have not been able to set up, essentially for want of resources, the bodies and methods required for such exchanges. (UNESCO 1988, Nos. 52)

The changed global constellation paved the way for the return of the idea of a universal convention for the recognition of higher education qualifications. Drawing on a resolution from 1968, UNESCO's General Conference at its 24th session in 1987 authorised the General Director to commission a feasibility study for an international convention (UNESCO 1987, Resol. 5.6). However, not all members were keen on establishing an international instrument; European states in particular wanted to keep a regional scope. A controversial debate ensued, leading to a neck-and-neck race between the two different options. Once again the proponents of a universal convention lost the battle, and this time it was the European region that defeated the international project.

EU members wanted to keep the regional scope, with a view to using this intergovernmental framework to improve the coordination of higher education policies at the European level without delegating competences in this field to the European Union (EU) (Hartmann 2008a). The fact that the US and Canada were both members of the European recognition convention certainly helped to strengthen this unilateral endeavour in the framework of UNESCO. The weakening of the organisation in the 1980s further facilitated the cooptation of the organisation's recognition instrument by one region. The European states finally gained support for their exclusionary reform project by promising to support the other regions in their own efforts to revise their regional conventions. A regional plan was agreed with the regional committees, whose task is to assist the implementation of their respective conventions. Accordingly, the UNESCO General Assembly justified its preference for the European project as follows:

> ... convinced that an efficient and operational convention in Europe would contribute to the objectives set out in the Joint Plan of Action of six regional committees for application of UNESCO's conventions in this field. (27 C/Resolution 1.13, 1993, No. 6)

However, this compromise turned out to be a weak one. Once the European countries had got what they wanted, they seemed to forget the commitment they had undertaken. This was noted with disappointment by the proponents of an international recognition convention:

> In the absence of such an approval [of the International Convention, E.H.], the issue of recognition at interregional level (and it is at this level that mobility has traditionally taken place) is brought literally to an impasse. (Bedrize 1996, 121)

UNESCO's role in an emerging global labour market

Nearly a decade later, at the beginning of the 2000s, the revision of the other UNESCO regional recognition conventions was put back at the top of UNESCO's agenda. This new interest in the UNESCO recognition instruments must be seen in the light of the emerging global knowledge-based economy and the low-income countries' interest in gaining access to the wealth of the North not only by exporting their products, but also by sending part of their skilled labour force abroad (Global Commission on International Migration 2005). In this context, well-established procedures for the recognition of foreign qualifications have become crucial. A case in point is the General Agreement on Trade in Services (GATS) and its regulation of temporary migration. GATS allows for mutual recognition agreements which do not include all WTO members. But it also urges its members to 'afford adequate opportunity for other interested Members to negotiate their accession to such an agreement or arrangement' (GATS, Art. VII.2) and recommends that 'recognition should be based on multilaterally agreed criteria' (GATS, Art.VII.5).

In the sectors where members have already undertaken commitments, the provisions are even stronger:

> In sectors where specific commitments regarding professional services are undertaken, each Member shall provide for adequate procedures to verify the competence of professionals of any other Member. (GATS, Art.VI.6)

GATS itself does not define the recognition standards or specify the procedures to be used to verify competence. It only states that the standards have to be standards of an international organisation whose membership is open to all WTO members (GATS Art. VI Fn.3).

In this context the UNESCO generic standards for the recognition of higher education qualifications have become a matter of great interest. From 2001 onwards, UNESCO organised workshops where education and recognition experts from all over the world were invited to discuss new strategies on how to facilitate recognition (UNESCO 2001, 2002). This strategy gained support from the UNESCO General Conference, which passed a resolution in 2003 urging all Members to use the UNESCO conventions as a normative educational framework to respond to the challenge of globalisation (UNESCO 2003). The resolution also invited UNESCO member states to:

> ... enhance national capacity for assuring quality and equity of higher education, promoting comparability between quality assurance systems through the use of transparent and appropriate criteria ... (UNESCO 2003, Para 1b)

Quality assurance of the higher education institution has become instrumental as a way of assessing the quality of a foreign qualification. However, to gain the support of the Northern UNESCO members the non-European regions had to establish a precarious alliance with the fractions seeking to enhance trade in educational services. A closer look at this alliance reveals how much the condensation of social forces within UNESCO, materialised into a specific selectivity, has changed today.

Precarious alliances for the global dimension

The 2003 UNESCO resolution also called upon UNESCO members to use the quality assurance mechanism in a similar way for foreign educational service providers (UNESCO 2003, Para 1b). Such an extension was presented as a way of preventing bogus foreign institutions from establishing themselves successfully. However, it can also be understood as an effort to regulate the market in trade in educational services and to put pressure on governments to reduce the restrictions placed on foreign providers.[5] International standards for controlling the quality of a higher education institution would help to ensure that the importing countries meet a major obligation of the GATS, which is to establish requirements for foreign providers that are 'not more burdensome than necessary to ensure the quality of the service' (GATS, Para VI.4). Hence, they can be used to challenge the adequacy of the domestic regulation of foreign education providers.

Subsequent to the resolution, the UNESCO secretariat further specified the resolution's recommendations by developing Guidelines for Quality Provision in Cross-Border Higher Education, in close collaboration with the Organisation for Economic Co-operation and Development (OECD) (UNESCO, and OECD 2005). A closer look at these guidelines reveals the interests underpinning this specification.

The guidelines are characterised by a threefold objective similar to the UNESCO resolution. They call upon UNESCO member states to further develop their regional convention and to establish an external quality assurance system in cooperation with national and international quality assurance agencies. But, as the title of the guidelines indicates, they put a major emphasis on the promotion of trade in education. In the very first recommendation, the guidelines call upon governments to:

> ... establish, or encourage the establishment of a comprehensive, fair and transparent system of registration or licensing for cross-border higher education providers wishing to operate in their territory. (UNESCO and OECD 2005, 13)

The proponents of the guidelines had anticipated that the UNESCO General Assembly would approve the guidelines with a view to giving them a more formal status. Such a formalisation would have increased the legitimacy of using them in a GATS dispute settlement designed to assess whether a given domestic regulation for foreign education providers was more burdensome than necessary. Hence, it would have strengthened the endeavour of the pro-trade lobby to instrumentalise UNESCO. However, this plan was thwarted by the resistance of some countries of the South. At the 171st meeting of UNESCO's Executive Board, representatives of these countries refused to recommend that the General Assembly should adopt the guidelines. They justified their position with the argument that the developing countries had not been sufficiently involved in the consultation process on the guidelines (UNESCO 2005b, 282). As a compromise, the Executive Board decided to publish the guidelines only as a document of the UNESCO Secretariat. The General Assembly confirmed this strategy by taking note of the guidelines but emphasising that they were 'neither a normative nor a standard-setting instrument' (UNESCO 2005a, 3).

As a non-normative instrument, the guidelines lack the legitimacy to be used in a dispute settlement process concerning the adequacy of a domestic regulation. In addition, the weakening of the guidelines helps to gain a reliable ally for the endeavour to strengthen a global recognition regime. It keeps the trade lobby interested in the revision of the UNESCO recognition conventions as a means to promote an external quality assurance system, which can then be used for the non-discriminatory regulation of foreign providers. Only this complex constellation of interests and the risk of enforcement can explain why the General Assembly was not asked to approve the guidelines. By contrast, there was little opposition to the use of the guidelines as a major reference. The Assembly even asked the Director-General to ensure the distribution of the guidelines and:

> ... to promote capacity-building for quality assurance at the regional level, using the draft Guidelines as a framework and calling upon the regional committees for the implementation of the conventions on the recognition of qualifications to act as consultative mechanisms. (UNESCO 2005a, Para 3b)

The involvement of the regional committees of the recognition conventions privileges a more bottom-up approach in the diffusion of the guidelines with a view to making the coalition underpinning this diffusion process more inclusive. In addition, the General Assembly also called upon its member states to provide extra-budgetary funding for capacity-building activities.

The latter request paved the way for the Global Initiative for QA Capacity-building (GIQAC). This initiative is interesting as it sheds light on the emerging role of

UNESCO. The initiative is a collaborative project between the World Bank and UNESCO, aiming at strengthening the different international and regional networks of quality assurance agencies. It can be understood as another effort to broaden the social base of the diffusion process. The collaboration treaty explains the rationale of this initiative as follows:

> It was agreed that this project would aim to consolidate a disparate set of World Bank DGF grants to establish a global support mechanism for regional networks. Through the DGF the World Bank has supported existing regional quality assurance networks in Africa, East Asia/South Asia and Latin America and the Caribbean. GIQAC will not only consolidate existing support, but open support opportunities to regional QA networks in Europe and Central Asia and the Arab States regions, thereby providing each region the opportunity to access resources. (UNESCO 2008, 2)

This initiative has not only extended the list of potential beneficiaries of the World Bank grants but has helped UNESCO to gain a new intellectual leadership in this field. Or, again in the words of the cooperation treaty:

> UNESCO, as the only UN organization with an explicit mandate in higher education, is linked with ministries, international agencies, implementing partners and partners in 194 countries, placing it in a position to achieve its mission to provide leadership, standard setting, and capacity building in higher education. GIQAC would aim to build on UNESCO's work through the Global Forum on International Quality Assurance and the UNESCO/OECD Guidelines for Quality Provision in Cross-border Higher Education. (UNESCO 2008, 2)

The major driving forces behind this initiative are European countries, with Germany, France, Norway and the Netherlands represented in the initiative's steering committee (UNESCO 2008, 3–4). These countries also ensured that the guidelines would become the major reference point of the new international strategy of the Bologna Process, which aims at fostering cooperation with other parts of the world (Bergen Communiqué 2005, 4; Leuven Communiqué 2009, 4; London Communiqué 2007, 4). Accordingly, the guidelines have become a major normative reference. But legally speaking, they are not a standard-setting instrument that could be used in a dispute settlement process of the WTO.

However, within the international higher education community not everyone was happy with the importance given to the guidelines, whose first recommendation is nevertheless the establishment of a comprehensive and transparent system for foreign education providers (UNESCO and OECD 2005, 13). The World Conference on Higher Education +10, which took place in July 2009, provided this fraction with a good opportunity to make their critique more visible. A first draft of the conference's communiqué included a reference to the guidelines which was eliminated in the final draft (World Conference on Higher Education 2009b, Para 35d). This can be seen as a reaction to the worries within UNESCO about a strong trade orientation. However, this concession did not go as far as permitting any official criticism of the GATS. Such a critique was put forward, in particular by the Latin American region, during the preparation process of the conference, and included in a first draft before it was eliminated in the final version (see also CRES Declaration 2008, Para B8; World Conference on Higher Education 2009a, No. 20). The elimination of the anti-trade criticism of GATS but also of the trade-oriented guidelines can thus be understood as a compromise between the competing interests of the pro-trade lobby and its critics, who are struggling with each other inside UNESCO.

Conclusion

The empirical findings presented in this paper have shown that the three different scenarios mentioned at the beginning do not exclude each other but co-exist. The interesting question then becomes: which of them will prevail? The study has shown that the second scenario, aiming at strengthening the global mobility of highly skilled people in the context of a global labour market, is at the top of the UNESCO political agenda. One can understand this strategy as an attempt to build transnational alliances between knowledge workers under the leadership of the fraction promoting global trade in services, notably through the multilateral framework of the GATS and other plurilateral free trade agreements.[6] However, the strengthening of the recognition regime can also be seen as part of the strategy to merge the regional higher education areas into one, in the framework of a global knowledge society as a new ethico-political project. As human beings, migrants are likely to strengthen the presence of the interests of the South in the North and to draw attention to the unequal distribution of wealth and environmental risks. However, climate change will be a major test of the solidity of such global solidarity. The case study has also shown that UNESCO is increasingly implicated in the emerging trade in education, which is at the heart of the third scenario. The failure of this last-mentioned fraction to get the guidelines adopted by the UNESCO General Assembly indicates, however, that the other regions have a certain capacity to block a simple capture of UNESCO. Nevertheless, these regions had to accept the now weakened UNESCO/OECD guidelines as the basis for international co-operation if they wanted to gain support for their endeavour to establish a strong recognition regime at a regional and global level.

In this sense it can be said that UNESCO has managed to play a role as a mediator between conflicting interests, but only to a limited extent and in a way that is characterised by a strong selectivity which privileges the interests of the major exporting countries in a global service-based economy. The historical comparison has shown that UNESCO's current role as a mediator is much weaker than it was in the 1970s, when this UN organisation became the mouthpiece for a new information order linked to a new economic order.

Notes

1. In his analysis, Poulantzas uses class in a narrow sense that defines the differences between the classes in relation to the economic structure. Accordingly, the bourgeoisie is characterised by its ownership of the means of production and the power to decide how to assign them and to allocate resources and profits. The relation of the fraction to capital defines the differences within the bourgeoisie. In this paper I use the concept of class in a broader sense, as the outcome of a classification process along the lines of property and allocation power, but also of gender, race, ethnicity and geographical location.
2. For an interesting analysis of the interdependency of these two political projects see Pavlić and Hamelink (1985).
3. *Convention on the Recognition of Studies, Diplomas, and Degrees concerning Higher Education in the States belonging to the Europe Region* (UN Treaty Series No. 20966).
4. Only 14 governments of the African region out of 53 had acceded to or ratified the *Regional Convention on the Recognition of Studies, Certificates, Diplomas, Degrees and other Academic Qualifications in Higher Education in the African States* by 1989. A similar situation prevailed in the Asia-Pacific region, where only seven governments had ratified or acceded to the *Regional Convention on the Recognition of Studies, Diplomas and Degrees in Higher Education in Asia and the Pacific* by 1989; see http://www.unesco.org/en/higher-education/conventions-and-recommendations.

5. Such restrictions could be, amongst others: limiting the foreign ownership of an institution to 49%, not recognising a degree issued by a foreign provider or even prohibiting the granting of degrees by foreign providers, or levying extra taxes on students attending such foreign institutions (Alderman 2001; Lenn 2002).
6. For an overview of other free trade agreements and their provision for the recognition of qualifications, see Hartmann (2008b).

References

Alderman, G. 2001. Higher education: Opinion: Ultimatums, taxes and absurd laws are just some of the barriers to free trade in education. *The Guardian,* January 9.

Bedrize, D. 1996. From regional conventions to a universal instrument: Steps forward and pitfalls. *Higher Education in Europe* 21, no. 4: 116–25.

Bergen Communiqué. 2005. The European Higher Education Area – achieving the goals. Communiqué of the Conference of European Ministers responsible for Higher Education, May 19–20, in Bergen.

Boron, A.A. 2003. Reforming the reforms. Transformation and crisis in Latin American and Caribbean universities. In *Meeting of Higher Education Partners. World Conference on Higher Education +5.* Paris: UNESCO.

Cox, R.W. 1987. *Production, power, and world order.* New York: Columbia University Press.

Cox, R.W. 1996. Social forces, states, and world orders: Beyond international theory (1981). In *Approaches to world order,* ed. R.W. Cox and S. Sinclair, 85–123. Cambridge: Cambridge University Press.

CRES Declaration. 2008. Declaration of the regional conference on Higher Education in Latin America and the Caribbean, Cartagena de Indias, Colombia, 4–6 June 2008, UNESCO, IESALC.

CSCE (Conference for Security and Co-operation in Europe). 1975. Conference on security and co-operation in Europe, final act, adopted on 1 August 1975, Helsinki.

Dosch, J., and J. Faust. 2000. *Diei ökonomische dynamik politischer herrschaft: Das pazifische asien und lateinamerika.* Opladen: Leske + Budrich.

GATS (General Agreement on Trade in Services). 1994. Geneva: World Trade Organisation.

Global Commission on International Migration. 2005. *Migration in an interconnected world: New directions for actions, 5 October 2005.* Geneva: Author.

Gramsci, A. 1978. *Selections from political writings (1921–1926).* London: Lawrence and Wishart.

Hartmann, E. 2008a. Der Bologna-Prozess und dessen durchsetzungskraft – im spannungsverhältnis legitimation, legitimität und legalität. Juridikum zeitschrift für kritik | recht | gesellschaft, no. 2, 85–90. Wien: Der Verlag Oesterreich.

Hartmann, E. 2008b. The role of qualifications in the global migration regime. GARNET Working paper, No: 39/08.

Hüfner, K. 1998. Die hochschulpolitik der weltbank in theorie und praxis. In *Deregulierung und finanzierung des bildungswesens,* ed. R.K. Von Weizsäcker, 287–306. Berlin: Duncker + Humblot.

Jessop, B. 2008. *State power. A strategic-relational approach.* Cambridge: Polity Press.

Lenn, M.P. 2002. The right way to export higher education. *Chronicle of Higher Education* 25, no. 25: B25.

Leuven Communiqué. 2009. Communique of the conference of European ministers responsible for higher education, Leuven and Louvain-la Neuve, April 28–29.

London Communiqué. 2007. Towards the European Higher Education Area: Responding to challenges in a globalised world, London, May 18.

Murphy, C. 1984. *Emergence of the NIEO ideology.* Boulder, CO: Westview.

Pavlić, B., and C.J. Hamelink. 1985. *The new international economic order: Links between economics and communications.* Paris: UNESCO.
Poulantzas, N. 1978. *State, power, socialism.* London: Verso.
Sewell, J. 1975. *Unesco and world politics: Engaging in international relations.* Princeton, NJ: Princeton University Press.
Spivak, G.C. 1998. *Critique of postcolonial reason: Towards a history of the vanishing present.* Cambridge, MA: Harvard University Press.
UN (United Nations). 1974. Declaration for the establishment of a new international economic order, adopted by the United Nations general assembly, 1 May 1974, a/res/s-6/3201.
UNESCO (United Nations Educational, Scientific and Cultural Organisation). 1945. Constitution of the United Nations Educational, Scientific and Cultural Organisation, adopted in London on 16 November 1945.
UNESCO. 1965. *Executive board, seventy-first session, 71 ex/ decisions, 29 November.* Paris: UNESCO.
UNESCO. 1968. *Resolutions, 15th session of the general conference.* Paris: UNESCO.
UNESCO. 1972. Intergovernmental conference on cultural policies in Europe, Helsinki, 19–28 June 1972, final report.
UNESCO. 1987. *Records of the general conference, twenty-fourth session, Paris, 20 October to 20 November 1987, vol. 1 resolutions.* Paris: UNESCO.
UNESCO. 1988. Preliminary study on the advisability of preparing an international convention on the recognition of studies, degrees and diplomas in higher education, 130 ex/9.
UNESCO. 1998. *World declaration on higher education for the twenty-first century: Vision and action, adopted by the World Conference on Higher Education.* Paris: UNESCO.
UNESCO. 2001. *Expert meeting on the impact of globalization on quality assurance, accreditation and the recognition of qualifications in Higher Education. Draft conclusion and recommendation ed-2001/hed/amq/05.* Paris: UNESCO.
UNESCO. 2002. Globalization and education, first global forum on international quality assurance, accreditation and the recognition of qualifications in higher education, 17–18 October 2002, final report, ed-2002/hed/amq/gf.1/11.
UNESCO. 2003. General conference thirty-second session, Paris 2003, item 5.17 Higher Education and globalization: Promoting quality and access to the knowledge society as a means for sustainable development, 32 c/72.
UNESCO. 2005a. Cooperation between UNESCO and OECD in drafting guidelines on 'Quality provision in cross-border Higher Education', item 5.8 of the provisional agenda, general conference 33rd session, Paris 2005, 33c/42.
UNESCO. 2005b. *Executive board, 171st session, Paris, 18–28 April 2005, summary records, 171 ex/sr.1–10.* Paris: UNESCO.
UNESCO. 2008. *Global initiative for quality assurance capacity (GIQAC), governance terms, UNESCO, Paris, January 2008.* Paris: UNESCO.
UNESCO. 2009. Item 8.4 of the provisional agenda, revision of the 1981 regional convention on the recognition of studies, certificates, diplomas, degrees and other academic qualifications in Higher Education in the African states and the 1983 regional convention on the recognition of studies, diplomas and degrees in Higher Education in Asia and the Pacific, general conference, 35th session, 35 c/48, 7 September 2009. Paris: UNESCO.
UNESCO, and OECD. 2005. *Guidelines for quality provision in cross-border higher education.* Paris: OECD.
Wells, C. 1987. *The UN, UNESCO, and the politics of knowledge.* New York: St. Martin's Press.
World Conference on Higher Education. 2009a. 2009 World Conference on Higher Education: The new dynamics of higher education and for societal change and development (UNESCO, Paris, 5–8 July 2009), draft communique (1st draft 26 June 2009).
World Conference on Higher Education. 2009b. The new dynamics of higher education and research. For societal change and development (UNESCO, Paris, 5–8 July 2009), communiqué, ed.2009/conf.402/2.

Index

academic freedom 32, 95
access 113, 115; globalisation 113
access (norming) 114, 116, 118; equality of opportunity 116, 118, 120; equality of rights 115, 119; inherited merit 115
actors 89
admission practices 117, 118
African Association of Universities (AAU) 102
African Network for the Internationalisation of Education (ANIE) 102
African Quality Assurance Network (AfriQAN) 107
African Union (AU) 106; harmonisation strategy 107, 108
agency 90
ALFA Tuning Project 58, 81
Apartheid: government 93; legacies 94
Asian universities 125
Atlas of Student Mobility 29
Attali, J. 42; report 42, 43, 44
Australia 66; Group of Eight 66

Becker, H.S. 118–19
Becker, R. 30; international branch campuses 32
Beijing 71; strategies 67; teaching materials 67–8
Bernasconi, A. 93; and Brunner, J.J. 82
blue-collar workers 17
Bologna 1
Bologna Policy Forum 1; participants 1; second meeting 1
Bologna Process 1, 4, 28, 53, 77; European ideas 81; normative power 84–5
Boron, A.A. 136
brainworkers 9, 17
branch campuses 30
Brazil 52; accreditation system 56; emerging economies 53; global economy 53; international indicators 53; market-university relations 53; republican challenges 52

Brazilian Humboldtian model 55
BRICs (Brazil, Russia, India and China) 52
Brint, S.: and Karabel, J. 119
Brunner, J.J. 81–2; and Bernasconi, A. 82
budgetary transparency 17

California University 12; lab funding 15
Cammack, P. 27
Campus France 40
capital accumulation 23; modes 90
capitalism: ecological dominance 24
Carr, E. 65
case studies: UK and USA 2–3
Centre for Development of Teaching and Learning (CDTL) 131
Centro Interuniversitario de Desarrollo (CINDA) 91
The challenge of establishing world-class universities (Salmi) 47
Chambers of Commerce and the Ministry of Foreign Affairs (MAE) 40, 41
Charlier, J-E.: and Croche, S. 110
Chen, Zhili 70
Chesbrough, H. 13
Chey, J. 67
Chile 91; ALFA Tuning Project 81; level playing field 92–3; public policies 81; QA systems 91, 92, 93; Valparaíso Declaration 81
China 65; case study 66; communication 73; culture 68; economic prowess 66; global affairs 67; government 70; higher educating policy 67; international exchange 73; long-term funding 72; scholar 131; soft power strategy 3, 73; university departments 72
The Chronicle of Higher Education 130
cognitive capitalism 8, 15; conflict 16; immiseration 16; inefficiency 16
college graduates 11
Commission of European Communities 120
community colleges 12
computer programmers 10
Conant, J.B. 116, 117

INDEX

Conference for Security and Co-operation in Europe (CSCE) 139
Confucius Institutes (CI's) 65, 67; criticism 67; headquarters 71; issues 71–2; leading group 70; network 65; program 73; rules and regulations 71; three kinds 71
Conservative Minister for Education (UK) 26–7
Coordination of Higher Education for Personnel Improvement (CAPES) 56
corporatisation 23
Council of Chancellors Chilean Rectors (CRUCH) 81, 82
Council of Higher Education (CHE) 94
Cox, R.W. 137
creative 130; class 9, 13; industries 131
Creative Community Singapore (CCS) 129
critical theory 24
Croche, S.: and Charlier, J-E. 110
cultural political economy (CPE) 89
curricular re-engineering 81, 83
cybernetics 126, 127

Dale, R. 1; higher educationism 1
de Wit, H.: and Knight, J. 105
Dearing, R. 27
decentralisation process 115
democratisation 93; qualitative 119; quantitative 119
Deng, Xiaoping 74
Department for Business, Innovation and Skills (BIS) 28, 33
Department of Education (DoE) 94
Department for Universities, Innovation and Skills (DIUS) 33
Dickhaus, B. 4
Diez, T. 80
diplomas 57
discourse of derision 26
Drucker, P. 9

eastern languages 130–1
economic depression 39
economic imaginary 23
education: Quasi-marketisation 53
Educational Testing Service (ETS) 117
efficiencies: sustainable 8
Ehrenreich, B. 17; and Ehrenreich, J. 8
Eisenhower, D. 67
Elite 10 competition (Germany) 12
emancipation 4
employability 12
ENADE exam 56–7
entrepreneurs 118–19
epistemic violence 80
equity: funding 120; policies 121
Eurocentric approaches 79

Europe 1; constitution 2
European Area of Higher Education 1
European authority 80
European Bologna language 84
European Credit Transfer and Accumulation System (ECTS) 43

For a European model of higher education (Attali) 42
European Quality Assurance Register (EQAR) 46
European Round Table (ERT) 42; knowledge economy 42–3
European Union (EU) 78
faculty members 12; non-tenurable 12
Fairclough, N.: Jessop, R. and Wodak, R. 79
Figueroa, F.E. 4, 77–85
Florida, R. 9
Fong, S.C. 132
foreign fee-paying students 3, 28
Foucalt, M. 2, 14; strategic dispositif 2
France 3; expatriate students 39; foreign students 39; foreign-backed campuses 41; *grandes écoles* 40, 43; new model 47; pre-revolutionary estates 17; reforms 38; thesis 38; university-industry nexus 3
French higher education system 41; three compartments 41

Gardner, R. 67
General Agreement on Tariffs and Trade (GATT) 43–4
General Agreement on Trade in Services (GATS) 136, 139
Germany: Elite 10 competition 12
global competition 3
global distribution 104
global equity 104
Global Initiative for QA Capacity-building (GIQAC) 142–3
global knowledge society 1
global league tables 31
global recession 37–8
global students 1–2
Global University 53
globalisation 2, 57; effects 89; relational view 24
Goastellec, G. 113–22
gold-collar workers 11
golden-age security 17
Gorz, A. 8, 15–16
Gramsci, A. 89; hegemony theory 136, 137
grandes écoles 40, 43; students 43; two-cycle structure 43

Hartmann, E. 4, 135–44; case study 4
Harvard Business Review 10

INDEX

Harvey, D. 26
hegemony: global 137; international ideas 53; powers 77; strategies 78
Heidegger, M. 126, 127, 128, 133; critique 127
high-tech industries 9; direct employment 9; mass layoffs 9
higher education (HE) 1; different functions 1; three-speed system 12
Higher Education Innovation Fund (HEIF) 30
Higher education in the learning society (Dearing) 27
Higher Education Quality Commission (HEQC) 94
Hood, C. 26, 45
Hoofd, I. 4, 125–34
Hu, Jintao 68
Hybrid Liberal University 55
Hybrid Silicon Laser 15

indirect modes 17
Indonesia 118; regional excellence seed 118
industrial state 8
inequalities 119
influence concept 84
infrastructures 32
Intel 14–15; advanced research projects 15; computer processors 14; staff 15
intellectual property 14
international academic collaboration 83
International Association of Universities (IAU): surveys 104
International Organisation for Standardisation (ISO) 44
international political economy (IPE) 1
international relations (IR) 1
international standards 4
international students 29
internationalisation agenda 105
internationalisation debates 103
internationalisation literature 105
internationalisation processes 37; short-term effects 83
internationalisation strategy 2

Jarratt Report 26
Jessop, B. 24–5; scales 89–90; *semiotic* in social action 25; spatio-temporal selectivities 25; strategic relational approach (SRA) 24–5, 88, 89, 90; strategic selectivity 137–8; structure and agency 24–5
Jessop, R.: Fairclough, N. and Wodak, R. 79
Junge, B. 87–96

Karabel, J.: and Brint, S. 119

Kehm, B.M.: and Teichler, U. 103
Khelfaoui, H. 108
Knight, J. 102; and de Wit, H. 105
knowledge: capitalism 8; commons 8; corporations 14; economy 7–8; industries 9–10; manager 11, 17; profitable 15; society 92
knowledge management (KM) 10; terms 15
knowledge types 10
knowledge workers 8, 11, 136; cognotariat 12
knowledge-based economy (KBE) 79

language 80; importance 84
Latin American Council of Social Sciences (CLACSO) 136
Lee, Boon Yang 128
Lee, B.Y. 129
Leite, D. 3, 51–62
leverage 14
Li, Mirmirani 68
Li-Hua, R. 68
Lisbon Agenda 28
Liu, Yandong 68, 70
Lu, Jianming 68
Luke, S. 65

McCutcheon, S.N. 69
Machtley, R.K. 69
Mamdani, M. 100
Mandelson, P. 33
Manners, I. 79, 80; NPE conception 79
Manovich, L. 128
marginality 126
massification process 114
maximally maintained inequality (MMI) 119
MECESUP projects 81–2
Merlinger, M. 80
Mexico universities 83
Microsoft 9, 14
Minister for Education (UK): Conservative 26–7
Minister for Information, Communication and the Arts (MICA) 128
Ministry of Education (MEC) 56
Ministry of Information and the Arts (MIA) 129
Mohamedbhai, G. 101
Munk, N. 11

National Accreditation System 81
National Centre of Evaluation for Higher Education (CENEVAL) 83
National Commission on Higher Education (NCHE) 94
National Committee of Inquiry into Higher Education 27
National Defence Education Act 114

INDEX

National Tuning Centre 82–3
nationalism 2
Neo-Gramscian scholars 137
neo-liberals 26
New Labour 27; competitiveness strategy 27
New Public Management (NPM) 24, 26, 48; strategies 38
Newfield, C. 2, 7–18
Normative Power Europe (NPE) 78, 79; conception 79; generations 79–80
Nye, J.S. 65

Office of Chinese Language Council International 70, 71
Office of Science and Technology (OST) 30
offshore campuses 3
Ogachi, O. 108
open innovation 13, 15; gurus 14; systems 14; theory 14
Organisation for Economic Co-operation and Development (OECD) 28, 29, 38
O'Shea, T. 68
Our competitive future: Building the knowledge driven economy (New Labour) 27
Overland, M.A. 130

paradoxical effect 38
Paris School of Economics (PSE) 47
Pearce, R. 68–9
People's Republic of China (PRC) 68
Pey, R. 82
Phelps, M. 14
political: dialogue 78; institutions role 90
Portuguese America 51
post-Cold War: architecture 1
post-colonial 51
Poulantzas, N. 137
Prime Minister's Initiative for International Education 28–9
privatism 82
professional-managerial class (PMC) 8–9
Program for Institutional Evaluation of Brazilian Universities (PAIUB) 56
public spending cuts 3

Qilan, Zhao 130
quality assurance (QA): collegial approach 96; critique 95; external 87, 93; framing 95; government perspective 88; introduction 88; meanings 88; policies 87
Quasi-marketisation of education 53

reality 84
Reichert, S. 108
Renaissance man 129
Research Assessment Exercise (RAE) 26, 31

Robertson, S.L. 3, 23–34, 79
Russia: public-private entrepreneur 44
Ryan, A. 26–7

SADC region 106
Salmi, J. 55
Salter, B.: and Tapper, T. 87
Sassen, S. 24
Sastry, T. 32
Sawyerr, A. 108
scales 89–90
scarcity 17
Scholastic Assessment test (SAT) 116
Schumpter, J.A. 52
Scott, P. 102
selectivity concept 96
Shanghai Jiao Tong 31
Shanghai Jiao Tong Ranking 55
Shavit, Y.: *et al* 119
Silver, H. 26
SINAES: quality evaluation process 56
Singapore: educational policies 126–7; government 130; students 130
Singapore Renaissance City campaign 127, 128, 131–2
Singh, M. 4, 99–109
skills: commodity 10; leveraged 10; proprietary 10
social scientists 118, 119
sociotechnic tools: diffusion 117
soft power 65
South Africa 93; Bologna influence 105; bridging the gap 106; funding framework 118; international partnership 101–2; opposition to QA 95–6; QA systems 94; revitalisation project 101
spatio-temporal selectivities 25
speed-elitism 126
Spivak, G.C. 78, 126
standardised examination test 116–17
STEM jobs 9
Stewart, T.A. 10
Storey, A. 80
strategic relational approach (SRA) 24, 88, 89; theoretical approach 90; variants 90
strategy: conflicting 2; innovation 13
student: fees 27; influxes 113
study programmes 2–3
Sub-Saharan Africa 4
subjugation 126
Sweden: academic interference 67

Tapper, T.: and Salter, B. 87
Teferra, D. 100
Teichler, U.: and Kehm, B.M. 103
Texas: University of 52
tiering blocks 13

translation: concept 89; process 90
Trow, M. 115

United Arab Emirates: strategy 30
United Kingdom (UK): higher education 28, 31–2
United Nations Educational Scientific and Cultural Organisation (UNESCO) 2, 4–5, 135–44; 1970's 138–9; General Assembly 140; recognition conventions 139; report 139
United States of America (USA) 7–8, 12; educational leadership 13; higher education 8; university system 9

Vinokur, A. 3, 37–48

Warwick: University of 31, 32
Washington consensus 52
wealth gap 12

Wesley, M. 66
white-collar labour 11
Wodak, R.: Fairclough, N. and Jessop, R. 79
workers: self-managed 11
World Bank 92; loans 78–9; pilot programme 92; report 47
World Class University 55; strategies 55
World Competitiveness Reports 42
Wright, T. 70

Xu, Lin 68

Yang, Rui 65–74
Yao, Xinzhong 70

Zgaga, P. 85
Zizek, S. 84

Contents Pages in Education

EDITOR:
Angie Davis, *Routledge Journals, UK*

Contents Pages in Education is a computer-based, international current awareness service that shows the contents pages of over 700 of the world's education journals.

Contents pages are arranged alphabetically by journal title and reset to a standardised and easy-to-read format.

Each issue of **Contents Pages in Education** contains:

- about 170 contents pages of the latest issues of the world's education periodicals
- comprehensive author and subject indexes
- an alphabetical listing of the journal titles in that issue
- a listing of new titles added to the service
- a full list of all journals covered by the service with subscription address, ISSN and frequency of publication

Additional bibliographical features of the service include:

- cumulative author and subject indexes in December
- cumulative indexes of journal titles in December

Every month **Contents Pages in Education** will give you access to all the major education journals in one comprehensive and up-to-date publication. No relevant journal is excluded through lack of space.

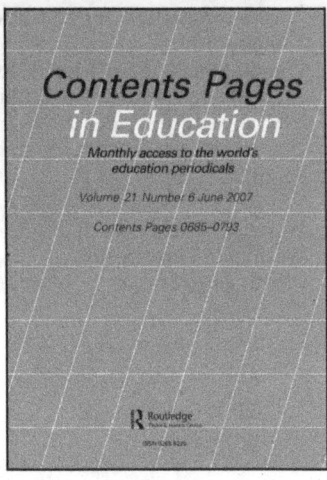

To sign up for tables of contents, new publications and citation alerting services visit www.informaworld.com/alerting

Register your email address at www.tandf.co.uk/journals/eupdates.asp to receive information on books, journals and other news within your areas of interest.

For further information, please contact Customer Services at either of the following:
T&F Informa UK Ltd, Sheepen Place, Colchester, Essex, CO3 3LP, UK
Tel: +44 (0) 20 7017 5544 Fax: 44 (0) 20 7017 5198
Email: subscriptions@tandf.co.uk

Taylor & Francis Inc, 325 Chestnut Street, Philadelphia, PA 19106, USA
Tel: +1 800 354 1420 (toll-free calls from within the US)
or +1 215 625 8900 (calls from overseas) Fax: +1 215 625 2940
Email: customerservice@taylorandfrancis.com

View an online sample issue at:
www.tandf.co.uk/journals/cpe